The Liberators of Pilsen

The Liberators of Pilsen

The U.S. 16th Armored Division in World War II Czechoslovakia

BRYAN J. DICKERSON

McFarland & Company, Inc., Publishers
Jefferson, North Carolina

Library of Congress Cataloguing-in-Publication Data

Names: Dickerson, Bryan J., author.
Title: The liberators of Pilsen : the U.S. 16th Armored Division in
   World War II Czechoslovakia / Bryan J. Dickerson.
Description: Jefferson, North Carolina : McFarland & Company, Inc.,
   Publishers, 2018. | Includes bibliographical references and index.
Identifiers: LCCN 2017052251 | ISBN 9781476671147 (softcover : acid
   free paper) ♾
Subjects: LCSH: United States. Army. Armored Division, 16th—
   History. | World War, 1939–1945—Campaigns—Czech Republic—
   Plzeň. | Plzeň (Czech Republic)—History, Military. | World War,
   1914–1918—Regimental histories—United States.
Classification: LCC D769.3053 16th .D53 2018 | DDC 940.54/
   213714—dc23
LC record available at https://lccn.loc.gov/2017052251

British Library cataloguing data are available

ISBN 978-1-4766-7114-7 (print)
ISBN 978-1-4766-2989-6 (ebook)

© 2018 Bryan J. Dickerson. All rights reserved

*No part of this book may be reproduced or transmitted in any form
or by any means, electronic or mechanical, including photocopying
or recording, or by any information storage and retrieval system,
without permission in writing from the publisher.*

Front cover image: citizens of Pilsen celebrating their liberation with
soldiers of the 16th Armored Division, May 6, 1945. Note the bottles of
Pilsner beer in the hands of the U.S. soldiers (National Archives); *inset*
the shoulder patch of the 16th Armored Division

Printed in the United States of America

McFarland & Company, Inc., Publishers
   Box 611, Jefferson, North Carolina 28640
      www.mcfarlandpub.com

*To the soldiers, living and deceased,
of the 16th Armored Division*

Map Symbols

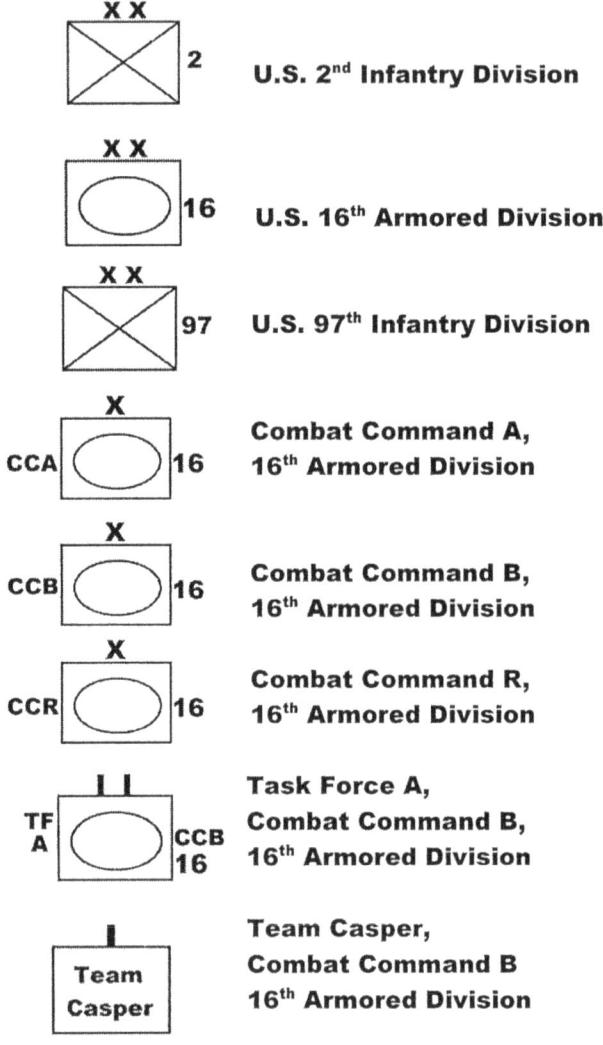

A Word about Names and Spellings

Bohemia, the western region of what is now the Czech Republic, has been home to both Czechs and Germans for centuries. As such, geographic places often have both German and Czech names and spellings. In many cases, they also have English spellings as well. For example, the city of Pilsen featured prominently in this book is spelled as Plzeň in Czech and Pilsen in German and English. The city of Cheb has both a Czech name (Cheb) and a German name (Eger). For this book, I have chosen to use English spellings of placenames with a few exceptions. Personal names are spelled with formal correctness.

For military ranks, I have chosen to use the rank as it is used by the military force in question. Thus American ranks are used when referring to American persons, e.g. colonel, lieutenant, etc. German ranks are used when referring to German persons, e.g. Generalfeldmarschal (field marshal), Oberst (colonel), etc. In this way, the reader can immediately recognize whether the person is part of the U.S. Army or the German Army.

Table of Contents

Map Symbols   vi
A Word About Names and Spelling   vii
Prologue   1
Introduction   3

1. Forming the 16th Armored Division   7
2. Training for War   32
3. Czechoslovakia's Long Years of Nazi Occupation   37
4. Summer and Fall of 1944   44
5. Deployed to Europe   53
6. First Battle for the 23rd Cavalry Squadron   64
7. The First Days of May 1945   79
8. Day of Decision   85
9. Pilsen and Prague on the Eve of Liberation   95
10. The Liberation of Pilsen   100
11. The Liberation of Pilsen Part 2   119
12. Ike Ordered Halt!   128
13. The End of the War in Europe   135
14. The Pratt Mission   139
15. V-E Day and Occupation Duties   147
16. The 16th Armored Division Shuffle   161

17. Returning Home and Deactivation	167
18. The Postwar Lives of the 16th Veterans	169
19. The Legacy of the 16th Armored Division	180
Epilogue	190
Chapter Notes	191
Works Cited	208
Index	217

Prologue

Pilsen, Czech Republic, Saturday 6 May 2000. On this warm sunny spring day, I was one of several hundred people who had gathered on Husova Street several blocks from Pilsen's Republic Square. Fifty-five years ago on this very day, soldiers of the U.S. 16th Armored Division had stormed into Pilsen and liberated the city and its long oppressed people from six long years of Nazi German occupation. Later in the day, other soldiers from the U.S. 97th Infantry Divisions had arrived to help secure the city. Today, the people of Pilsen had gathered to dedicate a new memorial in honor of their liberators from the 16th Armored Division. Among the crowd in attendance were many U.S. Army veterans. They included Vern Lewellyn, George Thompson, Gene Eike, Chuck Schaeffer, OJ Mooney and Charlie Savage of the 16th Armored Division.

The dedication ceremony featured representatives of the City Government of Pilsen, the Czech Government, and the Czech Armed Forces. 16th Armored Division Association President George Thompson was one of the featured speakers. "It is a great honor for me to accept this monument for the men of the 16th Armored Division, for those of us who are fortunate to be able to be here, for those who were not able to come because of health or other reasons, and for those who are no longer with us on this Earth," George said. He then thanked the various public officials and private companies who made the new memorial possible. After George's speech, the new memorial was unveiled. The memorial was a glass pyramid resting on steel supports. Etched into the glass were the 16th Armored Division's insignia and words of remembrance.

Fifty-five years after that historic day in May 1945, the people of Pilsen officially dedicated a memorial to honor and thank the American soldiers of the 16th Armored Division who liberated their city from Nazi oppression.

Introduction

During World War II, the United States Army organized, equipped and deployed sixteen armored divisions to the North Africa–European Theater of Operations. Armored divisions participated in the North African campaigns, the invasion of Sicily, the Italian campaigns, the liberation of western and central Europe and the conquest of Germany. The armored divisions brought tremendous mobility, firepower and organizational flexibility onto the battlefields. Despite having tanks with lesser armor and firepower than their German counterparts, American armored commanders were able to overcome these deficiencies through innovative combined arms tactics, and logistical superiority to defeat the vaunted German panzers.

When considering U.S. armored operations during the European Campaigns, several famed divisions immediately come to mind. The 4th Armored Division was one of the unstoppable armored spearheads of Patton's Third U.S. Army during the breakout from Normandy in late summer 1944. There was the stubborn defense of St. Vith by the 7th Armored Division and the relief of Bastogne by the 4th Armored Division during the Battle of the Bulge. The 9th Armored Division captured the only intact bridge across the Rhine River in March 1945. The 2nd and 3rd Armored Divisions encircled an entire German army group in the Ruhr in April 1945, forcing over 300,000 German soldiers to surrender.

Another U.S. Armored Division much less well known played a key role in the closing days of the war in Europe. Born and raised in Arkansas, the 16th Armored Division was the last armored division activated, the last one to deploy to the European Theater and the last one to see combat.

Arriving on the Continent in January 1945 and assigned to occupation duties, the 16th Armored Division very nearly missed out altogether in participating in combat operations. But at Patton's insistence, the division was rushed forward and sent into action. In its one and only combat operation, the 16th Armored Division liberated the city of Pilsen in western Czechoslovakia, freeing its residents from Nazi oppression and endearing itself to a grateful people who never forgot their heroes despite decades of subsequent anti–American Communist propaganda.

This book is the story of the 16th Armored Division, its brief, two-year existence, its one and only combat operation, and of the men who served in the division.

I first became involved with the story of the liberation of western Czechoslovakia and the story of the 16th Armored Division while pursuing a master's degree in American history at Monmouth University in West Long Branch, New Jersey. In the fall of 1997, I researched and wrote a paper on the U.S. decision not to liberate Prague in the closing days of the war in Europe for Dr. Jacqueline McGlade's American military history class. Ultimately, I researched and wrote my master's thesis on the emergence of the U.S.–Soviet Cold War as demonstrated by military and political events in Czechoslovakia during 1945. The 16th Armored Division played a prominent role in those events as well as in my master's thesis.

After graduation from Monmouth University, I continued to research the liberation of western Czechoslovakia. I spent numerous hours at the U.S. Army Military History Institute Archives at Carlisle Barracks, Pennsylvania and the National Archives II at College Park, Maryland, reviewing historical U.S. Army records. I got to know over a hundred veterans of the liberation and several Czech citizens through letters, phone calls and personal visits. I attended reunions of the 2nd Cavalry Association and the 16th Armored Division Association. In May 2000, I had the extraordinary opportunity and privilege to travel to the Czech Republic and experience the celebrations of the 55th Anniversary of the Liberation with many of the U.S. Army veterans who participated in the liberation. Utilizing my ongoing research, I wrote and presented papers on the topic at two history conferences and wrote articles that were published in historical journals, magazines, and online.

From April to December of 1945, the Third U.S. Army conducted operations in and around the western region of Czechoslovakia. Altogether, three of its corps (XII, V and XXII) and nine infantry divisions, four armored divisions and two cavalry groups participated in these operations. Some of the U.S. Army's most famous divisions served in Czechoslovakia at one time or another, including the 1st Infantry Division, the 2nd Infantry Division, the 90th Infantry Division, the 9th Armored Division, the 2nd Cavalry Group and the 4th Armored Division.

Introduction

The story of the liberation of western Czechoslovakia has been largely overlooked by both historians and the general public in our own country. Coming at the very end of the War in Europe, it is often overshadowed by the collapse of the Third Reich, Hitler's suicide, and the German surrender at Reims.

The purpose of this book is to honor the American liberators of western Czechoslovakia and in particular, those who served in the 16th Armored Division. Truth be known, the division was not the first American unit to enter Czechoslovakia; that honor belongs to the 358th Infantry Regiment of the 90th Infantry Division who did so more than three weeks earlier. But the 16th Armored Division's liberation of the city of Pilsen was one of the most important events of the U.S. Army's service in Czechoslovakia. It is an event that continues to be celebrated by the people of Pilsen to this very day.

As mentioned, nine infantry divisions, four armored divisions and two cavalry groups served in Czechoslovakia at various times between April and December 1945. In addition, there were numerous separate battalions and groups which were attached to the Corps and Army Headquarters. By focusing on the 16th Armored Division, I am not diminishing the role of these other units and the soldiers who served in those units. In this book, I discuss the other units as well. I have chosen to focus on the 16th Armored Division because their history has been neglected and theirs is a story that needs to be told. And it is my privilege to make an attempt to do so, an attempt which I hope will do them justice.

In the following pages, you will read about many veterans of the 16th Armored Division. Over 20,000 soldiers served in the division during its 27 months of existence. It is impossible to tell all of their stories in just one book—even if I could have collected stories about each one. Nevertheless, I have endeavored to tell as many of their stories as possible—generals and privates, tank commanders and truck mechanics, cavalrymen and radio operators.

The stories of the 16th Armored Division and its soldiers were compiled from numerous sources: official records preserved by the U.S. Army Heritage and Education Command Archives and the National Archives, published histories, interviews and correspondence with veterans, information provided by relatives (sons, daughters, others), obituaries, private letters, memoirs and written accounts. The soldiers mentioned in this book represent just a fraction of the total number who served with the division. Many stories are untold largely because they went unrecorded or were unknown to me. In short, the men who appear in this book are in the book because I *was* able to find information about them.

This book could not have been completed without the generous support and assistance of many people. These include the archivists at the U.S. Army Heritage and Education Center in Carlisle, Pennsylvania, and the National Archives II in College Park, Maryland, my professors at Monmouth University, Miloslava Vildova, Jaroslav Peklo, Vera Fiedlerova, Malvina Zajicova, 16th Armored Division veterans George Thompson, Dale Weaver, Harley Barrs, Ed Krusheski, O.J. Mooney, Sol Polish, William Smith, Jr., Charles Schaeffer, Gene Eike, Vern Lewellyn, and Mark Steece, George Schultz of the 2nd Infantry Division, and Clay Patterson and Kathy Hoffman whose fathers served in the 16th Armored Division. Kathy also provided many documents from the files of the 16th Armored Division Association. Dale Weaver's book on the 16th Armored Division provided many stories and background information for this book.

I would like to thank Margaret Lovecraft for her advice in preparing and marketing my manuscript. I also am indebted to my wife for her support and to Almighty God for His assistance in making this book a reality.

1

Forming the 16th Armored Division

When German panzer divisions surged across western Europe in the spring of 1940, the U.S. Army had exactly *zero* armored formations larger than brigade size, and no armored divisions at all.

Three years later, the U.S. Army had activated sixteen armored divisions, had deployed two to the North Africa / European Theater for combat operations and was preparing the remainder for the upcoming invasion and liberation of western Europe. Activated on 15 July 1943, the 16th Armored Division was the sixteenth and final armored division activated by the U.S. Army for service in World War II.

The shoulder patch of the 16th Armored Division. All U.S. armored divisions used this same format.

Development of the Armored Division in the U.S. Army

The U.S. Army lagged far behind the German Army in the creation, training and deployment of armored (Panzer) divisions. The first German panzer divisions were created in October 1935, nearly *five years* before the U.S. Army formed the 1st Armored Division at Fort Knox, Kentucky and the 2nd Armored Division at Fort Benning, Georgia on 15 July 1940. Both U.S. armored divisions were formed primarily from Regular Army cavalry units. By the time these first two U.S. armored divisions had been activated, the German Army had ten panzer divisions which had amassed considerable combat experience in conquering Poland, France and most of western Europe. By the end of the year, the German Army had formed ten more panzer divisions for a total armored force strength of twenty panzer divisions. In the months following the activation of the 1st and 2nd Armored Divisions, the U.S. Army struggled to form and train an armored force. Three more armored divisions were activated in 1941 before the Japanese attack on Pearl Harbor forced the U.S. into World War II. The following year, the U.S. Army activated nine more armored divisions. Their final two armored divisions were activated in 1943. In contrast, the German Army formed over forty panzer divisions during World War II and the Waffen–SS fielded seven SS panzer divisions as well.[1]

Forming and training armored division was no easy task for the U.S. Army. Indeed, the armored division underwent several major changes before the U.S. Army found the right organization and equipage. The 1st and 2nd Armored Divisions, and all subsequent armored divisions, were initially organized as what was later dubbed "heavy divisions." Each "heavy" division consisted of a Division Headquarters and Headquarters Company, an armored brigade, a reconnaissance battalion, an infantry regiment, a signal company, a medical battalion, a supply battalion and a maintenance battalion. The striking power of the "heavy" armored division was provided by the armored brigade consisting of two light tank regiments, a medium tank regiment, an artillery regiment and an engineer battalion. Barely four months later in November 1940, the armored division Table of Organization and Equipment (TO/E) was modified by adding an artillery battalion, moving the engineer battalion out of the armored brigade and giving the armored brigade a Headquarters and Headquarters Company.[2]

The U.S. armored division's TO/E remained more or less unchanged until March 1942. In that month, the TO/E was significantly changed in a further effort to streamline the armored division and make it more combat effective. The new reorganization gave the armored division a Division Headquarters, two Combat Command Headquarters (A and B), two armored regiments each consisting of a light tank battalion and two medium tank battalions, an armored infantry regiment, three artillery battalions, a reconnaissance battalion, an engineer battalion and Division Trains consisting of a maintenance battalion, supply battalion and medical battalion. The two Combat Command Headquarters were to coordinate the operations of subordinate combined arms task forces formed from

1. Forming the 16th Armored Division

the aforementioned tank, infantry, artillery and supporting arms units. These changes reflected the U.S. Army's growing realization that tanks were best employed in conjunction with other combat arms.[3]

The U.S. Army's armored divisions received their first test of combat in North Africa in 1942–43 and in the summer 1943 invasion of Sicily. As a result of experience gained during combat, the U.S. Army radically changed its organizational methods for the armored division. Ultimately, two methods were utilized for organizing its armored divisions, being known as "heavy" and "light" for the total number of tanks in each. At first, all U.S. armored divisions were organized with twice as many tank units as infantry units. This scheme later became known as the "heavy" armored division. Only the 1st, 2nd and 3rd Armored Divisions used this organization in combat. Though the 2nd and 3rd Armored Divisions retained the "heavy" organizational scheme throughout the war, battlefield experience further showed the Army that a greater balance of combat forces was needed within its armored divisions.[4]

The result was the creation of the "light" armored division adopted in September 1943. After the North Africa campaign, the 1st Armored Division was re-organized as a "light" armored division. With the exception of the 2nd and 3rd Armored Divisions, every other U.S. armored division (4th, 5th, 6th, 7th, 8th, 9th, 10th, 11th, 12th, 13th, 14th, 16th and 20th) was also re-organized as a "light" armored division and fought in combat as such. The "light" armored division employed a Division Headquarters, three Combat Command (A, B and Reserve) Headquarters and thirteen organic battalions. Each armored division contained three battalions each of tanks, armored infantry and armored field artillery as well as a mechanized cavalry squadron for reconnaissance, and armored engineer, armored medical and armored ordnance battalions. "Light" armored divisions were further bolstered by permanently assigning tank destroyer and self-propelled anti-aircraft artillery battalions and other support units as needed.[5]

The re-organization of the "heavy" armored divisions into "light" armored divisions resulted more than just structural changes. The re-organization significantly reduced the total number of personnel and tanks assigned to the armored divisions. The total number of personnel was reduced from 14,620 in the "heavy" division to 10,670 in the "light" division. Similarly the number of tanks in the "heavy" division was reduced from six battalions with a total of 390 tanks to three battalions containing 263 tanks in the "light" division.[6]

The "light" armored divisions had an authorized strength of 10,670 personnel. The division's primary offensive combat power was provided

The M4 Sherman medium tank armed with a 76mm gun was the primary tank of the 16th Armored Division's three tank battalions (author's photograph).

by its tanks and armored vehicles. The armored division was authorized 195 M4 Sherman medium tanks mounting either 75mm or 76mm guns, 77 light tanks, 54 self-propelled artillery pieces and 466 half-tracks. The light tanks were either M5s which mounted a 37mm main gun or the much improved M24 Chaffee which had a 75mm main gun. Artillery fire support was provided primarily by M7 self-propelled guns with 105mm howitzers. Each tank battalion also had a number of M4 tanks armed with short-barreled 105mm howitzers instead of 75mm or 76mm guns in their turrets. Half-tracks transported the infantry and performed a variety of support roles. The cavalry squadron contained light tanks, assault guns, and armored cars. Attached tank destroyer battalions were equipped with either the M10, M18 or M36 tank destroyers, mounting 75mm, 76mm or 90mm anti-tank guns respectively in open-topped turrets. Very late in the war, limited numbers of the heavy M26 Pershing tank entered service with several of the armored divisions in Europe. The M26 mounted a 90mm main gun, had heavier armor more comparable to that of the German tanks, and had a much improved suspension system. The new tank was also significantly heavier and wider than the standard M4 tanks, so much so that some units opted to retain their M4s.[7]

1. Forming the 16th Armored Division

Each tank company also included a M4 Sherman tank armed with a 105mm howitzer for additional fire support (author's photograph).

Thus the armored division entered into combat under the "heavy" organization scheme, but experience produced a new "light" organization scheme that became the standard for nearly all of the U.S. armored divisions which fought in World War II.

A Cadre Is Formed

By the spring of 1943, U.S. Army Ground Forces had a well-established procedure for organizing and training new divisions for combat and several years of experience in making it happen. The first two armored divisions (1st and 2nd) were both organized using cadres drawn from cavalry and other units. In turn, additional armored divisions were activated and organized using cadres drawn from its predecessors. Basically the process was as follows. First, a commanding general and his staff were selected. Then, a cadre was drawn from one or more parent armored divisions. This group could number up to 2,000 or more trained soldiers and officers. A group of cadre officers would then attend the New Divisions Course to learn the basics of organizing and operating a combat division. Following the cadre's formation, the division would be activated and brought up to authorized strength primarily with recruits. Most often, the new recruits would receive their basic and individual training with the new division. As the recruits became more proficient and their new units gained experience, training would expand to include larger unit exercises. After the division was considered trained, then oftentimes, a cadre would be extracted to form another armored division and the process would repeat.[8]

So it was for the 16th Armored Division. On 2 April 1943, the Adjutant General's Office of the War Department issued the Activation Orders for the 16th Armored Division. Per orders, the division would be activated on 15 July 1943 at Camp Chaffee, Arkansas, under the authority of the Chief of the Armored Force. Responsibility for providing the Division Cadre and a Supply Battalion was primarily with the Chief of the Armored Force. The Chief of Finance was directed to send a Finance Cadre of ten enlisted finance specialists from the 10th Armored Division on or about 15 April 1943. The Chief of Ordnance would provide personnel for the new division's Maintenance Battalion, which was to arrive at Camp Chaffee on 15 July 1943. The Postal Cadre would arrive at Camp Chaffee on 8 June 1943. The Bands of the 144th and 195th Field Artillery Regiments would relocate to Camp Chaffee on or about 10 July 1943. Upon activation of the 16th Armored Division, these bands would be de-activated and their personnel and equipment would become part of the Bands of the 5th and 16th Armored Regiments respectively. The remaining enlisted personnel to bring the division up to authorized strength would come from the Chief of the Armored Force and Army Ground Forces.[9]

Camp Chaffee was chosen to be the location for the activation of the U.S. Army's newest armored division. Camp Chaffee was a massive U.S. Army facility in northwest Arkansas not far from Fort Smith. The camp comprised 75,028 acres and could accommodate 2,491 officers and 41,330 enlisted soldiers. Camp Chaffee was primarily used by the Armored Force to activate and train armored divisions for war. The 6th Armored Division had trained here for much of 1942 and the 14th Armored Division had been activated here on 15 November 1942.[10]

Brig. Gen. Douglas T. Greene was selected as the new division's first commanding general. Greene was a graduate of the U.S. Military Academy Class of 1913 and had served as President of his class. In 1934, he was named as a Professor of Military Science and Tactics and Commandant of the Army Reserve Officer Training Corps (ROTC) program at the Drexel Institute of Technology (later Drexel University).[11]

A cadre staff was formed for the 16th Armored Division utilizing personnel drawn from various other commands. The cadre staff included Col. Richard A. Gordon as Division Chief of Staff, Maj. Ralph W. Gontrum as Assistant Chief of Staff G-1 (Personnel), Lt. Col. H. P. Holz as Assistant Chief of Staff G-2 (Intelligence), Lt. Col. James I. King as Assistant Chief of Staff G-3 (Operations), Lt. Col. Clealon V. Grafton as Assistant Chief of Staff G-4 (Logistics) and Maj. William W. Smith, Jr., as Division Engineer.[12]

Maj. Ralph W. Gontrum was assigned as the Cadre Assistant Chief of Staff, G-1 (Personnel). Gontrum had much experience with armored forces. In 1940, he had served as a Platoon Leader in the 1st Armored Division at Fort Knox, Kentucky and had taken a motorcycle operations class there with Maj. Gen. Adna Chaffee, Commanding General of the Armored Force. Later assigned to the 6th Armored Division, Maj. Gontrum was serving in California when he received orders transferring him to the cadre of the 16th Armored Division.[13]

Maj. William W. Smith, Jr., joined the 16th Armored Division as the Division Engineer Officer.

A 1938 graduate of the U.S. Military Academy, Smith had extensive experience with armored divisions. "You name an armored division and I was in it," he later recalled. "I was almost a professional cadre man." Smith was first assigned to the 2nd Armored Division's 2nd Armored Brigade in the summer of 1940. His brigade commander was Col. George S. Patton, Jr. Years later, Smith recalled his first encounter with Patton. Smith was with a group of the division's officers at a training class.

Patton walked out onto the stage and began his class by saying: "I was inspecting the guard the other night and I said 'Soldier, what's that rifle for?' And he said 'Sir, it's to walk guard with.' And I said, 'No, it's to shoot some son of a bitch in his guts before he can shoot you.'"

"And that was one session we all stayed awake through," Smith said. "That was our introduction to Patton and whatever else Patton was, he was a great actor."[14]

Smith remained with the 2nd Armored Division until he was transferred to the 3rd Armored Division in 1941. Later that year, he was transferred to the 5th Armored Division to help organize it. In 1942, he served with first the 8th Armored Division and then the 10th Armored Division. In 1943, he was assigned to the 12th Armored Division before finally being assigned to the newly activated 16th Armored Division.[15]

The other members of the 16th Armored Division cadre were primarily drawn from the 4th and 20th Armored Divisions. They also assembled at Camp Chaffee, Arkansas in the early summer of 1943. The cadre set up the administrative, logistics and training mechanisms for the divisions. The cadre brought with them much experience which they would impart to the new recruits. For instance, Maj. William Smith had previously helped organize six other armored divisions. When new recruits began arriving, the cadre then began training and integrating them into the new armored division. Unlike earlier armored divisions, the 16th Armored Division was not called upon to provide trained soldiers and officers for cadres to organize subsequent armored divisions because none were formed afterwards. However, the division would be called upon to provide combat replacements for other divisions once the European Campaign began in the summer of 1944.[16]

The 16th Armored Division was the sixteenth and final armored division activated for World War II. A total of twenty armored divisions were originally envisioned for wartime service. For reasons that are unclear, the U.S. Army did not activate the 15th, 17th, 18th and 19th Armored Divisions, and activated the 20th Armored Division on 15 March 1943 four months before activating the 16th Armored Division. The 16th Armored Division was one of seventeen divisions activated in 1943 and one of three activated on 15 July—the others being the 10th Light and 71st Light Divisions.[17]

Activation

The 16th Armored Division was officially activated in a ceremony held on 15 July 1943 at Camp Chaffee in the vicinity of Roberts Boulevard and 9th Avenue. The day was already very hot and humid when the ceremony commenced at 1000 in the morning. Col. Ralph W. Gontrum later described the activation ceremony:

> Following the arrival of the Division Commander, General Douglass T. Greene and party, and the presentation of troops, the Division Chaplain, Father Walsh, gave the Invocation. Major Schulten, Division Adjutant General read the Activation Order, then General Greene accepted command of the newly activated 16th ARMORED DIVISION. The Adjutant General read the order announcing the appointment of the staff. Next came the Presentation of colors and the National Anthem. Father Walsh gave the convocation and the colorful activation ceremony was over.[18]

As per the March 1942 the Table of Organization and Equipment, the 16th Armored Division was organized as a "heavy" armored division. The new 16th Armored Division had a Division Headquarters, two Combat Command Headquarters (A and B), the 5th and 16th Armored Regiments, and the 476th Armored Infantry Regiment. Each armored regiment consisted of a light tank battalion and two medium tank battalions. The Armored Infantry Regiment had three armored infantry battalions. Fire support was provided by the division's three artillery battalions: 393rd, 396th and 397th Armored Field Artillery Battalions. Other supporting units included the 96th Armored Reconnaissance Battalion, the 216th Armored Engineer Battalion and the Division Trains. The Division Trains consisted of the 137th Ordnance Battalion (Armored), a Supply Battalion and the 216th Armored Medical Battalion. The Division Headquarters Company operated the Division's Headquarters and had the Command and General Staff Section, Combat Command A Headquarters, Combat Command B Headquarters, Division Artillery, Chemical Warfare and Medical Detachment attached to it for administrative, mess and quartering purposes. The Table of Organization for the new division was thus as follows:

Division Headquarters
Combat Command Headquarters A
Combat Command Headquarters B
5th Armored Regiment
16th Armored Regiment
476th Armored Infantry Regiment
96th Armored Reconnaissance Battalion
216th Armored Engineers Battalion
216th Armored Medical Battalion
393rd Armored Field Artillery Battalion
396th Armored Field Artillery Battalion
397th Armored Field Artillery Battalion
137th Ordnance Battalion (Armored)
Supply Battalion
Signal Company (Armored)[19]

The key officers and staff of the new 16th Armored Division were:

Commanding General	Brig. Gen. Douglass T. Greene
Chief of Staff	Col. Richard A. Gordon
Assistant Chief of Staff, G-1 (Personnel)	Maj. Ralph W. Gontrum
Assistant Chief of Staff, G-2 (Intelligence)	Lt. Col. H. P. Holz
Assistant Chief of Staff, G-3 (Operations)	Lt. Col. James I. King
Assistant Chief of Staff, G-4 (Logistics)	Lt. Col. Clealon V. Grafton
Division Trains Commander	Col. C. H. Calais
Division Artillery Commander	Col. David G. Erskine

Adjutant	Maj. Leo E. Schulten
Division Chaplain	Maj. Eugene P. Walsh
Commander, 5th Armored Regiment	Col. Gerald B. Devore
Commander, 16th Armored Regiment	Col. Charles V. Bromley
Commander, 476th Armored Infantry Regiment	Lt. Col. William V. Gray
Commander, 393rd Armored Field Artillery Battalion	Maj. Herbert W. Semmelmeyer
Commander, 396th Armored Field Artillery Battalion	Maj. Mont Hubbard
Commander, 397th Armored Field Artillery Battalion	Maj. William D. Morgan (Lt. Col. Charles A. Symroski)[20]
Commander, 216th Armored Engineer Battalion	Maj. William W. Smith, Jr.
Commander, 137th Armored Ordnance Battalion	Lt. Col. Edward K. Purnell
Commander, 216th Armored Medical Battalion	Maj. Richard H. Ray
Commander, Supply Battalion	Maj. Philip E. Ware
Commander, 156th Signal Company	Capt. Stanley F. Ustach[21]

The 16th Armored Division was officially activated as a combat division of the United States Army but it was far from ready for combat. For starters, the division consisted only of the cadre at this point. Over the following weeks, the division would build upon this basic framework set up by the cadre. Every day, numerous new soldiers joined the division, many of whom had been civilians only a few weeks before. These soldiers were quickly integrated into the division's various units and basic training begun in earnest.

Col. Gerald B. Devore was commander of the 5th Armored Regiment. The 35th Tank Regiment of the 4th Armored Division provided the officers for the cadre responsible for organizing and training the new regiment. Most of the cadre's enlisted soldiers came from the 20th Armored Division.[22]

The 16th Armored Regiment was commanded by Col. Charles V. Bromley. The cadre for the regiment was drawn from the 195th Field Artillery Regiment, the 11th Armored Corps and the 20th Armored Regiment of the 20th Armored Division. The latter had only been activated the previous March.[23]

3rd Battalion, 476th Armored Infantry Regiment was activated at this time under the command of Maj. T. W. Drobek. At the time of activation, the battalion numbered eight officers and 126 enlisted men. The enlisted members of the cadre were drawn from the 20th Armored Division; the officers were from the 4th Armored Division.[24]

Reorganization

The 16th Armored Division had only been in existence for a couple of months when the U.S. Army Ground Forces implemented another major re-organization of its armored divisions. Beginning in September 1943, all but the 2nd and 3rd Armored Divisions were re-organized as "light" armored divisions using a new Table of Organization adopted that month. On 1 September 1943, Headquarters, Army Ground Forces issued "Memorandum for the Adjutant General, 322/5 (16 Armd Div)(R), dated 1 Sep 43, subject: "Reorganization of the 16th Armored Division." Accordingly two days later, the Division Headquarters issued its own memorandum to implement the division's re-organization per direction from Headquarters, Army Ground Forces.[25]

The 16th Armored Division began its re-organization immediately. On 3 September, the 5th Armored Regiment was broken up; its subordinate units were similarly re-organized and then reassigned. The 1st Battalion, 5th Armored Regiment became the 717th Tank Battalion and was relieved from assignment to the 16th Armored Division. That battalion would subsequently deploy to the European Theater and see combat with the 79th Infantry Division in Germany. The 2nd Battalion, 5th Armored Regiment and the Regiment Headquarters became the 5th Tank Battalion. 3rd Battalion, 5th Armored Regiment became the 26th Tank Battalion. The Reconnaissance Company became Troop D, 23rd Cavalry Squadron. The 5th and 26th Tank Battalions and Troop D all remained with the 16th Armored Division. The 5th Armored Regiment's Maintenance and Service Companies and its Band were all disbanded and their personnel reassigned elsewhere.[26]

The new 717th Tank Battalion underwent its own transformation several weeks later. Two of its light tank companies became medium tank companies. Lt. Col. Raymond W. Odor was placed in command of the new battalion. For the next several weeks, the new battalion remained attached to the 16th Armored Division for training and administration while it absorbed new personnel and filled out its ranks. Then in April 1944, the battalion was transferred to Fort Knox, Kentucky.[27]

On 10 September 1943, the 16th Armored Regiment was deactivated and its components reassigned and re-designated. The regimental headquarters and 1st and 2nd Battalions became the 16th Tank Battalion. The

3rd Battalion became the 787th Tank Battalion and was relieved of assignment to the 16th Armored Division. That battalion would deploy to France in March 1945 and would be briefly attached to the 86th Infantry Division during its drive into Austria. The regiment's Reconnaissance Company became Troop E of the newly activated 23rd Cavalry Squadron. The Regimental Band, Maintenance Company and Service Company were all disbanded and their personnel reassigned.[28]

As part of the division's re-organization, the 476th Armored Infantry Regiment was broken up on 10 September 1943. 1st Battalion became the 64th Armored Infantry Battalion. 2nd Battalion became the 69th Armored Infantry Battalion. 3rd Battalion and the remainder of the regiment became the 18th Armored Infantry Battalion.[29]

On 10 September 1943, the 96th Armored Reconnaissance Battalion became the 23rd Cavalry Reconnaissance Squadron [Mechanized]. In addition, two new units were added to the squadron. The 5th Armored Regiment's Reconnaissance Company became Troop D of the 23rd Cavalry and the 16th Armored Regiment's Reconnaissance Company became Troop E of the 23rd Cavalry.[30]

The new Table of Organization for armored engineer battalions eliminated Companies D and E (the treadway bridge company). Accordingly, the 216th Armored Engineers Battalion lost its Companies D and E. Company D was transferred to the Armored Command. Company E became the 998th Engineer Treadway Bridge Company and was attached to Second U.S. Army. Interestingly enough, the 998th Bridge Company would deploy to Europe before its former parent battalion and division.[31]

The 216th Armored Medical Battalion, the 137th Armored Ordnance Battalion, and the 393rd, 396th and 397th Armored Field Artillery Battalions remained intact during the re-organization.[32]

Altogether, the 16th Armored Division lost thirteen of its units through either transfer or deactivation. The Supply Battalion, Companies D and E of the 216th Armored Engineer Battalion, 1st Battalion / 5th Armored Regiment (aka 717th Tank Battalion), and 3rd Battalion / 16th Armored Regiment (787th Tank Battalion) were transferred from the division. The Headquarters, Maintenance and Service Companies, and Regimental Bands of the 5th and 16th Armored Regiments were deactivated and their personnel reassigned.[33]

In addition, the 16th Armored Division activated three new units: Military Police Platoon, Headquarters Reserve Command and Division Band. The Division Band was formed from the personnel and equipment of the deactivated 5th and 16th Armored Regiment Bands.[34]

After re-organization as a "light" armored division, the 16th Armored Division had an authorized strength of 594 commissioned officers, 53 warrant officers, and 10,293 enlisted soldiers. The new division's new Table of Organization was as follows:

Division Headquarters and Headquarters Company
Headquarters and Headquarters Company / Combat Command A
Headquarters and Headquarters Company / Combat Command B
Headquarters and Headquarters Company / Combat Command R
Headquarters / 16th Armored Division Artillery
Headquarters and Headquarters Company / 16th Armored Division Trains
5th Tank Battalion
16th Tank Battalion
26th Tank Battalion
18th Armored Infantry Battalion
64th Armored Infantry Battalion
69th Armored Infantry Battalion
393rd Armored Field Artillery Battalion
396th Armored Field Artillery Battalion
397th Armored Field Artillery Battalion
23rd Cavalry Reconnaissance Squadron
516th Counterintelligence Corps Detachment
216th Armored Medical Battalion
137th Armored Ordnance Maintenance Battalion
Military Police Platoon
216th Armored Engineer Battalion
156th Armored Signal Company[35]

At the head of this complicated fighting organization were the Commanding General and his Staff. The General's Staff included a Chief of Staff, and several Assistant Chiefs of Staff: G-1 (Personnel), G-2 (Intelligence), G-3 (Operations and Training), G-4 (Logistics), and G-5 (Civil Affairs). There was also a Division Adjutant General, Chaplain, and Division Medical Officer.

The Division Headquarters Company assisted the Commanding General and his Staff in the administration, training and operations of the 16th Armored Division. This company had a Headquarters Section, Maintenance Section, Command Vehicle Section, Traffic Control Section, Transportation Platoon, and an Administration, Mess and Supply (AM&S) Section.[36]

During this re-organization, Combat Command A and Combat Command B headquarters sections were removed from administrative control of the Headquarters Company and constituted as separate headquarters for their commands. The following February, Division Artillery became its own command headquarters as well.[37]

Combat Commands A, B and Reserve

When all of the re-organizations had been completed, the 16th Armored Division had five Commands to conduct its operations: Combat Commands A, B and Reserve, Division Artillery, and Division Trains. Combat Commands A, B and Reserve were the maneuver commands. Each had a Headquarters Company permanently assigned to it. Tank, armored infantry and armored artillery battalions were assigned as needed along with detachments of armored engineers, armored ordnance, armored medical, tank destroyer, anti-aircraft artillery and other supporting units.[38]

For much of its existence, Combat Command B (CCB) was led by Col. Charles Henry Noble, Jr. He was born on 30 October 1898 in Boise Barracks, Idaho to Charles H. and Mary Palmer Noble. His father was a brigadier general in the U.S. Army. He was raised and educated in Indianapolis, Indiana, and then attended Columbia Preparatory School in Washington, D.C. After receiving an at large presidential appointment, Noble attended the U.S. Military Academy and was graduated early on 1 November 1918. A month later, he returned to West Point as a second lieutenant and served there until June 1919. In 1922, Noble was one of the founding members of the United States Army Automobile Association, which two years later became United Services Automobile Association (USAA). In the post–World War I Army, promotions came slow and so Noble did not reach the rank of captain until 1 August 1935. He completed the U.S. Army Command and General Staff School in 1938. Noble was an accomplished horseman, polo player and competitive jump rider. He completed the U.S. Army Cavalry School Basic Equestrian Course in 1919 and the Advanced Equestrian Course in 1932. When the U.S. entered World War II in December 1941, Lt. Col. Noble was serving in a staff logistics position with the War Department. On 7 July 1942, he was assigned as a battalion commander with the 8th Armored Division. He was later promoted to colonel and placed in command of the division's 80th Armored Regiment. During his tenure, he oversaw the movement of the regiment first from Fort Knox, Kentucky to Camp Campbell, Kentucky, and then from Camp Campbell to North Camp Polk, Louisiana. In the summer of 1943, he was reassigned to the newly activated 16th Armored Division.[39]

The armored striking power of the 16th Armored Division was provided by its three tank battalions: the 5th, 16th and 26th. Each battalion consisted of a Headquarters Company, three medium tank companies (A, B, and C), a light tank company (D), and a Service Company. Each tank company had eighteen tanks including one that mounted a 105mm howitzer in place of the normal 75mm or 76mm gun. Including tanks serving with the Battalion Headquarters, a tank battalion had an authorized strength of 59 medium tanks and 17 light tanks.[40]

In reorganizing the U.S. armored division, Army leaders had greatly increased the number of the division's infantrymen and organized them into three armored infantry battalions. Each battalion consisted of a Headquarters Company, three Rifle Companies, and a Service Company and had an authorized strength of 1,001 soldiers. The Headquarters Company included the Battalion Reconnaissance Platoon, Mortar Platoon, Machine Gun Platoon and Assault Gun Platoon. The armored infantry rode into battle in half-tracks—a hybrid armored vehicle that had front wheels for steering, tracks in the rear for propulsion, an armored cab for the driver

Armored half-tracks were used to perform a variety of tasks in an armored division, including carrying armored infantry into battle (author's photograph).

and co-driver up front and an armored section in the rear of the vehicle to carry soldiers, supplies and/or heavy weapons. Upon entering the battle area, the armored infantrymen could either fight from the vehicle or dismount and fight on foot like traditional infantry. The 16th Armored Division's armored infantry battalions were the 18th, 64th and 69th.[41]

The 18th Armored Infantry Battalion had originally been formed as 3rd Battalion, 476th Armored Infantry Regiment on 15 July 1943. Its first battalion commander was Maj. T. W. Drobek. Its cadre was drawn from the 4th and 20th Armored Divisions. In September, 3rd Battalion, 476th Armored Infantry Regiment was re-designated and re-organized as the 18th Armored Infantry Battalion. The battalion also had a new commanding officer, as Maj. T. W. Drobek left and was replaced by Lt. Col. William H. G. Fuller on 10 September. On 22 October 1943, the first group of soldiers arrived to begin Basic Training with the battalion.[42]

Capt. Howard Painter joined the 16th Armored Division on 7 November 1943 and was initially assigned as a platoon leader with the 18th Armored Infantry Battalion's Headquarters Platoon. Not long after, the battalion's Company B was activated and Capt. Painter was placed in command. Per standard organization, Company B had four rifle platoons

This half-track has been configured to carry a quad .50 cal. machine gun mount for anti-aircraft defense (author's photograph).

and a motor pool, and was equipped with International half-tracks and machine guns. "Company B was blessed with a group of bright, dedicated soldiers who arrived from various army training centers throughout the United States," Painter later wrote.[43]

One of Company B's soldiers was Harley Barrs of Michigan. Barrs was deferred from military service because he had a job in a defense plant. Eventually he decided to enlist because many of his friends had enlisted or were drafted into military service. He was inducted into service at Fort Custer, near Battle Creek, Michigan. Initially, the induction center personnel tried to assign him to the U.S. Navy but Barrs insisted on joining the Army instead. After some initial training, Barrs was sent to Camp Chaffee where he joined the Anti-Tank Platoon of Company B, 18th Armored Infantry Battalion.[44]

Another of the 16th Armored Division's armored infantrymen was nineteen year old Private Edward Krusheski of Passaic, New Jersey. He left high school to go to work to support his mother and eight-year-old brother. On 26 May 1944, Krusheski was drafted into the Army. He completed Basic Training at Camp Wheeler, Georgia and joined the 16th Armored Division on 4 November 1944. Private Krusheski was assigned to Company A, 69th Armored Infantry Battalion.[45]

Division Artillery

The Division Artillery was originally part of the Division Headquarters Company. On 12 February 1944, Division Artillery became its own Command. Per the standard "light" armored division organization of September 1943, the 16th Armored Division included three armored field artillery battalions (AFAB): the 393rd, 396th and 397th. Each AFAB consisted of three firing batteries, a headquarters battery and a service battery. Each firing battery had six M7 self-propelled 105mm howitzers. Thus a standard armored division had a total of fifty-four M7 self-propelled howitzers for mobile artillery fire support for the division. Though standard organization assigned one AFAB to each Combat Command, overall direction of the division's artillery was performed by the Division Artillery Headquarters led by Col. David G. Erskine.[46]

The 393rd Armored Field Artillery Battalion was formed around a cadre drawn from the 412th Armored Field Artillery Battalion of the 20th Armored Division. Maj. Herbert W. Semmelmeyer was the battalion commander. Born 7 June 1900, Semmelmeyer entered the U.S. Military

The 16th Armored Division's three armored field artillery battalions were equipped with M7 self-propelled guns, which mounted a 105mm howitzer (author's photograph).

Academy in June 1917 as part of the Class of 1921 but was graduated early due to the exigencies of the First World War. Commissioned as a second lieutenant, he completed Field Artillery School in 1920 and became a battery commander. In 1922, he left the Army and entered the insurance business in California. When the U.S. entered World War II twenty years later, Semmelmeyer re-entered the Army as a field artillery officer. He subsequently served as such with the 8th and 20th Armored Divisions.[47]

The 396th Armored Field Artillery Battalion was formally activated on 15 July 1943 at Camp Chaffee. The officer cadre for the 396th Armored Field Artillery Battalion was drawn from the 4th and 9th Armored Divisions and the Field Artillery School at Fort Sill, Oklahoma. The 413th Armored Field Artillery Battalion of the 20th Armored Division provided the enlisted cadre. At the time of its activation, the battalion consisted of 37 officers and 115 enlisted men. The battalion was commanded by Maj. Mont Hubbard. He was born on 9 March 1910 in Pittsylvania County, Virginia to Mont and Emma Walker Hubbard. He was a 1932 graduate of Virginia Military Institute and a member of the Catholic faith.[48]

Private Oscar Jackson "O.J." Mooney, Jr., joined the 396th Armored Field Artillery Battalion a few weeks after its activation. He was born 2 December 1923 to Oscar Jackson Mooney, Sr., and Ettie Priscilla née McEwen on the family farm in Weogufka, Alabama. After high school, O.J. attended Alabama Polytechnic Institute (now Auburn University). Since participation was mandatory, Mooney was a member of the institute's Army Reserve Officer Training Corps (ROTC). In late winter 1943 of his freshman year of college, Mooney was drafted into the Army. Mooney's ROTC program was organized as an artillery unit, so he was sent to Fort Sill, Oklahoma for Basic Training. After completing Basic Training, Mooney was selected for the Army Specialized Training Program (ASTP). The ASTP was designed to train soldiers of high aptitude for specialized skills in the Army such as engineering and foreign languages. ASTP soldiers would attend college and earn a bachelor's degree in 18 months. O.J. Mooney, however, was not interested. "I was 21 years old and eager to be in the service," he later recalled. "I told the First Sergeant but it didn't make any difference." Against his wishes, Private Mooney was sent before a board of officers for selection into the ASTP. When the major in charge of the board suggested that he study engineering in the ASTP, Private Mooney replied that he'd prefer the infantry instead. Not long after, he was transferred to Camp Chaffee where he joined the 396th Armored Field Artillery Battalion.[49]

At the time of its activation, the 397th Armored Field Artillery Battalion's commander was Maj. William D. Morgan. His tenure was brief, however, as Lt. Col. Charles A. Symroski assumed command of the battalion the very next day. The battalion cadre was 54 officers and 115 enlisted soldiers drawn primarily from Camp Campbell and Fort Knox, both of which were located in Kentucky.[50]

Lt. Col. Charles A. Symroski was originally from Braddock, Pennsylvania. He graduated from the U.S. Military Academy as part of the Class of 1935 and was commissioned into the Field Artillery Branch. His first assignment was as a battery officer in the 84th Field Artillery Regiment at Fort Riley, Kansas. Later, he served at the Field Artillery School at Fort Sill Oklahoma first as a student and then as an instructor. He married Ann Rolfe in December 1942. After commanding pack artillery battalions at the Mountain Training Center in Colorado, Symroski was transferred to the 16th Armored Division to assume command of the 397th Armored Field Artillery Battalion.[51]

Division Artillery underwent a major organizational change on 17 March 1944 when Headquarters Battery was created. This new battery consisted of a Communications Platoon with a Message Center, Radio Section and a Wire Section, an Operations Platoon, a Meteorological Section, a Maintenance Section, a Survey Section, an armorer, two medics, a chaplain's assistant and two pilots for its L-4B light aircraft. A militarized version of the Piper Cub airplane, the L-4B was used for fire direction, artillery spotting and reconnaissance. Col. Erskine remained as Division Artillery Commander with Lt. Col. Barry D. Browne as his Executive Officer and Capt. Morris H. Stolz as Headquarters Battery Commander.[52]

Division Trains

The Division Trains Command provided the logistical support for the 16th Armored Division. Division Trains consisted of a Headquarters and Headquarters Company, a Military Police Platoon, the 137th Armored Ordnance Maintenance Battalion, and the 216th Armored Medical Battalion. Typically detachments from the latter two would be attached to the Combat Commands for operations. The Headquarters Company for the Division Trains was formed by a cadre of soldiers from the 4th and 20th Armored Divisions.[53]

Having over 2,650 armored vehicles and other vehicles, an armored division such as the 16th needed a good many soldiers to maintain and repair these vehicles. The 137th Armored Ordnance Battalion was the unit assigned to the 16th Armored Division to perform maintenance and repair of the division's vehicles. The battalion consisted of a Headquarters Company, and three Ordnance Maintenance Companies. Each Ordnance Maintenance Company had a Service and Supply Platoon, an Armament Platoon and an Automotive Platoon. Thus organized, the battalion could repair and maintain diverse items, from rifles to large trucks. The 137th Armored Ordnance Battalion was unique in that many of its original members had experience in the automotive industry prior to the war. The U.S. Army actively recruited such men for their automotive and mechanical skills, which were greatly needed to maintain the thousands of vehicles operated by armored divisions.[54]

The 137th Armored Ordnance Battalion had been established on 7 October 1942 at Camp Perry, Ohio. Since most of its members had little or no military training, the battalion first instituted Basic Training for these new soldiers. In July 1943, the battalion relocated to Camp Chaffee, Arkansas and became part of the newly activated 16th Armored Division. After Basic Training, the battalion's soldiers were sent to specialist schools or schools for advanced technical training required for the maintenance of the division's wide range of equipment, vehicles and weapons.[55]

One of 137th Armored Ordnance Battalion's vehicle maintenance soldiers was George Thompson. Originally from a farm in Kansas, Thompson joined the Army after graduating from high school in June 1943. After Basic Training, he completed vehicle maintenance school at Fort Knox, Kentucky and became proficient in repairing both wheeled vehicles and tracked armored vehicles. In December 1943, Thompson joined the 16th Armored Division and was assigned to Company C of the 137th Armored Ordnance Battalion in December 1943 as a wheeled vehicle mechanic.[56]

Also with the 137th Armored Ordnance Battalion was Verne Lewellen. Originally from the small town of Minatore in western Nebraska, Lewellen attempted to enlist in the Army Air Force and the Navy several times but was rejected for poor eyesight and being underage. In May 1943, he enlisted in the Army. He completed Basic Training and Mechanics School at Fort Knox, Kentucky. He was assigned to 16th Armored Division and became a parts clerk for the 137th Armored Ordnance Battalion.[57]

The 216th Armored Medical Battalion provided medical and casualty treatment support for the 16th Armored Division. The battalion consisted of a Headquarters Company, and three Armored Medical Companies. Each Armored Medical Company had a Company Headquarters, a Collecting Platoon and a Clearing Platoon.[58]

Other Divisional Units

Several other units were directly responsible to the Division Headquarters. Their components were attached to the Combat Commands as needed. Specifically they were the 216th Armored Engineer Battalion, the 23rd Cavalry Reconnaissance Squadron [Mechanized] and the 156th Armored Signal Company.

The 216th Armored Engineer Battalion provided combat engineer support for the 16th Armored Division. Its principal mission was to use engineer skills and equipment to facilitate the rapid movement of the armored division. Its tasks included reconnoitering roads and bridges, constructing and improving bridges and fords, constructing and removing obstacles, supporting assaults on fortifications and employing demolitions. The battalion was equipped and trained to fight as infantry if needed. Transportation for the battalion was provided by half-tracks, trucks and peeps.[59]

The 216th Armored Engineers Battalion was activated as part of the 16th Armored Division's activation on 15 July 1943. As organized, the battalion consisted of a Headquarters and Headquarters Company, four line companies (A, B, C, D) and a Treadway Bridge Company (E). The initial cadre was comprised of 100 officers and enlisted soldiers drawn from the 24th Armored Engineer Battalion, of the 4th Armored Division, 53rd Armored Engineer Battalion of the 8th Armored Division, the 220th Armored Engineer Battalion of the 20th Armored Division and the Armored Force School at Fort Knox, Kentucky. Maj. William W. Smith, Jr., was the battalion commander and Capt. "Shorty" Barrett was the Executive Officer. This cadre would be responsible for setting up the battalion and training and equipping the approximately 900 new soldiers who would be joining the battalion in the coming weeks to bring it up to authorized strength. During the September 1943 division reorganization, the battalion lost its Company D and Company E (Treadway Bridge).[60]

Around the first of August, a group of fifty new 2nd lieutenants joined the 216th Armored Engineer Battalion. They had just graduated from the Engineer Officer Candidate School at Fort Belvoir, Virginia. They were immediately distributed amongst the battalion's six companies. For a time, officers outnumbered enlisted in the battalion.[61]

In early 1944, 2nd Lt. Charles T. Schaeffer joined the 216th Armored Engineer Battalion. He was born on 10 July 1918 and raised in the Catholic faith in Milwaukee, Wisconsin. After graduating from Washington High School, he worked as a salesman selling commercial hardware for five years and was married to his wife Joyce. On 17 March 1943, Schaeffer enlisted in the Army as a volunteer Officer Candidate. Following Basic Training, he completed Officer Candidate School and was commissioned as a 2nd lieutenant in the anti-aircraft artillery in December 1943. Soon after, he was reassigned as an engineer officer and sent to Fort Belvoir, Virginia for engineer training. After completing engineer training, he was assigned to 216th Armored Engineers of 16th Armored Division. Upon arriving at the 216th Armored Engineer Battalion, 2nd Lt. Schaeffer was assigned to the Headquarters Company as Battalion Adjutant.[62]

The 216th Armored Engineer Battalion spent the rest of the summer and fall of 1943 training and incorporating the new joins. By October, the battalion was up to full strength. A great many of these new joins were new to the Army. The Division G-1 Officer and Adjutant General sought to place the new soldiers in units that best utilized their civilian occupational skills. Thus, soldiers who had civilian experience in the construction trades and heavy equipment operations oftentimes were assigned to the 216th Armored Engineers.[63]

Coordinating the operations of the division required a robust and efficient communications system. The 156th Armored Signal Company ensured that the 16th Armored Division had such a communications system. The company had a Company Headquarters, a Radio Platoon with medium and high power radio systems, and an Operations Platoon with a Message Center Section and a Wire Section. At the time of its activation, Lt. Col. Richard King was the Division Signal Officer and Capt. Frank Durham was commander of the 156th Armored Signal Company.[64]

Privates Solomon Polish and Herman Groff's journey to the 16th Armored Division began at Camp Funston, a sub-unit of Fort Riley, Kansas where both served in the 2nd Signal Company in 1941. The following year they were sent with a group to join the new 8th Armored Division at Fort Knox, Kentucky. While with the 8th Armored Division, Polish was promoted to staff sergeant and Groff was promoted to corporal. After several months with the 8th Armored Division, Polish and Groff were transferred again to help organize the new 20th Armored Division's 160th Armored Signal Company at Camp Campbell, Kentucky. Their stay with the 20th Armored Division was short-lived, however. In July 1943, Staff Sgt. Polish and Corp. Groff joined a cadre of ten officers and forty-two enlisted men to form the 156th Armored Signal Company of the new 16th Armored Division at Camp Chaffee, Arkansas. Polish became Division Message Center Chief with Groff serving as Assistant Chief. Later Polish would be promoted to Warrant Officer. In three short years, Polish and Groff helped organize signal companies in three different armored divisions.[65]

The 156th Armored Signal Company began with ten officers and forty-two enlisted men. Over the coming months, new soldiers were added to the company from fourteen military installations including Fort Bragg, North Carolina, Fort Dix, New Jersey, and Fort Meade, Maryland. Eventually, the company reached its authorized strength of 11 officers, three warrant officers, and 279 enlisted men.[66]

The 23rd Cavalry Reconnaissance Squadron (Mechanized) provided the Division Commanding General with a flexible, multi-function light armored force that could perform reconnaissance, and screening, offensive and defensive operations. The Squadron had a Headquarters, a Service Troop, three or four Reconnaissance Troops, a Light Tank Company, and an Assault Gun Troop. The Reconnaissance Troops (A, B, C and D) consisted of M8 armored cars, jeeps, and half-tracks. The Light Tank Company (F) was equipped with M24 light tanks. The Assault Gun Troop (E) was equipped with jeeps, half-tracks and M8 assault guns with turret-mounted 75mm howitzers.[67]

After experiencing combat in Europe, Capt. Howard P. Schaudt would later write about the effectiveness of the M8 armored car and the M24 light tank. "The M8 armored car is definitely a poor vehicle for pursuit operations as it is extremely road bound," he wrote in a paper while a student at the U.S. Infantry School's Advanced Officers Course. "The M24 light tank is an excellent vehicle for pursuit operations as it has fire power, maneuverability, speed and affords protection to the crew from small arms fire."[68]

Lt. Col. Raymond C. Adkisson would command the 23rd Cavalry during the European Campaign. Born on 6 June 1910 in Tennessee, Adkisson enlisted in the U.S. Army. In 1931, he was serving as a private in the 4th Field Artillery Battalion at Fort Robinson in northwestern Nebraska when he was selected to take the entrance exam for the U.S. Military Academy. He passed the exam and entered West Point as a cadet in 1931. He graduated from USMA with the Class of 1935 and was commissioned as a second lieutenant of cavalry. In 1938–1939, 1st Lt. Adkisson completed the Regular Course at the U.S. Army Infantry School at Fort Benning, Georgia. As part of his course study, he wrote a paper entitled *Night Marches: Action of Australian and Indian Units, Battle of Sari Bair (Gallipoli) 6–7 August 1915*, in which he critiqued a key Allied attack during the failed Gallipoli invasion in Turkey during World War I.[69]

Mark Steece served as Armorer for the Squadron's Troop B. He was born in 1924 in Parker, South Dakota. He was the oldest of four boys. His mother was a housewife; his father worked in an automotive mechanics shop. While in elementary school, the Steece family moved to Sioux Falls, South Dakota. In high school, he played basketball. After graduating from high school in June 1942, Steece originally wanted to attend college but expecting to be drafted, he decided to get a job instead. Nearly a year later, Steece was drafted in May of 1943 and sent to Fort Knox, Kentucky for Basic Training. After Basic Training, he was selected for the Army Specialized Training Program (ASTP). Steece worked around Fort Knox for several weeks with other ASTP selectees awaiting assignment to a college. But the Army decided instead to cut back on the program, so Steece and 20 other ASTP selectees were sent to Camp Chaffee in October 1943 to join the new 16th Armored Division. He was assigned to the 23rd Cavalry Squadron's Troop B. A month later, Steece was sent back to Fort Knox to attend Armorer School. Six weeks later, he completed Armorer School and returned to Troop B where he became an armorer in the Troop's Maintenance Section. As such, Steece was responsible for maintaining and repairing the Troop's weapons, primarily its Browning thirty-caliber and M2 fifty-caliber machine guns. "I spent a lot of time working with machine guns," Steece later recalled. "The biggest problem was keeping the Browning thirty-calibers firing in time."[70]

Included among the Special Troops assigned to the Division Headquarters was the Division's Military Police Platoon. During World War II, Military Policemen serving with combat units performed a wide variety of security and policing tasks including traffic control, rear area security and guarding prisoners of war. At its activation, the MP Platoon consisted of just three lieutenants and eleven enlisted soldiers. Building up the platoon took some time. By late October, the platoon had 48 enlisted soldiers and by January 1944, the platoon was up to 88 enlisted soldiers.[71]

Pfc. Charles R. Lemmons was one of the MPs assigned to the 16th Armored Division. Born on 1 March 1914 in Norwood, Ohio, his family moved first to Grayville, Illinois and then settled in Covington, Kentucky. After graduating from Holmes High School in 1932, Lemmons was employed in steel and iron work and later with a sign company. He married the former Pauline Juegl at St. Augustine Catholic Church on 3 August 1940. They had a son Robert three years later. In 1943, Lemmons received his draft notice. On 1 August 1943, he joined the Covington Police Department. Six weeks later, he was inducted into the Army and subsequently assigned as a Military Policeman with the 16th Armored Division at Camp Chaffee. "Aside from being away from his wife and son, Daddy enjoyed the physical side of basic training and all the 'problems they were given to resolve,'" his daughter Kathy Lemmons Hoffman later wrote.[72]

During its operations in the European Theater, the 16th Armored Division would have various units attached to it to assist in the accomplishment of its missions. These units included the 633rd Tank Destroyer Battalion (Self-Propelled), the 571st Anti-Aircraft Artillery (Automatic Weapons) Battalion (Self-Propelled), a platoon of the 994th Engineer Treadway Bridge Company, and Battery B of the 987th Field Artillery Battalion (155mm Gun).

Having spent several months organizing and then re-organizing itself, the 16th Armored Division set out in earnest to train its new members and prepare for war.

2

Training for War

Organizing, training and equipping a combat division for war was a tremendous undertaking. When the United States entered World War II on 7 December 1941, the U.S. Army had 38 divisions in existence, most of which were mobilized National Guard divisions. By war's end, the United States had 90 Army divisions. All but three of the Army's divisions deployed and saw combat. Though many of these divisions were mobilized National Guard or Army Reserve divisions, many more like the 16th Armored Division had to be created to meet wartime needs.

The 16th Armored Division was formed and trained for war at Camp Chaffee, Arkansas and spent most of its existence here. Located near the city of Fort Smith in northwestern Arkansas, Camp Chaffee was established in the fall of 1941. In addition to the 16th Armored Division, the 6th and 14th Armored Divisions also trained here at different times. The camp was named for Maj. Gen. Adna R. Chaffee, one of the U.S. Army's pioneers in the development of armored vehicles.

The 16th Armored Division spent the next year and a half training at Camp Chaffee and preparing itself for eventual deployment to the European Theater. The division was formed around a cadre of experienced officers and enlisted men gathered together from various other active units. Throughout the summer and fall of 1943, the division began to take shape as new members joined daily from other units and directly from recruit training centers. Since the majority of these new recruits had little or no military training, the division and its subordinate units conducted Basic Training for them.[1]

During its many months of preparation for war, the 16th Armored Division's soldiers went through six phases of training. The first phase was Basic Training of new recruits by the cadre members. During this phase, the new recruits were trained in the basic skills required for all U.S. Army soldiers. This included marksmanship, field hygiene, basic military knowledge, first aid and physical fitness. After completing Basic Training, the soldiers moved into Individual Training to learn the specific skills required for their specific military occupations. For example, medics learned medical training, tank crewmen learned how to operate tanks, and communications operators learned about communications equipment. Following this was Unit Training at the Platoon, Company and Battalion level. During this phase, the soldiers learned to fight and operate as units. Having completed Unit Training, the division undertook Combined Training whereby its combat commands trained to integrate and operate its subordinate units. The culmination of the training was the Division Maneuvers in which the entire division conducted exercises as one combat formation. After the Division Maneuvers, the 16th Armored Division conducted Post-Maneuvers training and prepared for deployment.

In addition to organizing and equipping the division, the cadre of the 16th Armored Division was expected to train the many thousands of new soldiers who would be arriving at Camp Chaffee in just a few short months. Most of these soldiers would be only a few weeks removed from civilian life. Thus the cadre underwent an intense period of "Train the Trainer."

The experience of the 3rd Battalion, 476th Armored Infantry Regiment was typical for the division's cadre during those first hectic months of the 16th Armored Division's existence. "Although each man of the cadre had already received his basic training, it was necessary for him to thoroughly review each phase of his training to enable him to better pass on this knowledge to the new men," recorded the battalion's history. The cadre conducted firings on all of the weapons ranges, performed bivouacs and attended classes on the various subjects required for new enlistees.[2]

On 22 October 1943, the 3rd Battalion, 476th Armored Infantry Regiment (now known as the 18th Armored Infantry Battalion) received its first group of new soldiers. Most had been civilians only a few weeks before. Under the instruction of the cadre, the new soldiers learned all of the basic skills necessary for serving in the mechanized U.S. Army. These skills included weapons firing and maintenance, vehicle maintenance, land navigation, living in the field, basic tactical maneuvers, first aid, and vehicle operation.[3]

The 18th Armored Infantry Battalion completed the Basic Training of its soldiers on 18 February 1944. The battalion progressed into unit level training. "Training was hard but rewarding," recalled Capt. Howard Painter, commander of the battalion's Company B. "It was gratifying to see that we were becoming a unit capable of making a contribution to the war effort of our country."[4]

Harley Barrs joined the 16th Armored Division's 18th Armored Infantry Battalion within a few weeks of enlisting in the Army. Like a majority of the division's soldiers, he completed his basic training with his battalion. "Then our training included driving all military vehicles from jeeps to half-tracks, care and cleaning of them and the firing and cleaning of the 37mm and 75mm cannon," Barrs later wrote.[5]

During the spring and summer of 1944, the 216th Armored Engineer Battalion progressed through a training program that developed the soldiers' skills in infantry and engineering tasks. Training exercises were held for squads, platoons and companies. Company level training included constructing several kinds of bridges, road building, demolitions and mine warfare. Since the battalion's bridge company had long since been transferred to Second U.S. Army, each of the line companies had to become proficient in bridge construction.[6]

In May 1944, the 216th Armored Engineers teamed up with the Arkansas Highway Department to put their training to practical use. As

M4 Sherman Tank crosses a treadway bridge erected by 216th Armored Engineer Battalion during a training exercise at Camp Chaffee, Arkansas. This Sherman is armed with a short-barreled 75mm gun (National Archives Photo).

a result of the war's diversion of manpower and resources, the Arkansas Highway Department was hard-pressed to maintain state bridges. The Department gratefully accepted the battalion's offer to re-build some of the small fixed bridges that served secondary roads. "Each such bridge job was handled as a tactical mission," Col. William W. Smith, Jr., later wrote, "with day and night construction giving all hands a lot of practical experience in the tactics, teamwork, use of tools and logistics involved."[7]

In the midst of this training, the 216th Armored Engineers had a shuffle of commanding officers. In late spring, Lt. Col. Smith left the battalion to attend the Command and General Staff College at Fort Leavenworth, Kansas. In his absence, Maj. Glen G. McConnell ran the battalion until he, too, left to attend Command and General Staff College on 4 June 1944. The Battalion S-3, Maj. Charles R. Surbey, assumed temporary command of the battalion until Lt. Col. Smith returned at the end of June. But then Lt. Col. Smith left again, this time for a temporary assignment at Second U.S. Army Headquarters. Maj. Surbey was back in command until 15 July 1944 when Lt. Col. Charles A. Symroski arrived to assume command. A field artilleryman, Lt. Col. Symroski commanded the 216th Armored Engineers until 19 August when he was reassigned to attend the U.S. Army Command and General Staff College. Maj. Surbey re-assumed command of the battalion until Lt. Col. Smith returned.[8]

Lt. Col. Frank Houlihan of the 137th Armored Ordnance Battalion later wrote about the training that his soldiers performed at Camp Chaffee. "Long, hard hours of day and night were spent on road marches, both mounted and on foot and with full field equipment to harden the men physically," he wrote in his history of the battalion. "Interminable, exhausting hours were required on obstacle courses, crawling under barbed wire with live machine gun fire above."[9]

Even training stateside could be dangerous. On 24 November 1944, 2nd Lt. Edward R. Bowlby's platoon of the 69th Armored Infantry Battalion was conducting training in using explosives to subdue enemy pillboxes. During the exercise, a ten-pound block of explosives prematurely detonated, killing Lt. Bowlby. He left behind a wife and three young sons. In the summer of 1944, Sgt. Ebensteiner of Company C, 216th Armored Engineers was killed by an accidental explosion during a demonstration of mine warfare for other units of the division. In February 1944, 2nd Lt. Edward S. Iwan and Private William R. Ballman of the 393rd Armored Field Artillery Battalion were killed when their observation aircraft crashed.[10]

The 137th Armored Ordnance Battalion had one fatality during training at Camp Chaffee. The accident occurred while the tank recovery unit was practicing the recovery of a damaged tank.

After having successfully recovered the tank, the unit was crossing a small bridge over a deep ravine on their way back to the rear area. Unfortunately they had not checked to see if the bridge could handle the weight of the recovery vehicle and the tank. The bridge gave way and Corp. Roby Rouse was killed.[11]

As 1944 progressed, the U.S. Army in England intensified its training and planning for the upcoming invasion of Normandy. Every month, new divisions arrived in England to participate in the invasion and subsequent campaigns ashore. Finally on 6 June 1944, the Allied Expeditionary Force landed in Normandy via parachute, glider and assault craft. Though taken by surprise, the Germans reacted violently and quickly the Normandy campaign devolved into a brutal slugfest. Both the Allies and the Germans suffered heavy casualties. The U.S. Army suddenly found itself in need of replacements for the losses suffered by its combat forces in Normandy. Tens of thousands of American soldiers in stateside units were sent overseas to serve as replacements. The 16th Armored Division was one of the many stateside divisions that provided soldiers as replacements. Between April and September 1944, some 2,947 soldiers were transferred out of the 16th Armored Division and sent overseas as replacements. Capt. "Shorty" Barrett left the 216th Armored Engineers to assume command of a battalion and was replaced as Battalion Executive Officer by Maj. Jack Bernstein.[12]

Throughout 1943 and 1944, the 16th Armored Division trained for its expected deployment to the European Theater of Operations and battle against the vaunted German Army. Throughout this time, no one—not anyone in the division or the U.S. Army or certainly in Czechoslovakia—expected that they would end up in that ill-fated nation which had endured six long years of Nazi occupation.

3

Czechoslovakia's Long Years of Nazi Occupation

Bohemia is the western province of what is now the Czech Republic. To the east lies the Czech province of Moravia. To its north and west, Bohemia is bordered by Germany. Poland is located on its northeastern border and Austria is to its south. Rugged mountains and thick forests ring much of Bohemia. Along the western border with Germany is the Cesky Les or Bohemian Forest. In the midst of this ring of mountains are the middle lands of the Vltava (Moldau) River basin. There are rich farmlands and deep gorges cut by streams. Nearly all of Bohemia's streams and rivers drain into the Vltava River and thence into the Elbe River. Ultimately the Elbe River empties into the North Sea in the vicinity of Hamburg, Germany.

Interspersed with the mountains, farms and forests are small villages, towns and some large cities, many dating back to medieval times. Due to its past history, these towns and cities often have both Czech and German names. In the northwest corner is Karlsbad (Karlovy Vary in Czech) a famous spa since the 16th Century, and Eger (Cheb in Czech) near the German border. The city of Pilsen is home to the famed Skoda Works industrial complex and the birthplace of Pilsner Urquell beer. In southern Bohemia is the town of Prachtice, where St. John Neumann was raised before leaving to become a missionary in America and eventually Bishop of Philadelphia, Pennsylvania. In central Bohemia astride the Vltava River lies Prague, the historic capital of the Czech Republic and one of the great cities of Europe. Prague is also home to the Church of Our Lady of Victory, in which is kept a small wood and wax statue of the Infant Jesus wearing royal robes and a crown. Known as the Miraculous Infant of Prague, this statue had inspired great faith and devotion to Jesus for people all over the world. In southwestern Bohemia is Budweis (Ceske Budejovice in Czech), a medieval city that dates back to 1265 and is known for its lager beer.

In 1938, Bohemia was part of Czechoslovakia, a country formed in 1919 by the Allied Powers from parts of the dismantled Austria-Hungarian Empire. Czechoslovakia was formed from the lands traditionally inhabited by the Czechs and the Slovaks. The fledgling democracy also contained several distinct ethnic minority groups, most notably Hungarians, Ruthenians and nearly 3 million Germans. Almost all of these ethnic Germans resided in the mountainous region along the German border known as the Sudetenland. Most significantly, these particular Germans had never historically been a part of Germany. Besides the German minority, the Sudetenland contained Czechoslovakia's strongest border defenses and fortifications, much of which had been patterned after France's famed Maginot Line. Much of the country's natural resources were also located in the region.

The story of Bohemia's liberation must begin with its subjugation. For many years, German Führer Adolf Hitler had lusted for the rich lands of Czechoslovakia. After forcibly annexing his native Austria in March of 1938, Hitler manufactured a crisis over the Sudeten Germans and escalated tensions to a point where war seemed imminent. The crisis came to climax at the Munich Conference on 29 September 1938. During this infamous conference, British Prime Minister Neville Chamberlain, French Premier Edouard Daladier, Italian dictator Benito Mussolini and Hitler decided Czechoslovakia's fate without bothering to include either its leaders or the Soviets, who by treaty were to have come to their aid had France done so first. At Munich, Hitler got everything he wanted ... except a war.[1]

Neville Chamberlain returned to a hero's welcome in England with the "assurances" that this would be Hitler's last land grab. From a second story window at 10 Downing Street, Chamberlain triumphantly declared to the world "I believe it is peace in our time." But not everyone was convinced. In a speech given in the House of Commons, Winston Churchill declared "We have sustained a total and unmitigated defeat.... We are in the midst of a disaster of the first magnitude." He then went on to predict the total subjugation of central Europe by Nazi Germany. But few in the world were listening.[2]

U.S. diplomat George F. Kennan arrived in Prague soon after the Munich Conference. Writing in his memoirs many years later, Kennan recalled that "...one of my first impressions of the post–Munich Prague was thus the sight of crowds of people weeping, unabashedly in the streets at this death knell of the independence their country had enjoyed for a brief twenty years."[3]

Miloslava "Milka" Vildova was twelve years old during the Munich Crisis. She lived with her family in the small village of Stenovice which sat on the line between the Sudetenland and the rest of Bohemia. She later described what happened when the first German soldiers arrived to occupy her village. "Everyone disappeared behind their doors," she recalled. "The streets were deserted.... We didn't want to see them."

A month later, a triumphant, gloating Adolf Hitler arrived in the Sudetenland on a tour of his newly seized lands. In the border city of Cheb, he received a thunderous ovation from Sudeten Germans who hailed him as their liberator.

Deprived of her formidable border defenses, Czechoslovakia had only a few more months to live independently after the Germans seized the Sudetenland. Poland and Hungary quickly carved off slices of the country for themselves. In March 1939, Hitler pressed the Slovaks into declaring their independence from Prague. Adolf Hitler massed German troops on the Czechoslovak border, prompting President Edvard Benes and Foreign Minister Jan Masaryk to seek a personal meeting with the German dictator in Berlin. At 1 a.m. on the morning of 15 March, Benes and Masaryk met with Hitler and several of his generals. Hitler had no intention of negotiating over the future of the hapless republic. He announced that German troops would be occupying Bohemia and Moravia beginning at 6 a.m. that morning. He demanded that the Czechoslovak Army be disarmed and confined to their barracks and warned that any attempt at resistance would be dealt with brutally. Then he offered the two Czechoslovak leaders an opportunity to consult via phone with their Government back in Prague. In addition, Reich Minister for Air Hermann Goering warned that he had orders to use his Luftwaffe (the German Air Force) to destroy Prague if the Germans encountered any resistance. Benes and Masaryk phoned Prague to discuss the situation. Seeing no alternatives, they complied with Hitler's demands.[4]

As declared by Hitler, German troops crossed the Czechoslovak frontier at 6 a.m. At 8:30 a.m., they began arriving in Prague. A triumphant Hitler declared "Czechoslovakia has ceased to exist!"[5]

Newspaper correspondent Harold Denny was in Prague when the German troops took over the city. "Hitler's tanks and trucks and scout cars rolled into the city among the stricken populace, who could only stand and look in grief on what seemed to be the death of their country," Denny later wrote. "They gathered spontaneously in St. Wenceslas Square and sang their anthem with tears running down their faces. They went into churches and prayed."[6]

In his memoirs, George F. Kennan also described the German takeover of Prague. "The entry of the German forces into Prague on March 15 was for all of us Americans who witnessed it and who experienced the stresses and excitements of that day, a harrowing experience," he wrote. "A stream of desperate persons was by this time arriving at the Legation, and we had to post a man down at the gate to turn those away whom we did not know well." After securing the city, the Germans imposed an eight o'clock curfew for the citizens. Around midnight, Kennan and several others from the U.S. Legation drove around the city. "It was strange to see these Prague streets, usually so animated, now completely empty and deserted."[7]

President Benes and Foreign Minister Masaryk returned to Prague about 8 p.m. and immediately met with the Council of Ministers. Benes was shocked to find out from them that Hitler and his Foreign Minister Joachim von Ribbentrop had already been in Prague for some time and were in fact in the Presidential Palace at that moment.[8]

Also on that tragic date, German troops rolled into the city of Pilsen and took control. Vera Fiedlerova was fourteen years old at the time. "That day March 15, 1939 I was going to school like any other day," she later recalled. "The school was occupied by German SS and we were told to go home. Later, during the day, we saw lot of tanks with soldiers ready to shoot and everywhere were German soldiers. People were shocked."[9]

The day after the German arrival in Prague, the German Government issued a lengthy decree establishing legal requirements of the Protectorate of Bohemia and Moravia. This decree was publicly announced by Foreign Minister von Ribbentrop. In the Preamble, the Reich used distortions and outright falsehoods to justify its establishing Bohemia and Moravia as a German protectorate. Among its outrageous assertions were the claims:

- that these lands traditionally belonged to the German people
- that the Czechoslovak government had failed to organize and maintain their state and safeguard the interests of the various nationalities artificially combined into it
- that the German Reich was acting in the interests of self-preservation and of safeguarding the peace and interests of all peoples living in the region.[10]

The 16 March 1939 decree had thirteen articles covered a wide range legal issues affecting the former Czechoslovak state and the new Protectorate of Bohemia and Moravia. A Reich Protector in Bohemia and Moravia would be appointed by Hitler to ensure the execution of his policies in the Protectorate. The German inhabitants of these lands were made citizens of the Reich. The Reich guaranteed military protection to the Protectorate and assumed full authority over its foreign relations. The latter meant that the Czechoslovak state's diplomats including Foreign Minister Masaryk were no longer representatives of their nation and peoples. The Reich had the power to issue legal regulations for the Protectorate and take "measures necessary for the maintenance of security and order."[11]

The U.S. Ambassador to Czechoslovakia was Wilbur J. Carr. A former Assistant Secretary of State, Carr had been appointed to the post in July 1937 by President Roosevelt and had been serving in Prague since September of that year. During this critical time, he sent regular messages to Secretary of State Cordell Hull on the situation in the doomed country. On 19 March 1939, he reported:

> The German secret police here are making hundreds and perhaps thousands of arrests in the usual Nazi manner; the Jewish population is terrified; as are the Social Democrats and also those persons closely associated with the former regime.[12]

The United States found the German actions completely unacceptable. In light of the German takeover of Czechoslovakia, Acting Secretary of State Sumner Welles advised Carr to formally request instructions for his future role in the country. Welles then informed Carr that after receiving this request from him, the State Department would direct him to close the Legation in Prague, turn over his files to Consul Gen. Irving Linnell and return to the United States. Carr complied with this instruction in a telegram that he sent about ten hours later. "There are consequently no officials of the Czechoslovak Government to which I am accredited with whom I can maintain relations for the protection of the interests of the United States and its citizens," Ambassador Carr somberly reported.[13]

Three days later, Acting Secretary of State Sumner Welles responded to Ambassador Carr's request for instructions. "In view of the situation as set forth in your telegram of March 17th, you are directed to close the Legation at Prague; to turn over the Government building, property and archives to the Consulate General; and at your convenience to leave Prague," Welles wrote. "The President has requested me to express to you his particular appreciation of the highly distinguished service you have rendered the Government as Minister to Czechoslovakia." At 5 p.m. the next day, Ambassador Carr reported "The Legation closed today as instructed."[14]

At noon Eastern Standard Time, Acting Secretary Welles announced to the press that the U.S. Legation in Prague was closing. In addition, he sent a message to the German chargé d'affaires Hans Thomsen in Washington regarding the Reich's establishing Bohemia and Moravia as a German Protectorate. "The Government of the United States has observed that the provinces referred to are now under the *de facto* [emphasis in original] administration of the German authorities," Welles wrote. "The Government of the United States does not recognize that any legal basis exists for the status so indicated."[15]

George F. Kennan remained in Prague only a few more months after the Germans took over. In late August, he filed what was to be his last report from Prague. "Work has gone on as usual.... But all other manifestations of human activity seem afflicted by a strange lethargy, almost a paralysis," he wrote. "Everything is in suspense. No one takes initiative; no one plans for the future. Cultural life and amusements continue in a half-hearted, mechanical spirit."[16]

As many other countries of Europe eventually learned, life under Nazi occupation was oppressive and dangerous. Churches, clergy and church leaders were persecuted. The synagogue in Pilsen, one of the largest in Europe, was closed and converted into a storage facility for the German Army. Universities and schools were closed. Young people were deported to Germany for forced labor. Jews were rounded up and sent to concentration camps where most ultimately died. The Nazis created a concentration camp at Theresienstadt to show the world how well they were treating the Jews but Theresienstadt was just that: a show. All forms of resistance were brutally crushed. After Czech partisans assassinated Reinhard Heydrich, deputy chief of the Gestapo and Acting Protector of Bohemia and Moravia, the Germans killed several thousand Czechs in reprisal and literally wiped the small village of Lidice from the face of the earth, killing nearly all of its inhabitants.[17]

Jaroslav Peklo, Milka Vildova, Malvina Zajicova, and Vera Fiedlerova all grew up in and around Pilsen during the Nazi occupation. Nazi oppression worked its way into all aspects of their lives. What should have been times of joy and hope for the future instead were times of fear, uncertainty and oppression. "Living under the German boot was very limited and sad. Everything was forbidden," Peklo later recalled. "The Germans told us what to do, when to do it and how to do it and you had better do it," said Vildova.[18]

The Germans vigorously suppressed education in Bohemia. Universities and schools were closed; teachers and professors were arrested. "My sister and future husband were enforced to work at the Skoda Works (as a part of so called Totaleinsatz) immediately after the secondary school because all higher education institutions were closed by Nazis since the beginning of the war," Zajicova recalled. In March 1942, the Germans came into Milka Vildova's school in Stenovice and took the whole school— some 250 girls—off to a concentration / work camp. The girls' parents were not informed what had happened to their daughters. At the camp, the girls were forced to cut up fallen trees and plant new ones. "There was no heat and no water in the camp and it was cold in the mountains," Vildova recalled. "You had to do exactly what they told you. There was very little food, only a little loaf of bread for breakfast and lunch." After six months, Vildova and all of the other girls were sent home to Stenovice.[19]

German penalties for so-called offenses were often death. "Practically every offense was punished by death, for instance, listening to foreign broadcasting, black market,helping parachutists, whispering anti–German propaganda, etc," remembered Jaroslav Peklo. "We listened to English or American broadcasts though capital punishment was threatened for it," Vera Fiedlerova remembered. "Every wireless set had to be equipped by notice 'Listening to foreign broadcast will be capital punished.' And the Germans really did it."[20]

Conditions in Bohemia worsened dramatically during the winter of 1944–1945. Hard pressed because of their military reverses, the Germans seized more and more of the area's agricultural products, foodstuffs and natural resources. As a result, food and fuel were in short supply. Peklo was 12 years old at this time. "The rations were very low," he recalled. "City people used to visit the country to ask the farmers for that good food. My father exchanged his only one Omega wrist watch for one goose. At that time each family lived in the kitchen because of heating."[21]

Life under the Nazis was harsh, and full of hardships and oppression. But the Thousand Year Reich and its stranglehold over Czechoslovakia was soon to end. Though no one knew it at the time, the U.S. Army and the 16th Armored Division were on their way to liberate Pilsen and western Bohemia.

4

Summer and Fall of 1944

On 6 June 1944, Allied forces launched Operation Overlord and invaded the Normandy region of France. After several weeks of heavy fighting, the Allies achieved a decisive breakthrough of the German lines and pushed across France with Blitzkrieg-like speed. Another Allied invasion force landed in southern France in August and pushed north to link up with them in eastern France the following month. Severe logistical difficulties, heavy autumn rains and stiffening German resistance halted the Allied advance at the German frontier. Then in mid–December, the Germans launched a surprise counter-offensive in the Ardennes region of Belgium, knocking a sixty mile "Bulge" in American lines before being halted by American reinforcements at the end of the month.

While Allied forces were fighting to liberate France, Belgium, Holland and Luxembourg, the 16th Armored Division was nearing the end of its training and preparing for deployment to the European Theater. During this time, the division completed its training and adjusted to numerous changes in leadership and personnel. At year's end, only the 13th, 16th and 20th Armored Divisions remained in the U.S., but each of them was scheduled to deploy the following year.

Changes in Leadership

In September 1944, Brig. Gen. John Leonard Pierce assumed command of the 16th Armored Division. He was born on 29 April 1895 to the former Isabella Archer and Frank Cusman Pierce in Dallas, Texas, and was the second oldest of eight children. His father was a lawyer and writer who subsequently moved the family to Brownsville in 1904. John L. Pierce was educated at the West Texas Military Academy (which later became the Texas Military Institute) in San Antonio and the Agricultural and Mechanical College of Texas (which later became Texas A&M University) in College Station. In 1911, he enlisted in the Texas National Guard. On 5 June 1917, Pierce was commissioned as a second lieutenant in the U.S. Army. Three months later, he was promoted to captain. On 29 June 1918, he married Kate Bodine Stone, with whom he would have daughters Jessie and Isabel and son John Jr. Assigned to the 8th Infantry Regiment of the 8th Division, Pierce departed with his regiment for France at the end of October 1918 but did not see combat as the Armistice was signed two weeks later. The regiment subsequently served on occupation duties in Koblenz, Germany. Capt. Pierce also served with the 83rd Infantry Division and 28th Infantry Division during the postwar occupation of Germany.[1]

After returning to the United States, Capt. Pierce remained with the Regular Army. Promotions were slow during the inter-war period and Pierce did not attain the rank of major until October 1934. When war broke out in Europe and it became necessary to greatly expand the Army, promotions came much quicker for Pierce. He was promoted to lieutenant colonel in July 1940, colonel in December 1941 and brigadier general in June 1943.[2]

Though commissioned into the Infantry Branch, Pierce eventually became involved with armored vehicles. Before assuming command of the 16th Armored Division, Pierce had served with the 2nd, 3rd and 9th Armored Divisions. In 1942, he participated in the Army's first large scale desert maneuvers held in southeastern California and Arizona and earned the Legion of Merit for his performance. He also served as Chief of Staff for first the II Armored Corps, and then Headquarters, Armored Command.[3]

After leaving the 16th Armored Division, Maj. Gen. Douglass T. Greene assumed command of the 12th Armored Division at Camp Barkeley, Texas. That division was preparing for deployment to the European Theater. Greene oversaw its movement to Camp Shanks, New York for embarkation but turned over command of the division to Maj. Gen. Roderick R. Allen in New York. It would be Allen, not Greene, who commanded the 12th Armored Division during its European campaigns.[4]

Brig. Gen. Pierce had been in command of the 16th Armored Division only a couple weeks when he suddenly found himself without a commander for the Division Artillery. Fortunately for him and the rest of the division, Pierce received a phone call from Army Ground Forces. The end result was the assignment of Lt. Col. Barksdale Hamlett, Jr., as the new Division Artillery commander.

Born on 30 December 1908 in Hopkinsville, Kentucky, Barksdale Hamlett, Jr., was the son of Barksdale Hamlett, Sr., and Daisey (Crume) Hamlett. He was raised in Kentucky and graduated from Adair County High School. After a year at Lindsey Wilson Junior College, Hamlett received an appointment to the U.S. Military Academy. He graduated with the Class of 1930.

Of the graduating class of 241 cadets, 62 would attain flag rank, including seven generals, eight lieutenant generals, twenty-eight major generals and nineteen brigadier generals. Hamlett was commissioned as a 2nd lieutenant of Field Artillery and posted to Fort Sam Houston, Texas at his request. There he served as an aide to Brig. Gen. Lesley J. McNair of the 2nd Infantry Division. A year later, he married Frances Valencia Underwood and together they had a daughter, Otila Crume. During the 1930s, Hamlett served as an artillery officer with the 12th Field Artillery Regiment at Fort Sam Houston, Texas, the 11th Field Artillery Regiment at Schofield Barracks, Hawaii, the 18th Field Artillery Regiment at Fort Sill, Oklahoma, and then back to Fort Sam Houston to serve first as Motors Officer and subsequently as Adjutant of the 15th Field Artillery Regiment. In 1940, Hamlett was promoted to captain. From 1940 until 1942, Hamlett served as an instructor in the Gunnery Department at the U.S. Army Artillery School at Fort Sill.[5]

Following the U.S. entry into World War II, Hamlett became Assistant Artillery Officer for II Corps Artillery Headquarters and went overseas to England on the staff of II Corps' commanding general, Maj. Gen. Mark Clark. Hamlett continued to serve with II Corps Headquarters after Clark was promoted and Maj. Gen. Lloyd Fredendall assumed command of the corps. During Operation Torch—the invasion of North Africa invasion, Hamlett landed with the 1st Infantry Division at Oran, Morocco. After the disastrous Battle of the Kasserine Pass, Fredendall was replaced by Maj. Gen. George S. Patton, Jr., as commanding general of II Corps. Hamlett was now Executive Officer for II Corps Artillery Headquarters. "I came to know Patton real well on the field of battle," Hamlett would later recall.[6]

In July 1943, Maj. Hamlett was brought back to the U.S. to serve with Lt. Gen. Lesley J. McNair at Army Ground Forces. There he was instrumental in developing training and doctrine for field artillery. Tragically, McNair was killed on 25 July 1944 near St. Lo, France, when a number of U.S. Army Air Forces heavy bombers supporting Operation Cobra accidentally dropped their bomb loads on American forces.[7]

McNair's death threw Lt. Col. Hamlett's future in doubt. In September

1944, he was appointed as Assistant Chief of Staff G-3 (Operations) for Army Ground Forces but he yearned to return to combat. Learning that the Division Artillery Commander for the 16th Armored Division was due to be transferred and knowing that the division was scheduled to deploy to Europe in a few months, Hamlett decided to seek out the position. In his oral history, Hamlett recalled what transpired when he called the division's commanding general to obtain the position:

> "General Pierce, you're losing your Division Artillery Commander, and you need another one." He said, "That's right. I certainly do." I said, "Well I'm volunteering for the job. My name is Hamlett. You've never heard of me," and I told him my background as a Field Artilleryman, and I said, "I want to be your Artillery Commander." Well he said, "If you can get the Ground Forces people to agree on it, get your orders out, and come on out here as fast as you can." And that's what happened.[8]

1st Lt. John C. Patterson joined the 16th Armored Division and was assigned to the 23rd Cavalry Squadron in July of 1944. Born on 9 September 1918 in Okmulgee, Oklahoma, Patterson was the son of Fanny nee Kenady and Ottis William Patterson. His father played semi-pro baseball and was a machine operator in the Coca-Cola Bottle Plant and later the Ball Brothers Fruit Jar Factory. He had an older brother Russell. John was an Eagle Scout and played baseball in high school. After graduating from high school, he attended the Oklahoma Military Academy and then went to the University of Wyoming on a football scholarship. In the spring of 1941, Patterson graduated from the University of Wyoming with a Bachelor's of Arts in Liberal Studies and was commissioned as a second lieutenant in the Army. On 23 July 1941, he married Dora Elizabeth Lebow, the younger sister of one of his OMA classmates. In July 1942, 2nd Lt. Patterson was assigned to the 26th Infantry Division's 26th Reconnaissance Troop. Nicknamed the Yankee Division, the 26th Infantry Division was a mobilized unit of the Massachusetts National Guard. For the next two years, Patterson served with the 26th Reconnaissance Troop in New England, South Carolina, Kentucky and Tennessee. From May to December 1943, 1st Lt. Patterson attended the Cavalry Mechanized Reconnaissance School at Fort Riley, Kansas. In July 1944, 1st Lt. Patterson joined Troop A of the 23rd Cavalry Squadron and the following month he was placed in command of Troop B. He and his wife had a young daughter by now and were expecting their second child.[9]

Also joining the 16th Armored Division in 1944 was Lt. Col. James Early Norvell. He was born on 19 December 1914 to Maj. B. P. and Bessie nee Carter Norvell in Muskogee, Oklahoma. James E. Norvell received a

Presidential appointment to the U.S. Military Academy in 1933 and graduated from there as part of the Class of 1937. His older brother Frank and younger brother Bill both were also USMA graduates. Commissioned as a second lieutenant in the field artillery, Norvell was first assigned to the 82nd Field Artillery Battalion of the 1st Cavalry Division at Fort Bliss, Texas. There he met and married Elizabeth "Betty" West, daughter of Col. William W. West. In 1940, Capt. Norvell was assigned to the 14th Field Artillery Battalion at Fort Benning, Georgia. Later he served at Camp Polk, Louisiana, and Fort Sill, Oklahoma. His duty assignments included command of the 440th Armored Field Artillery Battalion of the 7th Armored Division. When the 7th Armored Division was deployed to France in June 1944, Lt. Col. Norvell was in Camp Chafee, Arkansas with the 16th Armored Division.[10]

Lt. Col. Percy Harold Perkins, Jr., joined the 16th Armored Division in late August 1944 and assumed command of the 5th Tank Battalion. Born on 8 September 1905 in Metter, Georgia, he was the son of Percy Sr. and Bertha Mae nee Warwick. He was raised in the Methodist faith. After graduating from Claxton High School, he attended the College of Architecture at the Georgia Institute of Technology and served as a cadet in the Army ROTC program there. He graduated from Georgia Tech in 1927 and was commissioned as a 2nd lieutenant in the Army Reserve. He worked for several years as a draftsman for architecture firms in Atlanta and Fort Worth, Texas. In 1932, he completed the U.S. Army Infantry School at Fort Benning, Georgia.

On 5 November 1933, he married Mary Louise Martin, an aspiring painter and artist who had a bachelor's degree in the discipline. From 1933 to 1938, he served as an officer in the Civilian Conservation Corps and earned a promotion to captain in 1935. From 1938 until early 1941, he worked as an architect and served in the Army Reserve. On 10 February 1941, he was called to active duty and assigned to the 2nd Armored Division at Fort Benning. Soon after, he was assigned as Adjutant of the 760th Tank Battalion, Camp Bowie, Texas. After being promoted to major on 6 June 1941, Perkins was sent to the U.S. Army Command and General Staff College at Fort Leavenworth. After graduating on 14 February 1942, he became the Executive Officer of the 2nd Tank Group at Camp Bowie, Texas and later at the Desert Training Center in Indio, California. Following promotion to lieutenant colonel, Perkins was placed in command of the 191st Tank Battalion. In early 1943, he and his battalion deployed to North Africa and arrived in Casa Blanca, Morocco, on 9 March. Subsequently they relocated to Bizerte, Tunisia to prepare for the invasion of

Italy. In September 1943, Perkins' 191st Tank Battalion came ashore at Salerno, Italy and became the first U.S. tanks on the European Continent. They fought for 120 days in the front lines. In January 1944, the battalion participated in the Anzio invasion. Perkins left the 191st Tank Battalion in May 1944 and returned to the United States. On or about 26 August 1944, he was assigned to the 16th Armored Division and assumed command of the 5th Tank Battalion. He served as battalion commander until 8 October 1944 when he was transferred to Combat Command B Headquarters to become the command's Executive Officer.[11]

Lt. Col. Charles A. Symroski left the 16th Armored Division to attend the U.S. Army Command and General Staff College in late summer of 1944. Following graduation, he was assigned to the 12th Armored Division as Assistant Chief of Staff G-2 (Intelligence). His replacement as commander of the 397th Armored Field Artillery Battalion was Maj. John E. Weiler.[12]

Personnel Changes

The U.S. Army sustained heavy casualties during the summer fighting in Normandy. Divisions that had been training in the United States for deployment found themselves being called upon to provide trained soldiers to serve as replacements for the divisions in combat in France. This included the 16th Armored Division. Between April and September 1944, some 2,947 soldiers were transferred out of the 16th Armored Division and sent overseas as replacements.[13]

Enlisted soldiers were not the only members of the 16th Armored Division transferred to other units. On 19 August 1944, Lt. Col. Mont Hubbard was relieved of command of the 396th Armored Field Artillery Battalion and sent overseas. Over the next month, the battalion had a succession of three commanders until finally Lt. Col. James E. Norvell assumed command on 23 September. In the fall of 1944, the division Chief of Staff Col. Richard A. Gordon was sent overseas. On 14 December 1944, he assumed command of the 12th Armored Division's Reserve Command while it was operating as part of Seventh U.S. Army in the Bas-Rhins region of eastern France near the German border.[14]

Lt. Col. William H. G. Fuller had commanded the 18th Armored Infantry Battalion for ten months when he was relieved of his command and sent overseas. On 20 September 1944, he assumed command of the 7th Armored Division's 38th Armored Infantry Battalion. Maj. J. H.

Crawford assumed command of the 18th Armored Infantry Battalion after Lt. Col. Fuller's departure. Crawford's tenure as battalion commander was short. Over the next five months, the battalion experienced almost a new battalion commander each month until finally Lt. Col. Irving K. Hendren assumed command. Ultimately, Lt. Col. Hendren would lead the battalion into battle.[15]

With a deployment in the not so distant future, the 16th Armored Division needed to replace those soldiers sent overseas as combat replacements earlier in 1944. Gene Eike was one of those soldiers brought in to bring the division back up to authorized strength. He was born in a small town in Texas on 8 October 1924. He played end and tackle for his high school's football team. After the Japanese bombed Pearl Harbor, he and several of his teammates attempted to enlist in the Marine Corps but were turned down because of their age. After graduating from high school in June 1942, Eike went work in a defense plant making brass fuses for artillery shells. A year later almost to the day, he was drafted into the army at age eighteen. Following Basic Training, he completed infantry training at Camp Roberts located in central California. Then he was selected to attend Pasadena Junior College as part of a program to train future officers, but the program was canceled before he attended. Promoted to corporal, Eike instead became a training instructor at Camp Roberts. In December 1944, he was transferred to 16th Armored Division and made a squad leader.[16]

Hamlett in Command of Division Artillery

Lt. Col. Hamlett's transfer to the 16th Armored Division was approved by Army Ground Forces in early September. Soon after, he reported to Camp Chaffee. What he found was to his liking. "It was just the right size for our artillery," he later recalled. "It wasn't large enough for 155s [howitzers and guns], but all we had, of course, was the self-propelled 105 howitzers and it was just a great place for training a 105 outfit."[17]

Lt. Col. Hamlett joined the 16th Armored Division just as the division was completing its training program and preparing for overseas deployment. "See, we had just been filled when I went there, with brand new soldiers, but boy were they great!" recalled Hamlett. "We got all the people out of colleges…. Greatest bunch of enlisted people I have ever commanded. They were just great. And we had a lot of fine non-commissioned officers, because that division had been cadre'd three or four times." Many of his officers were excellent but not all of them. Later that fall, Hamlett was promoted to colonel.[18]

Fall Training and Maneuvers

Throughout 1944, the 16th Armored Division progressed inexorably towards the completion of its stateside training and its expected deployment to the European Theater of Operations. As part of the evaluation for the division's readiness for combat, all three of its armored field artillery battalions performed a series of tests to ensure mastery of the skills necessary to provide mobile fire support for the division. The 397th Armored Field Artillery Battalion's experiences were typical of the division's artillery. Between 3 October and 7 October, the battalion successfully passed three intensive tests conducted by evaluators from XXXVI Corps Artillery at Fort Riley, Kansas. Each of the battalion's firing batteries were tested in their abilities to rapidly occupy firing positions, plot fire missions, and accurately fire and adjust rounds onto targets. The battalion's Fire Direction Center was also vigorously tested on its ability to coordinate fires of the battalion. The 397th Armored Field Artillery Battalion passed all of its tests.[19]

Having completed individual and unit level training, the 16th Armored Division was ready to test its skills in a division-sized exercise. This exercise would determine if the 16th Armored Division was ready for combat. The division exercise was begun on 14 October 1944. "The war games staged were close to real and little was left to the imagination," wrote Lt. Col. Frank Houlihan of the 137th Armored Ordnance Battalion. "In fact, just about every situation encountered in actual combat was experienced."[20]

For the division maneuvers, the 216th Armored Engineer Battalion was broken up into its component companies with Companies A, B and C being assigned to the combat commands. Headquarters Company provided general support to the division's units, namely water supply, maps, and engineer reconnaissance.[21]

A month later, the 16th Armored Division completed its field exercise and was declared "combat ready." They were placed on alert for deployment to the European Theater. As part of the division's pre-deployment preparations, teams of inspectors from the U.S. Army Inspector General's Office in Washington, D.C., scrutinized the division's equipment and records. Meanwhile, members of the 137th Armored Ordnance Battalion were busily engaged in constructing the crates that would be used to ship the division's gear to Europe. Soldiers of the 216th Armored Engineer Battalion assisted the division's units in preparing their vehicles for rail shipment to the deployment embarkation port.[22]

It was expected that the 16th Armored Division would have to assault the German Siegfried Line of fortifications that guarded the German border after they arrived in Europe. In preparation for that expectation, the 216th Armored Engineer Battalion held a live-fire demonstration of assaulting fortifications for the division in December. Under the direction of S-3 (Operations) Officer Maj. Charles Surbey, members of the battalion constructed pillboxes and other fortifications and strung barbed wire. Then Company A conducted the assault demonstration using live explosives and artillery rounds. One soldier was injured by an errant artillery round, and required life-saving amputation of a leg.[23]

Following the Division maneuvers, the 18th Armored Infantry Battalion focused on gaining weapons proficiency and performing small unit tactical exercises, many of which involved live ammunition. Training was curtailed when the division received an alert for overseas movement. The battalion then turned all of its energies into preparing for deployment to the European Theater. For over a month, the battalion's personnel packed and crated its equipment. In addition, the battalion turned in all of its vehicles. The battalion would receive new vehicles after arriving in the European Theater.[24]

As 1944 came to a close, the 16th Armored Division was ready for deployment to war.

5

Deployed to Europe

One of the greatest logistical feats of the Second World War was the deployment of the U.S. Army's divisions from the United States overseas to the European Theater of Operations (ETO).

Moving a division overseas required a complicated coordination of trucks, trains, and ships to transport its 14,000 to 16,000 soldiers, its thousands of vehicles and tens of thousands of individual pieces of equipment. Getting them across the Atlantic Ocean safely required numerous naval escort vessels provided by the U.S. Navy, Royal Navy and Royal Canadian Navy and U.S., Canadian and British patrol aircraft to protect them from the German U–Boats still prowling about even as late as the fall of 1944.

On the eve of deployment, inspectors from Headquarters Fourth U.S. Army conducted intensive inspections of all of the 16th Armored Division's units to ensure its readiness for combat. These inspectors evaluated unit administrative records, supply procedures, training results and ordnance.[1]

16th Armored Division's long-awaited journey to the frontlines in Europe began in mid–January 1945. Having completed their training, the division left Camp Chaffee by train and travelled north through St. Louis, Missouri to Chicago, Illinois. Then they headed east to Buffalo, New York and continued on eastward across the state. On 28 January 1945, they arrived at Camp Shanks near Orangetown, New York. Occupying over 2,000 acres on the Hudson River about 30 miles north of New York City, Camp Shanks was the U.S. Army's largest Port of Embarkation in the U.S. Over a million soldiers passed through here on their way to the European Theater.[2]

Here at Camp Shanks, the soldiers of the 16th Armored Division made their final preparations for overseas movement. Equipment and weapons were inspected. New weapons were issued. Inoculations for various diseases were administered by medical personnel.[3]

Camp Shanks' proximity to New York City provided a limited number of 16th Armored Division soldiers with an opportunity for a quick visit to the city. New York native Warrant Officer Solomon Polish managed to get home for a quick visit with his family before embarking aboard ship for deployment to the European Theater.[4]

As the 16th Armored Division was completing its preparations for overseas deployment and travelling east to its Port of Embarkation, Allied forces in Europe were engaged in heavy fighting against the Germans amidst harsh winter conditions. By the end of January, Allied forces had repulsed both the German Counter-Offensive in the Ardennes and another one launched a couple weeks later against the Seventh U.S. Army and the French 1st Army in the Alsace-Lorraine region of France.

The 16th Armored Division's stay at Camp Shanks was brief. On 5 February 1945, the soldiers began embarkation on the ships that would take them to France. Col. Charles H. Noble's Combat Command B and the 216th Armored Engineer Battalion traveled aboard *USAT Santa Rosa*, a passenger ship pressed into wartime service by the Federal Government. Most of the division travelled aboard a U.S. Navy troop ship, *USS Hermitage*. *Hermitage* was an Italian cruise ship that had been seized by the U.S. Government and converted to a troop ship. Other units such as the 397th Armored Field Artillery Battalion embarked aboard *SS Marine Panther*, and *SS Marine Eagle*. Thusly embarked the division's passage across the Atlantic Ocean commenced.[5]

The voyage across the Atlantic was uneventful aside from the rough sea conditions which caused rampant sea sickness amongst the 16th Armored Division soldiers. The convoy containing the 16th Armored Division was escorted by U.S. Navy destroyers and an escort aircraft carrier as protection against German U-Boats. "The weather was over-cast and the sea unremittingly rough, but this seemed preferable to clear, calm weather when convoying through the submarine zone," Lt. Col. William W. Smith, Jr., of the 216th Armored Engineer Battalion later wrote. In a letter written to his wife, PFC Charles Lemmons later described the voyage. "It has been a long and monotonous voyage so far…. We had a few pretty rough days, at least, for us new seafaring men. I haven't noticed the rolling and rocking of the ship too much lately though. Don't worry about me honey, I'm just fine." Years later, 1st Lt. John C. Patterson of the 23rd Cavalry Squadron would recall the voyage to France. "The ocean was extremely rough," he wrote. "I don't know how the men on the destroyers could stand it. Their ships would disappear in the waves."[6]

Between 11 and 17 February 1945, the ships carrying the 16th Armored

Division's men and equipment arrived in the French port of Le Havre. An advance party of 16th Armored Division officers and soldiers met the division when they arrived in Le Havre. They were now part of the Fifteenth U.S. Army.[7]

Strategically located on the English Channel, Le Havre had been heavily fortified by the German Army as part of their Atlantic Wall defenses. Allied air forces had heavily bombed Le Havre and the city suffered further damage when British and Canadian forces had liberated it in September 1944. Mark Steece of the 23rd Cavalry Squadron later spoke of Le Havre's condition when his division arrived. "Big buildings were knocked down," he said. "They were able to use the port but the city was heavily damaged." Warrant Officer Solomon Polish of the 156th Armored Signal Company also described his experience with Le Havre. "It was a weird feeling, seeing the shattered buildings, most of which were hardly a shell," wrote Polish many years later. "The air was still filled with the smell of the fires that burned the city to dust."[8]

The 18th Armored Infantry Battalion's time in Le Havre was brief. Upon disembarking, the members of the battalion boarded a train and headed for the village of La Feuillie in Normandy. Battalion Headquarters was located in the village itself with its companies billeted in the nearby farms.[9]

Here in their temporary billets, the 18th Armored Infantry Battalion soldiers were issued new vehicles. The new vehicles included half-tracks made by the White Motor Company. "These White half-tracks proved to be much tougher than the International vehicle which we used at Camp Chaffee," Capt. Howard Painter later wrote. "We received our weapons and vehicles and spent days cleaning cosmoline from all the equipment," Harley Barrs later wrote. "This was a heavy, greasy coating used to protect it from weather and salt air during our trip across the ocean."[10]

The 18th Armored Infantry Battalion was not the only 16th Armored Division unit to receive new vehicles and equipment after arriving in France. The 5th Tank Battalion was equipped with new M4 Sherman tanks armed with 76mm main guns and various other vehicles.[11]

The soldiers of the 64th Armored Infantry Battalion arrived on USS *Hermitage* at Le Havre on 16 February and disembarked the following day. Due to the heavy damage sustained by the port facilities, the soldiers had to be ferried ashore by Navy LSTs (Landing Ship Tank). Once ashore, the soldiers marched through the city to a large pavilion located near a railroad station. At the pavilion, they were fed C-rations, coffee and doughnuts while an Army band played for their entertainment. Following this, the battalion boarded a train for Rourray, France some ninety miles away. Arriving the next morning, the battalion continued its journey by truck to an assembly area near Gournay. There, the soldiers were billeted in two old French chateaux and a farm. Meanwhile, the Battalion S-4 (Logistics) section and officers of the Advance Detachment were left in Le Havre to supervise the unloading of the battalion's vehicles and equipment. Accomplishing this task required a week. The 64th Armored Infantry Battalion remained in the vicinity of Gournay for the next two months training and preparing for combat.[12]

SS Marine Panther with the 397th Armored Field Artillery Battalion embarked arrived at Le Havre at 2100 on 16 February 1945. Due to the shattered conditions of the port facilities, the battalion did not disembark until just before midnight on 19 February. Their stay in Le Havre was brief; four hours later, they boarded a train for Lyons La Floret and arrived there at 1245. Headquarters and Service Batteries stayed in Lyons La Floret for billeting while Battery A moved on to billets at nearby Latronguay and Batteries B and C billeted at St. Lucien. For the next two months, Lt. Col. John E. Weiler and his battalion's 34 officers and 487 enlisted soldiers would remain here preparing themselves and their equipment and weapons for battle.[13]

Now in France, the 16th Armored Division continued to train for its eventual entry into combat. Staff Sgt. Gene Eike of the 18th Armored Infantry Battalion was one of many of the division's soldiers who participated in training exercises at the port of Dieppe located on the English Channel. On 19 August 1942, Dieppe was the scene of an ill-fated Allied amphibious raid. Nearly 60 percent of the mostly Canadian force were killed, wounded or captured. Part of Eike's training involved clearing the beaches of anti-personnel and anti-tank mines emplaced by the Germans to defend the vital port.[14]

The French coast had been heavily mined by the Germans as defense against Allied amphibious landings. Though the German Army had long since been forced back into Germany, thousands of the mines that they had emplaced were still buried on the beaches. Each of the 216th Armored Engineer Battalion's line companies were sent up to the vicinity of Fecamp about 25 miles north of Le Havre to clear the beaches of German mines. "Major Surbey, S-3, coordinated this excellent and hair-raising training, and though some of the mines were found by accident, fortunately there were no casualties," wrote Lt. Col. Smith.[15]

Once ashore, the 23rd Cavalry Squadron joined up with its vehicles which had travelled separately from the soldiers. They quickly set about preparing them for combat. "One of the first things done was to weld a ¼" inch steel plate on the bottom of the armored cars," 1st Lt. John C. Patterson later wrote. "The next was to install ring mounts and .50 caliber machine guns on the turrets of the cars."[16]

As the 16th Armored Division continued its preparations for entry into combat, Allied armies resumed their advance forward into Germany and reached the Rhine River. Supreme Allied Commander General Dwight Eisenhower's intention was for all of his armies to reach the Rhine before attempting to cross the last natural barrier into the heart of Nazi Germany. The capture of the only intact bridge across the Rhine at the town of Remagen by the 9th Armored Division forced a change in Eisenhower's plans. Other U.S. divisions were rushed across the bridge and subsequent bridges erected in the vicinity to exploit this fortunate opportunity. By the end of March, all of the Allied armies had crossed the Rhine.

The month of April witnessed the near collapse of the German Army forces in the west. Allied armored and mechanized forces rushed across central Germany. Allied forces discovered the atrocities of the Nazi concentration camps at such infamous places as Buchenwald, Bergen-Belsen and Dachau. By mid–April, the capture of Berlin seemed within reach of British and American forces but Eisenhower recognized that the Soviets were in a far better position to capture the city. So he directed his forces to halt well short of the city. American and French forces overran southern Germany and pushed into Austria. Throughout this time, the 16th Armored Division remained in Theater Reserve in the vicinity of Elbeufren-en-Bray, in the Seine-Inferieure region of France until mid–April 1945.[17]

To help prepare the division's leadership for entry into combat, a number of senior commanders and staff officers were sent to the frontlines as observers. Lt. Col. James Norvell of the 396th Armored Field Artillery Battalion and Lt. Col. John Weiler of the 397th Armored Field Artillery Battalion spent several days in March with First U.S. Army. Col. Noble was sent to the Seventh U.S. Army in Germany, temporarily leaving Lt. Col. Perkins in command of Combat Command B. While serving with Seventh Army, Noble and his driver were nearly killed when they got ahead of U.S. lines and were fired upon by the Germans.[18]

After Col. Noble returned to Combat Command B, Lt. Col. Perkins was sent forward as an observer with Combat Command B of the 9th Armored Division. While with the 9th Armored Division, Perkins participated in the reduction of the Ruhr Pocket. On one occasion, he disabled an abandoned German artillery piece with a thermite grenade. On the way back to 16th Armored Division, Perkins spent the night in Paris.[19]

As it prepared for combat, the 16th Armored Division continued to experience changes in personnel. On 9 April, the commanding officer of the 64th Armored Infantry Battalion, Lt. Col. Edward E. Cruise, was transferred to Headquarters, Fifteen U.S. Army. Lt. Col. Richard E. Horrocks assumed command of the battalion. In addition, Maj. Donald W. Mather replaced Capt. Arjenter B. Cardwell as the Battalion S-3 (Operations) Officer. Capt. Cardwell was transferred to Division Headquarters. Horrocks' tenure as Battalion Commander was brief; on 22 April, he was transferred to assume command of the 69th Armored Infantry Battalion.[20]

Recognizing the importance of having experienced combat leaders in his division, Brig. Gen. John L. Pierce requested that some officers with combat experience be transferred into the 16th Armored Division. One of these new officers was Maj. George B. Pickett, Jr., who had formerly served as Executive Officer of 42nd Tank Battalion, 11th Armored Division during the Battle of the Bulge. Pickett joined the 16th Armored Division in mid-April and assumed command of the 64th Armored Infantry Battalion on 22 April 1945.[21]

George Bibb Pickett, Jr., was born in Montgomery, Alabama on 20 March 1918. He was a distant descendant of Confederate Maj. Gen. George E. Pickett who was one of the leaders of the failed Pickett / Pettigrew Charge at the Battle of Gettysburg. Pickett Jr. graduated from the Tennessee Military Institute in 1936 and earned a surveyor's license. He went to work for his father as a civil engineer. The following year, he accepted an appointment to the U.S. Military Academy. After graduating from USMA in 1941, he was commissioned as a second lieutenant and then married Beryl Robinson. In 1942, he completed the Armored Force School and in 1943 he completed the General Staff Course of the U.S. Army Command and General Staff College. He rose rapidly through the ranks. In the winter of 1944–45, Maj. Pickett served as the Executive Officer of the 42nd Tank Battalion, 11th Armored Division and fought in the Battle of the Bulge. He was awarded the Silver Star for valor.[22]

Another new arrival to the 16th Armored Division was Col. A. Worrell Roffe. The son of Mr. and Mrs. Thomas I. Roffe, A. Worrell Roffe was born in Blue Springs, Missouri on 6 November 1890. He earned his undergraduate and law degrees from the University of Missouri. On 29 November 1916, Roffe received a direct commission into the U.S. Army in the Cavalry Branch as a first lieutenant. Several months later, he saw service with first the 14th U.S. Cavalry Regiment and then the 96th

5. Deployed to Europe

Infantry Division on the Mexican border. For this, he received the Victory Medal and the Mexican Border Ribbon. On 5 August 1917, Roffe was promoted to captain. In February 1918, he married Viola Chasten with whom he had a son and a daughter. On 26 June 1918, Roffe was promoted to major. He did not deploy overseas for World War I.[23]

After the war, Roffe remained with the Regular Army. At various times, he served with the Cavalry School and the 2nd, 3rd and 7th Cavalry Regiments. He also attended and completed the Cavalry Troop Officers School in 1920, the Advanced Equitation Course at the Cavalry School in 1924, the French Cavalry School at Samur, France in 1927, the U.S. Army Command and General Staff School in 1931 and the U.S. Army War College in 1937. In 1928, he competed in the Amsterdam, Holland Olympic Games as part of the U.S. Olympic Team. He was promoted to lieutenant colonel on 1 August 1938 and colonel on 14 October 1941. In May 1940, he was assigned to the General Staff Corps.[24]

Col. Roffe's most important wartime service occurred in 1944–45. In May 1944, he was ordered to the European Theater of Operations and assumed command of the 2nd Infantry Regiment of the 5th Infantry Division on 10 July 1944. Less than a week later, Col. Roffe and his regiment were engaged in the brutal fighting in the Normandy hedgerows. During the drive across France, Col. Roffe's regiment liberated the city of Reims and participated in the capture of Metz. In December 1944, Col. Roffe accepted the surrender of Fort Driant, one of the fortresses that guarded Metz. The regiment later participated in the reduction of the Ardennes Salient in Luxembourg and the reduction of the Ruhr Pocket in Germany. For his combat leadership, Col. Roffe was awarded the Silver Star, the Bronze Star twice and the French Croix de Guerre with Palm. On 30 April 1945, Col. Roffe became the Assistant Division Commander of the 16th Armored Division.[25]

A month after arriving in the European Theater of Operations, the 16th Armored Division received a new Chief of Staff at Division Headquarters. On 21 March, Col. Thomas V. Webb was replaced by Col. Edwin C. Greiner. Greiner was born 8 July 1901 and was a graduate of the U.S. Military Academy Class of 1922. On 15 April 1941, Maj. Greiner became the first commanding officer of the 3rd Reconnaissance Battalion (later 83rd Armored Reconnaissance Battalion) of the 3rd Armored Division at its activation at Camp Beauregard, Louisiana. Afterwards, he commanded the 2nd Group, Armored Replacement Training Center at Fort Knox, Kentucky and then served as G-2 (Intelligence) Officer for XXIII Corps. He was promoted to colonel on 12 March 1943.[26]

By the end of March 1945, the Allied armies had breached the Rhine River barrier in multiple locations and had begun pouring across into the heart of the Third Reich. The 16th Armored Division was hastily moved forward. On 16 April, the division arrived in the vicinity of Reims in northeastern France. The following day, the division crossed into Germany and was assigned to Third U.S. Army. Upon entering Germany, the division found a country devastated by war.

"The first view of Germany for all members of the Battalion proved to be very encouraging due to the utter and complete ruin of the majority of the cities and towns," stated the 64th Armored Infantry Battalion's Unit History. The Division Headquarters was set up temporarily at the city of Kaiserslautern. From here they continued eastward to the city of Mainz. After remaining near Mainz for a week, the division continued on to Wurzburg.[27]

Lt. Col. Houlihan of the 137th Armored Ordnance Battalion later wrote about the division's rapid movement across Europe to catch up with the war. "We moved as much as 400 miles in one 24 hour period and it should be kept in mind that during most of this time, we were in support of the fighting units of the 16th Armored Division," he wrote. The battalion's soldiers were responsible for maintaining the thousands of vehicles in the division and repairing them when they broke down.[28]

The 16th Armored Division's stay in Wurzburg was short. Next they moved to the city of Nuremberg and relieved the 71st Infantry Division on 28 April. Nuremberg had been the scene of various massive Nazi Party rallies during the 1930s. The 71st Infantry Division had been performing security and occupation duties here so now the 16th Armored Division assumed these responsibilities. Capt. Howard Painter's Company B, 18th Armored Infantry Battalion was tasked with guarding a weapons collecting depot, a bakery and a winery. "We were at Nurnberg for about one week," Painter later wrote. "That portion known as the old or walled part of the city was completely destroyed." In addition, they conducted patrols to maintain order. Occasionally the American soldiers were fired on; indeed one Company B soldier was wounded by small arms fire. "For several days in Nurnberg we continued our preparations for combat and did some rubble clearing in the streets and a little patrolling," wrote Lt. Col. William W. Smith, Jr., of the 216th Armored Engineer Battalion.[29]

The closer that the division got to the front lines, the more signs of the battle that they came across. Lt. Col. Houlihan later wrote of a scene he witnessed outside of Nurnberg. A glance along the roadside told us of very recent heavy fighting in the area. German rifles by the dozen stood at attention, their bayonets sticking in the ground, plasma bottles still attached to the up end. Meanwhile, the spot where gravely wounded soldiers had been was clearly indicated. For others, it was too little too late, as we saw regulation gray German blankets covering bodies as they awaited the coming of identification and grave registration teams.[30]

While in Nurnberg, the Division's Military Police Platoon was kept busy with occupation and policing duties. The MPs provided traffic control, maintained law and order and processed enemy prisoners of war.[31]

On 4 May 1945, military policeman PFC Charles Lemmons wrote home to his wife describing the conditions he encountered in Germany. He wrote:

> This is a sorry sight. The people just mill around not knowing where or what to do. I don't know how they exist but they do. I know that Hitler's super race begs for food. I've never seen such systematic destruction. They must have used pattern bombing on all of Germany. I'm glad there is 3000 miles of water between the US and these nations over here.[32]

Maj. George B. Pickett's 64th Armored Infantry Battalion was also tasked with maintaining security in Nuremberg. Platoons from both B and C Companies were tasked with guarding Displaced Persons Camps in the city. During the several days that they guarded the DP Camps, the armored infantrymen had several instances of sniper attacks upon the camps. Other soldiers of the battalion patrolled the ruined city streets, engaging in several firefights with snipers. Fortunately, no members of the battalion were wounded in these engages which resulted in the deaths of two German snipers and the wounding of several others.[33]

With the 16th Armored Division's personnel stationed in and around Nuremberg, the 216th Armored Medical Battalion detached subordinate units to provide medical support. A and B Companies were attached to the Headquarters of Combat Commands A and B respectively. C Company was tasked with operation the Division Holding Station, where they treated patients and evacuated ones needing higher echelon care.[34]

During their hurried movement across France and Germany, the 16th Armored Division picked up two new units as attachments and detached its 23rd Cavalry Reconnaissance Squadron [Mechanized] to serve with the 86th Infantry Division temporarily. The two new units were the 571st Anti-Aircraft Artillery Automatic Weapons Battalion (Self-Propelled) and the 633rd Tank Destroyer Battalion (Self-Propelled).

The 571st AAA AW Battalion (SP) was attached to the 16th Armored Division on 20 April while the division was in Mainz. The battalion (Self-Propelled) consisted of a Headquarters Battery, four firing batteries (A,

B, C, and D) and a Medical Detachment. The battalion used armored half-tracks mounting quad-fifty caliber machine guns for defense against low altitude enemy aircraft. It had been activated at Camp Edwards, Massachusetts on 10 June 1943 and had entered the European Theater in France on 22 December 1944.[35]

On 1 May, the 633rd Tank Destroyer Battalion (Self-Propelled) was attached to the 16th Armored Division while the division was serving on occupation duties in Nuremberg, Germany. The battalion had been formed on 16 December 1941 at Camp Forrest, Tennessee with personnel reassigned from the 122nd, 123rd and 124th Field Artillery Battalions of the 33rd Infantry Division. The battalion consisted of a Headquarters Company, three companies of tank destroyers (A, B, and C) and a Reconnaissance Company. As a tank destroyer battalion, the 633rd was equipped with lightly armored vehicles that mounted anti-tank guns in an open turret. Their mission was to destroy enemy tanks, yet their thinly armored vehicles put them at a major disadvantage when engaging the larger German tanks. Initially, the 633rd Tank Destroyer Battalion was equipped with M10 tank destroyers which had 75mm guns but later these were replaced by M18 Hellcat tank destroyers with more powerful 76mm guns.[36]

The 633rd Tank Destroyer Battalion spent nearly the entirety of the war as "School Troops" at stateside postings in Texas, California, Washington and Oregon. As School Troops, the battalion was involved with training of tank destroyer crews. Finally, in January 1945, the battalion received orders to deploy to the European Theater. Overseas movement did not actually commence until 31 March; they arrived in France on 12 April. For two weeks, the battalion remained in France and then was assigned to Third Army with orders to proceed rapidly to Nuremberg, Germany. Advance elements of the battalion arrived there on 3 May 1945 and the battalion was officially attached to the 16th Armored Division. Unfortunately, most of the battalion's armored vehicles would not arrive in time for it to participate in the upcoming drive into Czechoslovakia.[37]

While the 16th Armored Division was engaged in military occupation duties, to the east Gen. George S. Patton, Jr.'s, Third U.S. Army was busily overrunning southern Bavaria. On 18 April, elements of the 90th Infantry Division reached the 1937 Czechoslovak-German border and crossed into the Nazi-occupied Allied nation. Lt. Col. Charles B. Bryan's 3rd Battalion, 358th Infantry Regiment was the first Allied unit to enter into Czechoslovakia. Eisenhower's primary focus, however, was to prevent the formation of the "National Redoubt" area of last ditch fanatical Nazi resistance rumored to be occurring in southern Germany and western

5. Deployed to Europe

Austria. So after reaching the Czechoslovak border, Eisenhower turned Third U.S. Army to the southeast and pointed it towards Austria.[38]

For the rest of the month, XII Corps of Third U.S. Army advanced parallel to the Czechoslovak border as it protected the army's left flank during the drive to Austria. XII Corps also conducted several important cross-border operations. The 2nd Cavalry Group liberated the border town of Asch and the 97th Infantry Division liberated the city of Cheb. 2nd Cavalry Group also undertook two daring raids to rescue Allied prisoners of war and to rescue the famed Lippizzaner performing horses of the Spanish Riding School from behind enemy lines. The 90th Infantry Division liberated the Flossenbürg Concentration Camp. By month's end, Third U.S. Army held positions along and over the Czechoslovak border and were driving into Austria.[39]

At the end of April the 23rd Cavalry Squadron was detached from the 16th Armored Division and assigned to the 86th Infantry Division. As part of that division, the Squadron engaged in combat operations from the Isar River to Wasserburg, thus becoming the first 16th Armored Division unit to see combat in the European Campaign, albeit as part of another division. The story of the 23rd Cavalry's operations with the 86th Infantry Division are detailed in the following chapter.

6

First Battle for the 23rd Cavalry Squadron

On 28 April 1945, the 23rd Cavalry Reconnaissance Squadron [Mechanized] was detached from the 16th Armored Division and temporarily attached to the 86th Infantry Division. This assignment would last until 3 May 1945 and garner the Squadron its first combat experience.

The Black Hawk Division

Like the 16th Armored Division, the 86th Infantry Division was a newcomer to the European Theater of Operations. Unlike the 16th Armored Division, the 86th Infantry Division dated back to World War I. Though the division had deployed to France in August 1918, it did not see any combat action and was inactivated after the war. After two decades of inactivity, the division was re-activated on 15 December 1942. The "Black Hawk" Division was training in southern California for amphibious warfare in the Pacific Theater when its mission was abruptly changed by the German Counter-Offensive in the Ardennes. Instead of the Pacific Theater, the division was sent to the European Theater, arriving in France on 4 March 1945. In April, the division participated in the reduction of the Ruhr Pocket as part of First U.S. Army. On 19 April, the division was reassigned to Third U.S. Army and participated in III Corps' drive through southern Bavaria and into Austria. The division crossed the Danube River, the Amper Canal, and the Isar River in rapid succession. This was part of Gen. Eisenhower's intention to occupy the rumored "National Redoubt" region and prevent to the establishment of a last ditch Nazi stronghold—a stronghold which existed only in the minds of the Nazi

Propaganda Minister Josef Goebbels and the senior leadership and staff of SHAEF (Supreme Headquarters Allied Expeditionary Force).[1]

The 86th Infantry Division was organized per the standard Table of Organization and Equipment for U.S. Army infantry divisions. Maj. Gen. Harris M. McLasky was the Commanding General. He was assisted by a Division Staff and a Headquarters Company. There were three infantry regiments: 341st, 342nd and 343rd. The Division Artillery consisted of four field artillery battalions. Three of these battalions were equipped with 105mm howitzers: the 331st, 332nd and 911th. The 404th Field Artillery Battalion employed 155mm howitzers. Other organic units included the 86th Cavalry Reconnaissance Troop (Mechanized), the 311th Engineer Combat Battalion, and the 311th Medical Battalion. The Division Special Troops consisted of the 786th Ordnance Light Maintenance Company, the 86th Quartermaster Company, the 86th Signal Company, a Military Police Platoon, and the Division Band. During the last weeks of the war in Europe, the 86th Infantry Division was augmented with a variety of attached units including the 839th Anti-aircraft Artillery Automatic Weapons Battalion (Mobile), the 787th Tank Battalion, the 95th Chemical Mortar Battalion, the 281st Field Artillery Battalion (105mm Howitzer), the 254th Field Artillery Battalion (155mm Howitzer), the 807th Tank Destroyer Battalion (Self-Propelled) and of course, the 23rd Cavalry Squadron.[2]

23rd Cavalry Attached to the Black Hawk Division

On the morning of 28 April, the 23rd Cavalry received orders attaching it to III Corps of Third U.S. Army. At this time, the Squadron was bivouacked six miles northeast of Nuremberg. Upon reporting to III Corps Headquarters that afternoon, Squadron Commander Lt. Col. Raymond C. Adkisson learned that his unit had been attached to the 86th Infantry Division. He subsequently reported to that division's Headquarters and received orders to protect the right flank of the division, which also happened to be the right flank of both III Corps and Third U.S. Army.[3]

At this time, the 86th Infantry Division and III Corps were engaged in pursuing the disintegrating and retreating German Army south. Overall, there was no discernible front-line, only pockets of resistance wherever and whenever the Germans decided to fight. The 23rd Cavalry's mission was to support this drive by maintaining contact for the 86th Infantry

Division with the 14th Armored Division on its left and the Seventh U.S. Army on its right.[4]

As Adkisson travelled about to get more details on his Squadron's exact mission, his troop commanders and staff officers were busily getting the Squadron on the move to join up with the 86th Infantry Division. The Squadron Executive Officer was Maj. Carl O'Dowd. 1st Lt. John C. Patterson commanded Troop B. Troop C was commanded by Lt. Roy L. Dedmon. The Troop D commander was Capt. John A. Pindar and Troop E was commanded by Capt. Joseph Kolesar. Company F's commander was Capt. Russell B. Alexander. Service Troop was commanded by Capt. Harris R. Freal. Capt. Howard P. Schaudt served as Squadron Motor Officer.[5]

While attached to the 86th Infantry Division, the 23rd Cavalry Squadron would be operating in an area that extended from the Danube River valley south to the foothills of the Alps Mountains. "We were in rural Germany, mainly small towns," Mark Steece of Troop B later recalled. Three major rivers—the Danube, Isar and Inn—crossed this area from west to east along with several canals. "This terrain can be characterized as flat and rolling with numerous well defined stream and ridge lines," Capt. Schaudt later wrote. "As a whole the terrain is well suited for defense and delaying actions due to the excellent observation over the relatively flat areas, the well-defined ridge lines and numerous river, canal and stream lines."[6]

Late in the afternoon of 28 April, the 23rd Cavalry Squadron left the vicinity of Nuremberg, with Company F in the lead of the squadron column. Moving the 23rd Squadron to join up with the 86th Infantry Division proved to be quite difficult. Retreating German forces had destroyed numerous bridges along the route of advance. The movement was further complicated by the cold, and near constant rainfall which made the unimproved roads slippery and muddy. "It was very cold, rainy and miserable," Mark Steece of Troop B later recalled. Fuel shortages also posed a serious problem. "The movement of Allied troops during the last phase of the War had been so rapid, that gasoline dumps had not been able to displace forward fast enough to keep up," Capt. Schaudt later wrote. The Squadron went into an assembly area near the south bank of the Danube River in the early hours of 29 April and bivouacked for a couple hours. Meanwhile Adkisson and his officers planned the employment of the Squadron and its troops.[7]

Maj. Arnold J. Hoebeke, USA, was Regimental Supply Officer for the 343rd Infantry Regiment at this time. "Gasoline was a major problem and at one time required a haul of one hundred and thirty-five miles," he wrote after the war. He also noted that the Germans had successfully destroyed bridges over the Danube and Isar Rivers and canals. However, their hastily formed units were not strong enough to offer determined resistance to the American advance and lacked the necessary logistical support for sustained operations.[8]

In the early hours of 29 April, the 23rd Cavalry Squadron arrived in the 86th Infantry Division's area of operations and assembled near Ingolstadt. The first day of the 23rd Cavalry's attachment to the 86th Infantry Division was plagued by fuel shortages and some confusion as to the employment of the Squadron. Troops A, C, and D conducted patrols on the division's right flank, seizing several key towns and numerous prisoners in the process. Troop B worked with the 342nd Infantry Regiment, maintaining contact for the regiment with the adjacent 14th Armored Division. 2nd Platoon of Troop E and 1st Platoon of Company F were attached to the 342nd Infantry Regiment. Troop E's 3rd Platoon and Company F's 2nd Platoon Company F were attached to the 343rd Infantry Regiment. By the time these platoons joined up with the infantry, they were low on fuel and consequently were not used. The rest of Troop E and Company F were immobilized by lack of fuel. Throughout the day, Service Troop scoured the fuel dumps around Nuremberg and obtained enough to refuel Troop E and Company F that night. The Squadron Medical Detachment assigned medical teams to Troops A, B, and C. That morning, the Medical Detachment acquired a disabled Italian Fiat panel truck and managed to return it to running condition. Henceforth, the "liberated" Fiat would serve as a command car and ambulance for the Squadron Surgeon. "The closed cab protected driver and passenger very nicely from the unpredictable elements," recorded the Squadron After Action Report.[9]

Operations on 30 April 1945

The confusion over the Squadron's employment was sorted out by the morning of 30 April. Troop B and the borrowed platoons from Troop E and Company F were relieved of their attachments to the 86th Infantry Division's infantry regiments and reverted back to Squadron control. The Squadron re-assembled that afternoon. The new plan was to utilize the 23rd Cavalry Squadron's mobility and firepower to conduct semi-independent operations in support of the Black Hawk Division's advance. Bad weather and fuel shortages continued to be a problem as well as the numerous bridges that had been destroyed by the retreating Germans. Fortunately, Lt. Col. Adkisson was able to get his Squadron across the Isar River courtesy of a crossing secured by the nearby 106th Cavalry Reconnaissance Group [Mechanized].[10]

Throughout 30 April, the 23rd Cavalry Squadron pushed on deeper into southern Germany. Troop A made contact with the 106th Cavalry Reconnaissance Group [Mechanized]. Technician 5 Paul Weissman of Troop A was slightly wounded in action near Eching. Troop C's platoons captured several German towns while working to secure the 86th Infantry Division's right flank. Troop B, Troop E, Company F and the Squadron Medical Detachment accompanied the Squadron Headquarters south to Nieder-Neuching covering over fifty miles through periodic rain and hail. Encountering determined German resistance outside the town around 1800, the Squadron halted for the night. At 2000, Lt. Driscoll took a dismounted patrol of 21 men several miles behind the German lines and spent the night in the village of Pretzen. Meanwhile, Service Troop was busy trying to obtain fuel for the Squadron and managed to get 5,000 gallons of the precious fluid. That afternoon, Maj. Julius K. Lawwill from Division G-4 joined Service Troop with 12 trucks on loan from division. Service Troop ended the day astride the Autobahn near Eching.[11]

Of the 23rd Cavalry Squadron's seven subordinate units, Troop D was the most engaged that day. In early afternoon, Troop D reported back to Lt. Col. Adkisson and was soon after reinforced by the M24 light tanks of Lt. Robert F. Bartley's 1st Platoon of Company F and Lt. Richard E. David's 4th Platoon of M8 assault guns from Troop E. Leaving Troop D's Trains with the Squadron Headquarters, Capt. Pindar and his reinforced Troop D sped down the Autobahn in the direction of Freising. They crossed the Isar River on a bridge that had been captured intact by the 106th Cavalry Group and turned south. Outside the town of Fischerhausen, Capt. Pindar was wounded in the right elbow by a sniper's bullet. Pindar's men returned fire, wounding one sniper and capturing another. Troop D's Executive Officer Lt. Edward C. Burke assumed command. Capt. Pindar was evacuated to the Medical Detachment for treatment where he was heard to remark "I would have to be the first!" He was later evacuated further to the rear for additional medical treatment.[12]

With Lt. Burke now in command, Troop D (Reinforced) pressed onward. Outside the town of Moosinning, they came upon a force of approximately 100 German soldiers who were busily engaged with elements of the 106th Cavalry Group. Troop D deployed for battle and opened fire on the unsuspecting Germans. Caught by surprise by this new American force, the Germans quickly surrendered. This helped the 106th Cavalry to capture Moosinning. Altogether, the two American cavalry forces captured over 90 German soldiers. Next Troop D crossed the Isar Canal and continued on to Reixing. Meanwhile Troop D's Trains had stocked up on ammunition and fuel and set out to rejoin their parent troop. Unfortunately, they made a wrong turn and ended up on the outskirts of Munich. Troop D Trains backtracked and eventually caught up with Troop D late that night.[13]

Operations on 1 May 1945

On the 1st of May 1945, the 23rd Cavalry Squadron battled against poor roads, poor weather conditions, fuel shortages, and pockets of determined German resistance. Several times during the day, Troops B and D found themselves temporarily halted by lack of fuel. Towards the end of the day, heavy snow began to fall which severely hindered road movement. Overcoming these obstacles required initiative, determination and creativity on the part of Lt. Col. Adkisson and his cavalrymen.

Adkisson had most of his 23rd Cavalry with him in the vicinity of Indorf near where they had been halted the previous evening by stiffening German resistance. The Squadron's operations on the 1st of May can be grouped into three distinct efforts by Troop A, Troop B and Troop D and the remainder of the Squadron. Troops A and B independently struck out to bypass the German resistance in front of the Squadron. Both Troops overcame pockets of German resistance that they encountered. Troop D also bypassed Indorf, followed by Adkisson with the remainder of the Squadron. Troop D and Adkisson's group together then became engaged with the Germans in Dorfen that afternoon.

Early on the morning of 1 May, Adkisson sent Troop A to reconnoiter routes to bypass the Germans blocking his Squadron's advance. Despite the poor roads and near continuous rain, Troop A's patrols completed their mission and reported back to Adkisson a few hours later. He then sent the troop to bypass Indorf and cut off the German retreat to the Inn River. Troop A passed through several towns, then took Highway 15 due south towards the Inn River. In doing so, they drove German soldiers towards Dorfen and the main body of the Squadron. Troop A fought several small firefights and captured some prisoners along the way. They also liberated a German labor camp that was holding about 540 persons, most of whom were Polish. Arriving in Armstorf (Arestodt) in the early evening, the troop halted for some much needed rest. At 2039, however, Adkisson ordered them to continue southward. They bypassed two undefended roadblocks, then one of their armored cars slid off the road and into a ditch. After pulling the armored car out of the ditch, Troop A pressed on and captured four German trucks, a prime mover towing an artillery piece and a group of German soldiers hiding in a barn. Next they entered Haag and captured numerous German soldiers, several vehicles and a tank. In the early hours of 2 May, Troop A finally halted and caught some much needed sleep.[14]

Early that same morning, 1st Lt. John C. Patterson's Troop B linked up with Lt. Driscoll's patrol, and gained some important intelligence on the Germans opposing the Squadron. Lt. Col. Adkisson next sent Troop B on a mission to get around the Germans in front of the Squadron. Troop B captured the town of Pretzen, killing four Germans and capturing another sixty-one while losing one peep and sustaining no casualties themselves. Afterwards, Lt. Stanley M. Staszak's 1st Platoon of M24s from Company F and Lt. Harvey M. Perryman's platoon of assault guns from Troop E were attached to Troop B. "I had a lot of firepower in the Reconnaissance Troop and had a platoon of light tanks attached along with a platoon of self-propelled 75mm artillery," Patterson later wrote. The reinforced Troop moved on to Kirchasch but had to halt for six hours while fuel was brought forward for them.[15]

Having been refueled, Troop B (Reinforced) resumed its advance, and arrived in Lengdorf around 1430. Not long after, a company-sized German force was spotted approaching the town from the north. In response, Patterson deployed his force astride the road leading into town. Lt. Perryman's assault guns and two platoons of dismounted cavalrymen took up position on the left side of the road and Lt. Staszak's tanks were sent to the right of the road. The Americans opened fire with howitzers, tank guns, machine guns and rifles. Unfortunately, the tanks ran into trouble. One tank got stuck in a ditch and the batteries in Lt. Staszak's tank went dead.[16]

Despite the tankers' travails, American firepower inflicted numerous casualties on the Germans and destroyed their supply vehicles. Many of the survivors surrendered here. Others tried to escape to nearby Schrafstetten. They were pursued by the Americans. After receiving machine gun fire, the attached assault guns opened up on the town and then ordered the town to surrender. Faced with irresistible firepower, these soldiers surrendered as well, for a grand total of over sixty Germans captured including two officers.[17]

With fuel running low, Troop B returned to Lengdorf and re-grouped. While arranging for their German prisoners to be transported to the rear,

6. First Battle for the 23rd Cavalry Squadron

Troop B met up with elements of the 342rd Infantry Regiment. From them, Patterson and his soldiers learned that the 23rd Cavalry Squadron's mission had been changed again. They remained in the town for the night awaiting confirmation of the news from the Squadron Headquarters.[18]

After having already sent Troops A and B on missions to get around the Germans to his front, Lt. Col. Adkisson sent Troop D out on a similar mission. Reinforced by 4th Platoon of Troop E and a platoon of tanks from Company F, Troop D set out at 0630. An M8 assault gun of 4th Platoon's 1st Gun Section had engine trouble and so had to be left behind. The assault gun later caught up with Troop D near Hecken but subsequently ran onto the soft shoulder of the road and overturned. Again, it had to be left behind. After leaving 1st Gun Section behind, Troop D (Reinforced) did not get too far. In the town of Kinzlbach, they were halted by low fuel.[19]

For most of the morning, Lt. Col. Adkisson had his Headquarters, Troops C and E, Company F and Service Troop with him near Indorf while Troops A, B and D conducted advances designed to get around the German opposition and force them to retreat. At around 1200, he received orders for the Squadron to join Task Force Polk—a provisional force comprised of infantry, tanks, cavalry and artillery drawn from the 341st Infantry Regiment and other units of the 86th Infantry Division. Task Force Polk's mission was to seize crossings over the Inn River in the vicinity of Wasserburg, a picturesque medieval town situated where a hairpin bend in the river forms a near peninsula. At 1400, Adkisson led Troop E and Company F to support Troop A while the Squadron Headquarters and Troop C followed behind to provide reinforcements if needed. While Adkisson's group headed forward, Service Troop's Transport Platoon headed to the rear to obtain more fuel and the Squadron Maintenance Section worked on recovering several disabled U.S. vehicles.[20]

Troop D waited in Kinzlbach for four hours until the Troop's Trains arrived with more fuel. After refueling, Troop D Trains again headed for the rear for more fuel and supplies and again, Troop D with its attached tanks and assault guns pressed forward. Between Kinzlbach and Bockhorte, Troop D engaged some German infantry in the nearby woods.[21]

The Fight for Dorfen

Ahead of Troop D was the town of Dorfen, which would figure prominently in the 23rd Cavalry Squadron's operations this day. Dorfen was located on the Isen River some thirty miles east of Munich. In addition to Troop D, Lt. Col. Adkisson, Squadron Headquarters, Troop C and the main bodies of Company F and Troop E were also heading for Dorfen. About two miles north of Dorfen, Pfc. Joseph Rufrano, Jr., of Troop D was slightly wounded in action.[22]

Troop D was the first 23rd Cavalry unit to encounter Dorfen. On the outskirts of the town, the troop captured two German motorcyclists. Next, Lt. Henry H. Whiting in his M8 armored car cautiously led his platoon into Dorfen. At first, the town looked peaceful. A few German civilians appeared waving white flags. Still the town's narrow streets made maneuvering the American armored vehicles difficult.[23]

In the center of town, Lt. Whiting came across a German Sturmgeschütz III (StuG III) assault gun. The StuG III featured a long-barreled 75mm gun mounted on a Panzerkampfwagen (Pz) III tank chassis. Instead of a revolving turret, the StuG III's 75mm gun was mounted in an armored casemate that required the entire vehicle to turn in order to aim the weapon. Lt. Whiting charged the StuG III with his armored car but quickly abandoned the effort when the StuG III began turning in his direction. Whiting's thinly armored M8 could not have sustained a hit from the 75mm gun. With his gunner firing a fifty-caliber machine gun at the StuG III, Whiting's armored car backed away and got behind some cover. He then guided a nearby M24 tank into position to prevent the StuG III from advancing this way. While this was occurring, other German soldiers opened fire on the Troop D column from nearby buildings. For the next fifteen minutes, a fierce gun battle raged.[24]

From another direction, Company F and Troop E entered Dorfen. The lead tank commanded by Lt. Seekins came across four German StuG IIIs, one of which fired at the Americans. In attempting to seek cover, his tank became stuck and had to be abandoned. He and his crew climbed aboard the other Company F tanks. The whole force then withdrew from Dorfen and went into firing positions about 1.5 miles outside of the town. Along the way, a peep and a M10 trailer were also lost.[25]

By now, Lt. Col. Adkisson had arrived outside Dorfen with Squadron Headquarters. Piecing together the confusing situation in Dorfen, Adkisson ordered all of his units out of the town so that it could be shelled. Despite the difficulties of turning the armored vehicles around in the narrow streets, Troop D with elements of Troop E and Company F were all pulling out of Dorfen. A heavy snowfall now began to fall, severely restricting visibility in the fading light. At 1930, a four-gun battery of M8 assault guns from Troop E began shelling Dorfen from a range of 2,000 yards.

Twenty-five rounds were fired before deteriorating light and weather conditions ended the barrage. Troop E's commander Capt. Joseph Kolesar and Corp. Patrick R. McLain then entered Dorfen and discovered that the enemy had fled.[26]

After learning that the enemy had evacuated Dorfen, Lt. Col. Adkisson ordered his forces to bypass the town and push on to Wasserburg. Their advance was hindered by periods of heavy rain and snow. Heading west to bypass Dorfen, Troop D soon encountered poor road conditions. Most of the troop's vehicles got stuck in the mud. Troop D spent a most miserable night trying to clear their vehicles, all the while contending with bitter cold and a heavy snowfall. Meanwhile Troop D Trains had secured more fuel and ammunition for their troop but got caught in a severe snowstorm near Erding. The Headquarters of the 86th Infantry Division happened to be located in Erding, so the Headquarters staff put the wayward cavalrymen up for the night.[27]

Operations on 2 May 1945

Most of Adkisson's squadron was on the move under harsh cold and snow conditions as 1 May turned into 2 May. As part of Task Force Polk, the 23rd Cavalry Squadron was maneuvering with Wasserburg as its objective.

Troop A began 2 May in the vicinity of Haag where they had halted for a few hours rest. As Troop D was still struggling with the mud, Adkisson sent Troop C to join up with Troop A and support its advance south. Troop C bypassed Dorfen around 0200. About an hour later, the Troop C column got separated into three groups because of the heavy snow and darkness. The first group was led by the Troop Commander Lt. Roy L. Dedmon and contained seven armored cars, a half-track and three peeps. Outside of Haag, they destroyed two towed German 88mm anti-tank guns and searched a German hospital train preparing to depart. Soon after, they located Troop A in Haag. Dedmon met with the Troop A commander to coordinate their operations. At 0400, Troop A left Haag followed by Dedmon and his group from Troop C. Soon after leaving Haag, the Dedmon group surprised a German force in bivouac and captured fifty of them. Troops A and Troop C continued southward to Wasserburg which was less than ten miles distant.[28]

The second Troop C group consisted of 2nd Platoon and the Troop Headquarters Section. At 0800, they met up with Troop B and followed

The German 88mm Gun was the most lethal anti-tank weapon of the war. Fortunately, these guns were not a factor in the liberation of western Czechoslovakia (author's photograph).

them to St. Wolfgang where they captured fifty German soldiers. At 1300, Squadron Headquarters ordered them by radio to proceed to the Squadron's Assembly Area near Haag. Outside Haag, 2nd Platoon / Command Section fought a firefight with some Germans in a wooded area, killing several and capturing seventy-five. Afterwards they rejoined the Squadron.[29]

The third group from Troop C consisted of 3rd Platoon. This group further fragmented when Sgt. George Morrow and his armored car got separated from it. After some time, 3rd Platoon joined up with Troop E, Company F, and elements of the Squadron Headquarters and continued with them towards Haag. Outside Haag, the combined column encountered two German self-propelled 88mm guns and a personnel carrier. The Squadron Communications Officer, Capt. Vincent R. Schmidt, led two enlisted men on a bold flank attack which completely took the Germans by surprise. The Germans quickly surrendered. Capt. Schmidt then led the column in clearing out the town, capturing some 400 German soldiers. The column then left Hagg and headed for Wasserburg. Sgt. George

Morrow and his armored car spent most of the day trying to find Troop C. Eventually they rejoined Troop C outside of Haag.[30]

At 0445 on the morning of 2 May, Troop B left Lengdorf with orders to proceed to Wasserberg via Route 15. 2nd Platoon Leader Lt. Victor Driscoll's armored car led the column, followed by 1st Lt. John Patterson in a peep. Near the town of Schwindau, the column encountered a roadblock. While attempting to drive around the roadblock, Driscoll's armored car struck a land mine. "I was in a jeep [peep] just back of it and watched the front wheel go up until it was just a speck in the sky," recalled 1st Lt. Patterson. "Fortunately the iron plate they had added protected the crew." The armored car was disabled and Driscoll, Technician 4 Runion, Technician 5 Riatau and Technician 5 Shaw all suffered shock from the blast. Reducing the roadblock took three hours. Thirty-one Germans were captured and the troop pushed south. About two miles north of Wasserburg, Troop B rejoined its parent Squadron.[31]

Two of Troop E's platoons were temporarily serving with Troops B and D. The rest of Troop E led by Capt. Joseph Kolesar accompanied part of the Squadron Headquarters moving on Wasserburg. At 0600, this force entered the outskirts of Haag. In Haag, one soldier was injured by a ruptured fifty-caliber machine gun cartridge and another was wounded by friendly fire. Both were taken to a local military hospital where the 3rd Platoon Leader accepted the surrender of the hospital and the town. Troop E also destroyed two German 88mm anti-tank guns with grenades. They left Haag at 1100 bound for Wasserburg.[32]

With two of his platoons temporarily attached to Troops B and D, Capt. Russell Alexander was left with 3rd Platoon and the Company F Headquarters. Accompanying the Squadron Headquarters, Capt. Alexander's part of Company F reached the outskirts of Haag around 0930. After a brief firefight, they took several German medical personnel as prisoners. In Haag, one American soldier was wounded in the hand by small arms fire. Continuing on, Alexander's group had several more small firefights with the Germans, killing several of them and capturing another 30 or so.[33]

Troops A and Lt. Dedmon's group from Troop C were the first American units to approach Wasserburg. On the outskirts of this picturesque Bavarian town, the Americans encountered numerous German soldiers. Many surrendered without a fight, but several firefights occurred with those who were intent on resisting. Lt. James W. Struber from Troop A was wounded while trying to get four heavy German trucks moving up a hill after they had become stuck. One group of Germans in particular attempted to fight a delaying action with anti-tank guns and machine guns. This group fired on the head of the American column, then hastily withdrew to a new position and opened fire again. After withdrawing a second time, the Germans set up a roadblock augmented by mines on some high ground overlooking Wasserburg. Troop A halted and sent a party forward to check out the roadblock. By now, the Germans had decided to further resistance was futile. They surrendered and the roadblock was overcome.[34]

Dedmon came upon Troop A held up outside Wasserburg. He led a team with a peep and an armored car to find a way around the roadblock. In doing so, they found four German trucks hauling arms and equipment. Two Germans were captured and the Americans set fire to one of the trucks. Further on, they captured another 75 Germans. After that, they contacted elements of the 121st Cavalry Reconnaissance Squadron [Mechanized] of the 106th Cavalry Group and returned back to the Troop A / C column.[35]

From captured German soldiers and local civilians, Troop A's commander learned that Wasserburg was strongly held by SS troops. He radioed Lt. Col. Adkisson for additional tanks and assault guns to continue the drive into town. Not long after, Adkisson arrived on scene, who informed him that the Commanding General of the 86th Infantry Division Maj. Gen. Harris M. McLasky had decided to use his infantry instead to capture the town. The cavalrymen were to stand aside while the rest of Task Force Polk passed through them to attack Wasserburg. Later that afternoon, Task Force Polk did indeed pass through Troops A and C and capture Wasserburg.[36]

In early afternoon, Company F arrived outside Wasserburg. Adkisson joined them and inquired of their fuel situation. Capt. Alexander informed his commanding officer that his tanks were nearly out of gas. Adkisson directed them to remain there and have chow. As chow was being served, the Germans fired artillery at Company F. The company was relocated to a more secure location where they remained for the rest of the day.[37]

At 1430, Troop E arrived in the area northwest of Wasserburg. A four-gun battery of M8 assault guns took up a position and began firing on the town at 1530. A total of 95 rounds of 75mm artillery ammunition were fired at Wasserburg from ranges between 2,400 to 4,000 yards. After completing their fire mission, Troop E went into bivouac for the rest of the day.[38]

Troop D spent much of the morning of 2 May struggling to extricate

6. First Battle for the 23rd Cavalry Squadron   77

several of its armored cars from the mud. 4th Platoon of Troop E assisted with this effort. They were able to free the armored cars and got moving again around 0800. They bypassed Dorfen. In the town of Geislbach, the attached tanks of 2nd Platoon / Company F began running low on fuel and so the platoon was left here to await a resupply. Troop D and 4th Platoon / Troop E continued on without them. Near Esterndorf, Troop D met a Frenchman who informed them that a group of 150 Germans wanted to surrender. The Americans rounded up the surrendering Germans and sent them back to Geislbach to be guarded by 2nd Platoon / Company F. Troop D then continued on to link up with the rest of their Squadron in the vicinity of Wasserburg. Unfortunately, 4th Platoon of Troop E's vehicles ran out of fuel at St. Wolfgang. Left behind by Troop D, 4th Platoon waited for several hours until fuel was brought to them around 2300.[39]

On the morning of 2 May, Troop D Trains learned that the 23rd Cavalry Squadron was advancing on Wasserburg. So Troop D Trains set out to rejoin them in that location. They passed through Dorfen without incident but encountered small arms fire in Haag. There were no American casualties. Soon after, they contacted the Squadron Headquarters Forward Echelon and joined up with them in heading forward. Along the way, they were fired on by a group of twelve soldiers. In the ensuing firefight, three Germans were killed and several more were wounded.[40]

By nightfall, the 23rd Cavalry Squadron had more or less reconstituted itself in the vicinity of Wasserburg. Troop B rejoined the Squadron near Wasserburg at 1600. Troop A and Lt. Dedmon's group of Troop C rejoined the 23rd Cavalry Squadron outside of Wasserburg at around 1700. The main body of Troop E was in bivouac northwest of Wasserburg; its 2nd and 4th Platoons would rejoin it the next day. Twenty-four hours after leaving their parent troop, Troop D Trains found its parent Troop on a roadside near Soyen. The Trains re-supplied Troop D's vehicles with fuel and passed out rations to the cavalrymen. Then the re-constituted Troop D proceeded to Soyen where they billeted for the night. Early in the morning of 3 May, 4th Platoon / Troop E rejoined Troop D. Company F was re-united with its 1st Platoon at 1900 and spent the night outside Wasserburg. Company F's 2nd Platoon were finally refueled at 2200 but decided to spend the night at Geislbach guarding the German prisoners and catching up on their sleep. They would rejoin their company the following afternoon. On 3 May, Squadron Maintenance retrieved Company F's abandoned M24 tank and peep from Dorfen.[41]

2 May was the last day of the 23rd Cavalry Squadron's combat operations with the 86th Infantry Division. The following day, the Squadron

reverted back to the 16th Armored Division's control and departed from III Corps' area of operations. They weren't the only ones leaving III Corps. Also that day, the 86th Infantry Division was transferred to Seventh U.S. Army.

Though the 86th Infantry Division lost one 16th Armored Division unit, it soon gained another former unit of the division. On 6 May 1945, the 787th Tank Battalion became part of the division in Erding, Germany. Later that day, the battalion crossed into Austria and served with the division for the few remaining days of the war in Europe. It did not see any combat action.[42]

During its five days with the 86th Infantry Division, the 23rd Cavalry Squadron gained valuable experience in combat operations. Though often hampered by insufficient fuel supplies and poor weather and roads, the Squadron covered 150 miles, fought numerous small firefights and captured numerous towns and villages and several hundred German soldiers. The Squadron operated as mechanized cavalry was designed; it used its mobility and firepower to conduct reconnaissance, secure objectives, guard prisoners and support advances by the infantry. For his leadership during the Squadron's first combat operation, Lt. Col. Raymond Adkisson was later awarded the Bronze Star. "Most of the opposition consisted of fanatical SS troops who seemed determined to give their lives for the Fatherland and their Führer," Capt. Howard Schaudt would later write. "The 23d Cavalry tried to help them with this effort."[43]

7

The First Days of May 1945

As the month of May began, the Third Reich was only days away from oblivion. On 30 April, Adolf Hitler, his wife Eva Braun and a number of his senior Nazi leaders committed suicide in an underground bunker in Berlin. The Western Allies and the Soviets were rapidly overrunning what was left of the Third Reich.

The Situation in Early May 1945

The 1937 Czechoslovak-German border region was mountainous and heavily wooded which channelized vehicular movement through defensible mountain passes and gaps. Once through these mountains, the terrain leveled out into rolling farmland and the road network improved significantly. The region's most important city was Pilsen, with its massive Skoda Works industrial complex and a large airport utilized by the remnants of the German Luftwaffe.

Since the middle of April, Third U.S. Army had been advancing parallel to the border. Its XII Corps with 2nd Cavalry Group and the 90th and 97th Infantry Divisions were screening the ever-lengthening Third Army left flank. XII Corps' other divisions—26th Infantry, 5th Infantry and 11th Armored—were already into Austria. Concerns over this flank prompted Twelfth U.S. Army Group (Gen. Omar Bradley) to have First U.S. Army send its 1st Infantry Division south to the Czechoslovak border so that XII Corps could tighten up its lines. Plans were also in the works to transfer V Corps from First U.S. Army down to Third U.S. Army to further aid the drive into Austria.[1]

The Protectorate of Bohemia and Moravia (as the Nazis had renamed these regions of Czechoslovakia) operated under a somewhat complicated system of military and political governance. The civil government for the Protectorate was headed by Reichsminister Karl Frank. The military command structure was more complicated. The German Army garrison forces in Prague and Pilsen reported to Gen. Rudolf Toussaint, commander of Wehrkreis (Military Area) Prague. The German 7th Army commanded the field forces confronting Patton's Third U.S. Army along the 1937 Czechoslovak-German border. Army Group Center commanded by Generalfeldmarschall (field marshall) Ferdinand Schörner was fighting against the Soviets driving westward from Moravia.

The German forces defending the Czechoslovak border belonged to Gen. Hans von Obstfelder's 7th Army. Having been devastated during the Normandy Campaign and again in the Ardennes Counter-offensive, the German 7th Army was a shell of its former self. It consisted of the severely depleted 2nd Panzer Division, Wehrkreis XIII (a training and replacement command absorbed into the 7th Army), an engineer brigade, an Officer Candidate School, and the 11th Panzer Division. Only the 11th Panzer Division was near its authorized manpower strength, but like the 2nd Panzer Division, it was short of tanks. Supplies in general were lacking. An acute shortage of fuel rendered the two panzer divisions virtually immobile. Lacking sufficient forces to cover the entire border, 7th Army's defense consisted only of strong points and roadblocks. A counter-attack using the 2nd and 11th Panzer Divisions had been ordered against Third U.S. Army's left flank in late April but lack of fuel prevented it from being launched.[2]

German Army garrison forces in the vicinity of Prague and Pilsen were under the command of Gen. Rudolf Toussaint, commander of Wehrkreis (Military Area) Prague. His forces consisted of two regional defense divisions, which were tasked with guarding various installations around the city. The German garrison in Pilsen also fell under his supervision.[3]

The German forces in the city of Pilsen and its vicinity were under the direct command of Generalmajor (brigadier general) George von Majewski. The Pilsen garrison was a mixture of German forces. Just outside of Pilsen, the Luftwaffe maintained an air base with assorted military aircraft grounded here due to lack of fuel. Several German anti-aircraft artillery units were stationed in and around the city to protect the Skoda Works industrial complex. Generalmajor von Majewski also had some infantry units and an artillery replacement battalion.[4]

On 29 April 1945, Generalmajor Gerhard Müller reported to Gen. Rudolf Toussaint, commander of German forces in Wehrkreis (Military

Area) Prague and was in turn ordered to report to Pilsen to assist Generalmajor von Majewski in conducting a defense of that city. Born on 21 September 1895 in Magdeburg, Germany, Müller had first joined the German Army in March 1914. During World War I, Müller had commanded an engineer platoon, and served as a battalion adjutant and staff officer. After the war, the victorious Allies forced a massive downsizing of the German Army. Müller was able to remain in the much reduced Army but was transferred from the engineer branch to the artillery. During the 1920s and early 1930s, Müller steadily ascended through the ranks, reaching the rank of major by 1933. In 1937, he became a General Staff Corps officer and was promoted to lieutenant colonel. During World War II, Müller served in a variety of staff and command positions. He commanded a regiment during the France campaign of 1940, and was later promoted to colonel. From 1943–1944, he was a corps artillery commander. In 1944, he was promoted to generalmajor.[5]

Upon arriving in Pilsen, Generalmajor Müller soon discovered the poor condition of German forces in the city. Machine guns and small arms were in short supply. Von Majewski had organized his forces into alert units. "In addition to these forces there were some antiaircraft artillery batteries placed around Pilsen, but there were too few tractors to move the guns into antitank defense positions quickly enough to ward off an attack by armor," Generalmajor Müller wrote after the war. "The commander [von Majewski] knew that with these weapons and means a town like Pilsen could neither be pacified in case of an uprising nor defended against well-equipped hostile troops."[6]

In Prague, Gen. Toussaint realized the hopelessness of his command's situation. As April came to a close, he discussed the situation with Reichsminister Frank and proposed to contact Gen. Patton via the International Red Cross. Frank agreed but efforts to establish this contact failed. So on 3 May, Toussaint sent his Chief of Staff Gen. Max Ziervogel and Protectorate Minister Bertsch by car to attempt to contact the American forces directly. On the way, they were captured by Czech partisans and later turned over to the Soviet Army.[7]

Gen. Toussaint was in a precarious situation. He had no desire of continuing the fight but he would not surrender to the Czech partisans. He ordered his troops not to resist the Americans whenever they showed up.[8]

All German forces opposing the Soviets in central Czechoslovakia were under the command of Generalfeldmarschall Ferdinand Schörner and Army Group Center. The relentless drive by the Soviet Army was pushing Army Group Center back at the same time that Patton's Third Army was pressing against the German 7th Army along the Czechoslovak border. As a result, German forces were being steadily pressed into a pocket in western Czechoslovakia. An estimated 141,000 German troops were believed to be in this pocket, the vast majority of whom were confronting the Soviets in an effort to enable German civilians and other German forces to escape Soviet capture by fleeing west towards the Americans. In late April, Schörner assumed overall command of all German forces in the Czechoslovak Pocket. This included the 7th Army and Gen. Toussaint's Wehrkreis Prague.[9]

Ferdinand Schörner was a fanatical Nazi and a notoriously brutal commander. He was born in Munich, Germany on 12 June 1892. He initially served as a soldier in the Infantry Leib Regiment in Munich from 1911 to 1912 before leaving the army to attend universities in Munich, Germany; Lucerne, Switzerland and Florence, Italy. When World War I broke out, Schörner rejoined the German Army and was commissioned as a Leutnant (2nd lieutenant) in the Infantry Leib Regiment. During the war, he fought in campaigns in France, Italy, Serbia and Rumania, earning the Pour Le Merite military award for heroism and a promotion to Oberstleutnant (1st lieutenant) in March 1918. After the war, Schörner remained in the truncated German Army. During the 1920s, he served as a company commander in the 41st and 19th Infantry Regiments, covertly attended the Fuehrergehilfenschule (German staff officer school) which had been outlawed by the victorious Allies and earned a promotion to Hauptmann (captain). From 1932 to 1935, he served as an instructor at the Infantry School Dresden and was promoted to major. From 1935 to 1937, he served on the German Army General Staff in Berlin and was promoted to Oberstleutnant (lieutenant colonel). He commanded the 98th Mountain Infantry Regiment in the Poland and France Campaigns, and earned promotions to Oberst (colonel) and generalmajor in rapid succession. From 1940 to 1942, he commanded the 6th Mountain Infantry Division during campaigns in the Vosges Mountains of France, Norway, Greece and Finland. He then earned another series of rapid promotions, first to Generalleutnant (major general) and then to General der Gebirgstruppe (lieutenant general of Mountain Troops). From 1942 to 1943, he commanded the XIX Mountain Corps in Norway and Finland and was promoted to Generaloberst (general). Next he was assigned as Chief of the National Socialist Indoctrination of the Army responsible for instilling Nazi ideology in the German soldiers. This assignment proved both unsuccessful and brief. In April 1944, he assumed command of Army

Group South and then assumed command of Army Group North four months later. In January 1945, Hitler placed him in command of Army Group Center and then promoted him to Generalfeldmarschall (field marshall) in April 1945. He was both a fanatical Nazi and a fanatical anti–Communist.[10]

Soon after assuming command of all German forces in the Czechoslovak Pocket, Generalfeldmarschall Schörner ordered the 11th Panzer Division to leave the Czechoslovak border areas and head east to fight the Soviets. The order was virtually impossible to carry out due to the serious fuel shortages within the German Army. The 11th Panzer Division's commander, Gen. Wend von Wietersheim, knew full well what Schörner's orders to head east to fight the Soviets meant for his soldiers: death on the battlefield or years of captivity in a Soviet prisoner of war camp with little chance of survival. With the assistance of 2nd Cavalry Group's commander, Col. Charles H. Reed, Gen. von Wietersheim surrendered the bulk of his division to Brig. Gen. Herbert Earnest and the 90th Infantry Division on 4 May 1945. The 2nd Infantry Division played a supporting role in processing the German surrender. Several days later, the remainder of the 11th Panzer surrendered to the 26th Infantry Division in southwestern Czechoslovakia. The effect was an unmitigated disaster for 7th Army. "The unexpectedly hurried departure of the 11th Pz [Panzer] Div [Division] meant the exposure of our southern flank and clearance of the Taus-Pilsen road for the Americans," Gen. Karl Weissenberger, commander of Wehrkreis XIII, later wrote.[11]

With Third U.S. Army operating along and over the 1937 Czechoslovak border, many Czechs were eagerly hoping that the Americans would push further east and liberate them before the Soviet Army did so. Already, the Soviet Army had established a frightful reputation for brutality against the peoples of the lands that it captured. Everywhere the Soviet Army operated, its soldiers committed atrocities and depredations against the local populations, including pillaging, rapes, deportations and murder. Soviet brutality was not restricted to the Germans and their allies, as the people of Poland, Ruthenia, the Baltic States and the Slovak region of Czechoslovakia could readily attest to.

Czechoslovak President Eduard Benes was especially exuberant over the possibility of an American liberation. As his personal secretary and legal advisor Edward Taborsky later wrote,

> I shall never forget the deep emotion with which Benes, who always hated to bare his feelings, received the news of Patton's armies crossing the border into Czechoslovakia. "Thank God, thank God," he said when I rushed in to tell him that Patton

was at long last on Czechoslovak soil. Unable to control his excitement he began to pace his study, and to judge by the expression in his eyes he was already visualizing the beneficial political consequences of this event.[12]

With a collapsing German Army and a powerful American Army on its western border, western Czechoslovakia's deliverance from its nightmare of Nazi occupation seemed at hand and a bright postwar future seemed possible.

8

Day of Decision

The life of the Third Reich and its armed forces was coming to a rapid and violent end. Only days remained in its brutal, evil existence. The remaining German forces were inexorably being squeezed into a pocket that covered parts of western Czechoslovakia and Austria. With Third U.S. Army and its newly gained V Corps massing just over the 1937 Czechoslovak border, the Supreme Allied Commander Gen. Eisenhower finally decided to push eastward and liberate part of that Allied nation. As part of this effort, the 16th Armored Division was rushed forward from Nuremberg to join in the final offensive of the war in Europe.

Debate over Czechoslovakia

For the last several weeks, debate had been raging at the highest levels of the Allied High Command over whether or not to liberate western Czechoslovakia and more specifically, the capital city of Prague. British Prime Minister Winston Churchill, the British Chiefs of Staff, the British Foreign Office, the U.S. State Department and pro-democracy Czechs and Slovaks pressed for Third U.S. Army to liberate Prague and as much of western Czechoslovakia as possible as a counter-balance to Soviet machinations to install pro–Soviet Czech and Slovak Communists in power in the liberated country. Supreme Allied Commander Gen. Dwight D. Eisenhower, however, did not want to hazard American lives for postwar political purposes and did not want to offend the Soviets. U.S. President Harry S. Truman, U.S. Army Chief of Staff Gen. George C. Marshall and the other U.S. Chiefs of Staff supported Eisenhower's decision as the Theater Commander in Europe. Soviet Premier Josef Stalin, the Soviet High Command and Czech and Slovak Communists all wanted a pro-Soviet Communist government installed in Czechoslovakia and thus were opposed to Patton liberating Prague.[1]

By early May, Gen. Eisenhower was satisfied that the National Redoubt was nothing more than a figment of Nazi propaganda. The rapid and minimally opposed occupation of the National Redoubt area by Third and Seventh U.S. Armies had proven that fact beyond any doubt. The complete capitulation of Nazi Germany was only days away. Adolf Hitler and several of his senior leadership had already committed suicide. The Soviets had captured Berlin. In the north, British Field Montgomery Sir Bernard Montgomery's forces had driven to the Baltic Sea at Lübeck and linked up with Soviet forces when they arrived there several hours later. In the center, First U.S. Army had linked up with Soviet forces on the Elbe River the week before. To the south, U.S. and French forces were nearing to juncture with other Allied forces driving up from Italy. The only remaining German forces of any appreciable size were in central and western Czechoslovakia and parts of Austria.[2]

Eisenhower decided to send Third U.S. Army to help the Soviets clear the remaining German forces out of Czechoslovakia. On 4 May, he sent a message to the Soviets informing them of his decision to send Third U.S. Army eastward to the line Karlsbad–Pilsen–Budweis with a possible further advancement to the west bank of the Vltava River. Since the Vltava River flowed through Prague, this implied a possible advance to liberate at least part of the Czechoslovak capital. Eisenhower also sent orders to Gen. Bradley for Third U.S. Army to conduct the operation.[3]

At 1930 hours, Bradley telephoned Patton with Eisenhower's orders to attack to the Karlsbad–Pilsen–Budweis line. In addition, Bradley was transferring First U.S. Army's V Corps to Third U.S. Army for Patton to use in his offensive. V Corps was already in the process of moving its forces south to support Third Army's operations along the Czechoslovak border. Patton immediately called V Corps' commanding general, Maj. Gen. Clarence Huebner, and ordered him to attack the following morning with the intention of securing the city of Pilsen. The new 16th Armored Division would be given to V Corps for the attack on Pilsen. Patton's Chief of Staff Maj. Gen. Hobart Gay called XII Corps commanding general Maj. Gen. S. LeRoy Irwin and ordered his corps to advance on Prague with the 4th Armored Division and the 5th and 90th Infantry Divisions. Irwin's 11th Armored and 26th Infantry Divisions would cover the corps' right flank as they advanced northeast into Czechoslovakia. Both V and XII Corps were to attack the following morning with their infantry divisions to open up routes for their armored divisions to pass through.[4]

Maj. Gen. Huebner asked to use the more experienced 9th Armored

Division for the Pilsen attack instead of the 16th Armored Division. This was not a slight against the 16th Armored Division. The 9th Armored Division was well-experienced and battle-tested, having had fought in the Ardennes Counter-Offensive, seized the Remagen Bridge and driven across central Germany. With the war in Europe winding down, Patton, however, wanted to get the new 16th Armored Division into the final fight. So, 16th Armored Division would drive on Pilsen, and the 9th Armored Division would detach its Combat Command A to spearhead 1st Infantry Division's drive on Karlsbad while the rest of the 9th Armored Division was held in reserve.[5]

Opposing V Corps along the Czechoslovak border was a conglomeration of miscellaneous German Army units belonging to the 7th Army. Facing the 1st Infantry Division and CCA of 9th Armored Division were the 404th Training Division, the 413th Training Division, several battalions of officer candidates, and several kampfgruppen. Opposing the 97th Infantry Division was the 2nd Panzer Division, the 665th Engineer Brigade, a battalion of Volkstrum (Home Guard), and several kampfgruppen. The 2nd Infantry Division was opposed by several kampfgruppen and the 13th Engineer Construction Replacement Battalion. All of these units were under-strength, lacking fuel and short on artillery.[6]

At 2200 on 4 May 1945, Col. S. B. Mason, V Corps Chief of Staff, issued a Letter of Instruction on behalf of Maj. Gen. Huebner for V Corps' advance into western Czechoslovakia. Per this Instruction, the 97th Infantry Division was to undertake V Corps' primary effort on the morning of 5 May with an advance along the Bor-Pilsen axis. The Trident Division's mission was to prepare the way for the 16th Armored Division's advance on Pilsen. On the 97th Infantry Division's right, the 2nd Infantry Division was to attack along the axis Klener-Pilsen. On the 97th Infantry Division's left, the 1st Infantry Division was to maintain contact between that division and the VIII Corps of First U.S. Army on V Corps' left. Combat Command A of the 9th Armored Division was attached to the 1st Infantry Division but could only be committed by order of V Corps Headquarters. The remainder of the 9th Armored Division constituted V Corps' reserve. The 16th Armored Division was ordered to assemble at Waidhaus and to be prepared to pass through the forward positions of V Corps and secure the city of Pilsen. Perhaps, most significantly, Col. Mason concluded by writing "PILZEN will be secured with the utmost speed."[7]

Third U.S. Army Attacks on 5 May 1945

On the morning of 5 May 1945, the infantry divisions of V and XII Corps began the attacks to open up the routes for the armored divisions to exploit. In the north, 1st Infantry Division pushed eastward from the vicinity of Cheb and the 97th and 2nd Infantry Divisions pushed east to open up the main routes to Pilsen. On V Corps' right, XII Corps sent 90th and 5th Infantry Divisions and the 2nd Cavalry Group to open up the mountain passes that the 4th Armored Division would use for its advance on Prague. At first, the Americans were coldly greeted by Sudeten Germans but after entering into the area populated by the Czechs, each town and village exuberantly greeted the Americans as liberators. The people turned out to greet the Americans dressed in their finest attire and bearing gifts of food, beverages and alcohol. For many American soldiers, the scenes were reminiscent of liberating France the previous summer.[8]

V Corps' attacks on 5 May went exceedingly well with significant advances made by the infantry. Based on these successes, Maj. Gen. Huebner issued a revised Letter of Instruction for his corps via his Chief of Staff, Col. Mason. In V Corps' north sector, the 1st Infantry Division was to attack early on the morning of 6 May with the objective of capturing Karlsbad. Combat Command A of the 9th Armored Division would spearhead 1st Division's attack. V Corps' primary mission continued to be the liberation of Pilsen. Accordingly, the 97th Infantry Division was to continue its advance per the preceding day's Letter of Instruction. In addition, they were to allow two combat commands of the 16th Armored Division to pass through their lines for a drive on Pilsen on 6 May. The Trident Division would also maintain contact with the adjacent 1st and 2nd Infantry Divisions. On the 97th Infantry Division's right, the 2nd Infantry Division would continue its advance and permit one of 16th Armored Division's combat commands to pass through its forward lines. The remainder of 9th Armored Division remained as V Corps reserve while the 102nd Cavalry Reconnaissance Group [Mechanized] (Reinforced) would mop up the corps' rear areas for bypassed pockets of German resistance and maintain contact between the 1st and 97th Infantry Divisions. V Corps' primary effort thus became the 16th Armored Division's drive on Pilsen. The 16th Armored Division was to pass through the forward lines of the 97th and 2nd Infantry Divisions along the Bor-Pilsen axis and secure the important city. After occupying towns, all V Corps units were to establish roadblocks leading into those towns with the purpose of screening military and civilian traffic.[9]

16th Armored Division Heads for the Front

While V and XII Corps were attacking into Czechoslovakia, the 16th Armored Division was still over a hundred miles to the west at Nuremburg. Having completed its temporary assignment with the 86th Infantry Division, the 23rd Cavalry Squadron was back with the 16th Armored Division. After being relieved of their security responsibilities, the 16th Armored Division rushed its units eastward to Waidhaus, Germany with Combat Command B in the lead. CCB departed for Waidhaus at 0600 on the morning of 5 May and completed its movement at 1900. Division Headquarters was established in an old railroad car in Waidhaus, and the combat commands took up positions that night inside Czechoslovakia in the rear of the U.S. infantry's front lines.[10]

When Company C of the 137th Armored Ordnance Battalion rolled into Nyrany, they were the first Americans to enter the Czech village. Some German soldiers attempted to resist the Americans but were quickly subdued. "I can remember some firing and having rifle bullets come too close for comfort to me," recalled Sgt. George Thompson. He marched a group of German prisoners through the village and turned them over to Military Policemen for transport to a prisoner of war camp. While doing so, Sgt. Thompson and his soldiers had to prevent the Czech villagers from exacting revenge on their German oppressors.[11]

Preparing for Battle

Late on 5 May 1945, the 16th Armored Division completed its movement into the V Corps area of operations. Brig. Gen. John Pierce assembled his key commanders and staff and briefed them on the division's upcoming operation. Their mission was to pass through the forward lines of the 2nd and 97th Infantry Divisions and push eastward to liberate Pilsen, western Bohemia's largest and most important city. All three of the division's combat commands would be involved. Col. Charles Noble's Combat Command B (CCB) would make the main effort down the Bor-Pilsen Road and seize the high ground west of the city. On a parallel road to their south, Lt. Col. Thoss B. Beck's Reserve Command (CCR) was to cover CCB's flank and seize high ground east of Pilsen. Lt. Col. Shelby F. Williams' Combat Command A (CCA) was to follow Noble's forces in support and reserve. Completion of these movements would put the division in position to liberate the city.[12]

On the eve of its first combat offensive, the 16th Armored Division was organized as follows:

Division Headquarters
  Division Artillery Headquarters
  Division Trains
Combat Command A—Lt. Col. Shelby F. Williams
  5th Tank Battalion
  18th Armored Infantry Battalion
  393rd Armored Field Artillery Battalion
  Troop A, 23rd Cavalry Reconnaissance Squadron [Mechanized]
  Company A, 216th Armored Engineer Battalion
  Company A, 216th Armored Medical Battalion
  Battery A, 571st Antiaircraft Artillery [Automatic Weapons] Battalion
Combat Command B—Col. Charles B. Noble
  64th Armored Infantry Battalion
  16th Tank Battalion
  396th Armored Field Artillery Battalion
  Battery B, 571st Antiaircraft Artillery [Automatic Weapons] Battalion
  Troop B, 23rd Cavalry Reconnaissance Squadron [Mechanized]
  Company B, 216th Armored Engineer Battalion
  Company C, 137th Armored Ordnance Battalion
  Company B, 216th Armored Medical Battalion
Reserve Command—LtCol. Thoss B. Beck
  26th Tank Battalion
  69th Armored Infantry Battalion
  397th Armored Field Artillery Battalion
  Company C, 216th Armored Engineer Battalion
  Troop C, 23rd Cavalry Reconnaissance Squadron [Mechanized]
  Battery C, 571st Antiaircraft Artillery [Automatic Weapons] Battalion[13]

The key commanders and staff officers were as follows:

  Commanding General—Brig. Gen. John L. Pierce
  Assistant Division Commander—Col. A. Worrell Roffe
  Artillery Commander—Col. Barksdale Hamlett
  Chief of Staff—Col. Edwin C. Greiner
  Assistant Chief of Staff G-1(Personnel)—Lt. Col. Ralph W. Gontrum
  Assistant Chief of Staff G-2 (Intelligence)—Lt. Col. Everett G. Hahney
  Assistant Chief of Staff G-3 (Operations)—Lt. Col. James M. Worthington
  Assistant Chief of Staff G-4 (Logistics)—Lt. Col. Philip L. Elliott

8. Day of Decision

Assistant Chief of Staff G-5 (Civil Affairs)—Maj. Julian P. Anderson
Adjutant General—Lt. Col. Leo E. Schulten, Jr.
Commander, Combat Command A—Lt. Col. Shelby F. Williams
Commander, Combat Command B—Col. Charles H. Noble
Commander Reserve Command—Lt. Col. Thoss B. Beck[14]

Of the 16th Armored Division's key commanders and staff officers, only the Division G-1, Lt. Col. Gontrum, and the Division adjutant general, Lt. Col. Schulten, had been with the division since its activation nearly two years beforehand.

To support the 16th Armored Division's advance into Czechoslovakia, the 216th Armored Engineer Battalion was broken up and its line companies were assigned to each of the combat commands. Company A was attached to Combat Command A, Company B was attached to Combat Command B and Company C was attached to Reserve Command. A section of Headquarters Company's Reconnaissance Section and Water Supply Section were also attached to each combat command. The remainder of Headquarters Company was attached to the Division Headquarters. Anticipating that rivers and streams would have to be crossed, the Assistant Division Engineer Capt. Schullen arranged to borrow a platoon of the 998th Engineer Treadway Bridge Company and attach it to the 216th Armored Engineers. This company had previously been the battalion's Company E back at Camp Chaffee.[15]

Like the 216th Armored Engineer Battalion, subordinate units of the 23rd Cavalry Squadron were temporarily detached from the Squadron and assigned to the Combat Commands. Troop A was attached to Combat Command A. Troop B was attached to Combat Command B. Troop C was attached to Reserve Command. Troop D with 2nd Platoon of Troop E attached was tasked with screening the division's right flank for the drive into Czechoslovakia. Squadron Headquarters and the remainder of Troop E travelled together. Company F accompanied Service Troop, the Squadron Rear Echelon and Medical Detachment.[16]

Standard procedure for U.S. armored divisions was to form combined arms task forces within their combat commands for operations. Several days prior, each of the 16th Armored Division's three combat commands accordingly formed several task forces consisting of tanks, armored infantry, armored field artillery, engineers, medics, and communications and supply troops.

For his combat command's assault, Col. Noble formed three task forces:

Task Force A (Maj. George B. Pickett)
   64th Armored Infantry Battalion (minus Company B)
   Company A, 16th Tank Battalion
   1 platoon, Company D, 16th Tank Battalion
   Troop B, 23rd Cavalry Squadron
   1 platoon, Company B, 216th Armored Engineers Battalion
Task Force B (Lt. Col. L. F. Lewis)
   16th Tank Battalion (minus Company A)
   Company B, 64th Armored Infantry Battalion
   1 platoon, Company B, 216th Armored Engineers Battalion
Task Force R
   CCB Headquarters
   396th Armored Field Artillery Battalion (Lt. Col. James E. Norvell)
   Company B, 216th Armored Engineers Battalion (-)
   Company B, 216th Armored Medical Battalion
   Company C, 137th Armored Ordnance Maintenance Battalion
   Battery B, 571st Antiaircraft Artillery [Automatic Weapons] Battalion[17]

Similarly Reserve Command formed its task forces as such:

Task Force Horrocks (Lt. Col. Richard E. Horrocks)
   69th Armored Infantry Battalion (minus Company B)
   Company B, 26th Tank Battalion
   One Platoon, Company C, 216th Armored Engineers Battalion
   One Platoon, Battery C, 571st Antiaircraft Artillery [Automatic Weapons] Battalion
Task Force Baker (Lt. Col. William O. Baker)
   26th Tank Battalion (minus Companies B and C)
   Company B, 69th Armored Infantry Battalion
   One Platoon, Company C, 216th Armored Engineers Battalion
   One Platoon, Battery C, 571st Antiaircraft Artillery [Automatic Weapons] Battalion
Task Force "R"
   Reserve Command Headquarters
   397th Armored Field Artillery Battalion
   Company C, 26th Tank Battalion
   Company C, 216th Armored Engineers Battalion (minus two platoons)
   Battery C, 571st Antiaircraft Artillery [Automatic Weapons] Battalion (minus two platoons)[18]

8. Day of Decision

After Brig. Gen. Pierce issued his orders for the next day's attack towards Pilsen, these orders flowed down through the subordinate commands. Through the night, plans were formulated and preparations made to execute those plans.

Having received the warning orders about the next day's attack, Combat Command B proceeded further east to an assembly area near Bor, Czechoslovakia. The 64th Armored Infantry Battalion was the first to arrive at Bor at 2040 followed by the 396th Armored Field Artillery Battalion. CCB's Forward Command Post was set up in Bor at 2135. Later that night, the 16th Tank Battalion and the remaining elements of CCB arrived in and around Bor.[19]

Col. Barksdall Hamlett, Jr., the commander of 16th Armored Division Artillery, later recalled some confusion as to Czechoslovakia's status. In his 1976 Oral History, Hamlett remembered:

> Our last mission was to secure Pilsen, Czechoslovakia, and we went in there with no orders as to how to treat the civil population. A very confusing thing. We didn't know whether we were invading enemy territory or friendly territory. And there's a great deal of difference. But the Czechs took this into their own hands and made if [sic] friendly territory. And I'll never forget.[20]

In the early evening, Maj. George Pickett and his staff of the 64th Armored Infantry Battalion received the Situation Overlays and Order of Battle Notes from Combat Command B Headquarters for the next day's attack on Pilsen. At 2130, Maj. Pickett issued oral orders to his staff and company commanders for that attack.[21]

The 16th Tank Battalion was commanded by Lt. Col. L. F. Lewis. The battalion included several of the new M26 Pershing heavy tanks which boasted a high velocity 90mm gun capable of taking out the German Tiger and Panther tanks. At 1900, the battalion received a verbal order for the following day's attack. Forty minutes later, the Battalion S-3 (Operations) Officer and a section of the Recon Platoon headed out to reconnoiter the routes to the Assembly area. At 2000, Lewis issued orders to his commanders and staff to move the battalion into an assembly area six miles east of Waidhaus beginning at 2230. The Battalion Trains would remain in place until being called forward. The 16th Tank Battalion's movement to the new Assembly Area commenced on time and was completed at 0500 on the morning of 6 May.[22]

Now part of the 16th Armored Division, Lt. Col. Floyd R. Brisack was ordered to break up his 633rd Tank Destroyer Battalion (Self-Propelled) and assign his tank destroyer companies to support the division's combat commands. Company A was attached to Combat Command A,

Company B was attached to Combat Command B, and Company C was attached to Reserve Command. The Reconnaissance Company was assigned to provide security for the Division Administrative Center. Unfortunately for the battalion's soldiers, they would not be participating in the next day's advance into Czechoslovakia. Their 36 M18 Hellcats and three M32 recovery vehicles were still in transit by rail. They did not join up with the battalion in Waidhaus, Germany until early on the morning of 6 May 1945.[23]

The commanding general's orders for the 16th Armored Division's advance into Czechoslovakia included attaching the 216th Armored Medical Battalion's companies in support of the three combat commands. Company A was attached to CCA, Company B was attached to CCB and Company C was attached to Reserve Command. The Battalion Headquarters and Headquarters Company were attached to the Division Trains. Third U.S. Army attached its 583rd Ambulance Company to the battalion to augment its capabilities. The company's ambulances in turn were distributed to the battalion's three companies. The battalion's plan was for each of its companies to operate clearing stations for the combat commands to which they were attached. Any casualties requiring higher echelon care would be transported by the attached ambulances of the 583rd Ambulance Company from the clearing stations to Third U.S. Army's 39th Evacuation Hospital at Weiden, Germany.[24]

Throughout the night of 5–6 May, units steadily pulled into the Division Assembly Area near Waidhaus. Moving an armored division with nearly 11,000 personnel, nearly 800 tracked armored vehicles and over 1,100 other vehicles nearly 90 miles from Nuremberg to the Czechoslovak border was a major logistical undertaking. Nevertheless, the 16th Armored Division accomplished this task in less than 18 hours.

9

Pilsen and Prague on the Eve of Liberation

Third U.S. Army had been operating along the 1937 Czechoslovak border for over two weeks now and the Soviet Army was pushing eastward from central Czechoslovakia. To the Czech people, there were unmistakable signs that the Third Reich was only days away from total oblivion. All across the region, the Czech people anxiously awaited their liberation. There were also fears of what the German soldiers and in particular, the SS and the Gestapo, might do in their waning days of power.

Despite the Nazi stranglehold on mass communications, people in Bohemia were very much aware of the impending end of the war. In May 1945, Malvina Zajicova was sixteen-years-old and living in Pilsen with her parents and sister. "The foreign broadcasting (listening to which was punished by death penalty)—namely "BBC London Calling" and Voice of America—informed us regularly in the Czech language on the situation on the fronts," she later recalled. "We followed their move with anxiety and hoped that they would reach Pilsen sooner than the rumors that the Germans want to change Pilsen into fortress and defend it would turn true. The whole night of 4 May the German motorcades passed darkened Pilsen from the north to south with permanent rumble and BBC announced that 3rd Army of General Patton entered already the Czechoslovak territory."[1]

Another resident of Pilsen awaiting the American Army was twenty-year-old Vera Fiedlerova. "As the front was coming nearer—and we knew it because our family as well as the others was listening to foreign broadcasts, e.g. Voice of America or BBC—the tension increased," she later wrote. "I remember that my father did not sleep too much that time. He knew better than I what dangers threatened because he had his experiences from the WWI."[2]

Jaroslav Peklo also recalled the anticipation of the Americans' arrival. Peklo was twelve-years-old at the time and living in Pilsen. "We knew that the GIs were near, on the border, and since the end of April even their artillery was heard when they shelled Domazlice, the city only 30 miles southwest of Pilsen," he wrote years later.[3]

The end of Czechoslovakia's long occupation by Nazi Germany was now at hand. Many of the Czechs decided to take matters into their own hands. In numerous Bohemian towns, Czechs began uprisings against the Germans. Czech flags were displayed for the first time in six years. German language signs and propaganda billboards were torn down. Czechs armed themselves and prepared for battle. Most of the Germans had no interest in fighting but refused to surrender to the Czechs. Thousands of German soldiers and civilians started heading west to surrender to the Americans. Many others chose to remain in place instead. So in those towns, a tense and uneasy stalemate ensued as both sides waited for the Americans to arrive and settle the matter.

In the capital city of Prague, however, the Czech people rose up against the German occupiers. They took to the streets, erected barricades, and seized the radio station and other key buildings in the city. The German garrison in Prague had no interest in fighting; they just wanted to escape west and surrender to the Americans. So, an understanding was reached between the city's garrison commander, Gen. Rudolf Toussaint, and the Czech patriots to not fire on each other. Toussaint had been trying unsuccessfully for several days to contact Gen. Patton to negotiate a surrender of his forces.[4]

Early on in their uprising, the Czechs were aided by a division of Russian defectors under the command of former Soviet Generals Andrei Vlasov and Sergei Bunyachenko. These soldiers had been captured by the Germans, and then defected to fight against the Soviets. Now with the end in sight, they decided to defect again—this time to the western Allies. At first the Czech leaders welcomed their assistance. Then they realized the possible postwar political ramifications of collaborating with these Soviet defectors and requested that the defectors leave Prague immediately.[5]

Unlike most other German commanders, Generalfeldmarschall Ferdinand Schörner had no intention of surrendering, nor did he countenance Gen. Tousssaint's de facto cease-fire agreement with the Czech partisans in Prague. Upon learning of the uprising, he dispatched nearly ten thousand SS troops to crush the Czechs. These troops included the 4th "Der Führer" Panzer Grenadier Regiment of the 2nd SS Panzer "Das Reich" Division, which had fought fierce battles on both the Western and Eastern Fronts. When these SS troops arrived in Prague, there would be no mercy for the brave Czech partisans.[6]

This tragic episode in Prague demonstrated how brutally fanatical Schörner was. Even in the midst of a titanic struggle with the Soviet Army, he sent 10,000 of his best troops to crush this uprising by the citizens of Prague.

With the arrival of the U.S. Army imminent, resistance fighters in Pilsen also sought to liberate themselves from German occupation. On the morning of 5 May, they began tearing down German signs and raising Czechoslovak flags. A crowd also set fire to a large billboard on Republic Square that read "Führer befiehl, wir folgen!" (The Führer Leads, We Follow!). In response to the billboard being set afire, several German soldiers fired on the crowd, wounding several civilians.[7]

In other areas of Pilsen, the residents passed a quiet but tense morning. "The morning of 5 May was unexpectedly quiet in the streets," Malvina Zajicova later wrote. "Here and there the Czechoslovak flags appeared on the houses after six years."[8]

Later that morning, a group of partisans in a truck attempted to storm the Kommandantur building on Klatovska Avenue where Generalmajor von Majewski had his headquarters. A German soldier guarding the building fired a Panzerfaust anti-tank rocket at the truck, destroying it and killing three of the partisans and wounding several others. An angry crowd quickly assembled. Generalmajor von Majewski himself appeared before the crowd in an effort to calm down the situation but he failed to do so.[9]

Events in Pilsen quickly escalated. Several blocks away at Republic Square, a group of civilians went into City Hall and forced the city German-appointed Mayor, Dr. Walter Sturm and his deputy, Mr. Wild, to resign and hand over control of the civilian government to a new Revolutionary National Committee headed by Jindra Krejcik. Soon after, Dr. Karel Krepinsky and other representatives of the Revolutionary National Committee appeared at Generalmajor von Majewski's headquarters. During the ensuing negotiations, the representatives demanded that the Germans surrender. Von Majewski adamantly refused, saying that he would only surrender to the Americans. However, he issued orders for the soldiers under his command to remain in their barracks and not offer any resistance to the Americans when they arrived. Generalmajor Müller also issued orders halting German patrols in the city so as to avoid unnecessary violent confrontations between the soldiers and the civilians. The negotiations ended with the situation in the city still very much unresolved.[10]

According to Malvina Zajicova, the displaying of Czechoslovak flags and other acts of defiance against the Nazis inspired some of the young

Czech men to try and seize weapons from the Hitlerjugend (Nazi youth organization) in Pilsen. Included amongst them was her future husband Joseph Zajic "At that time I was 20 years old and my hope of gaining liberty from the German occupation was very strong," Joseph Zajic later wrote."[11]

Joseph Zajic and the other men went to the Hitlerjugend's building in Pilsen and found it abandoned. They did, however, find guns and Panzerfausts (anti-tank rockets). "Unfortunately only a few of them in fact really knew how to handle the guns," Malvina described. "The boys were very lucky." Zajic and his associates promptly brought the weapons to the Revolutionary National Committee at City Hall.[12]

While negotiations were underway between the Revolutionary National Committee and the German Army commanders, the Germans in control of the local radio transmitter and phone cables with Prague began preparations to destroy these vital communications links. Fortunately, a group of Czech policemen were able to capture the communications equipment and prevent their destruction. At 12:35 pm, the following message was broadcast in Czech: "This is Pilsen, the free Pilsen calling. We call on you, the citizens of Pilsen and all of West Bohemia. We want to let you know that we have ended the German oppression And from now on, we are free!"[13]

The words of that broadcast were brave but the situation in Pilsen was still quite dangerous. The German garrison in Pilsen was still heavily armed and unwilling to surrender to anyone but the Americans. The partisan forces were steadily gaining in numbers but they lacked sufficient weapons to battle the Germans in Pilsen. More ominously, rumors spread of Generalfeldmarschall Schörner having dispatched forces to suppress the uprising in Pilsen. Periodically throughout the city, shootings occurred between Czech partisans and German soldiers. The local German Gestapo force reportedly had turned its building into a fortress.[14]

According to Malvina Zajicova, the Germans began to re-assert their authority in Pilsen in the early afternoon. She wrote:

> But later, around noon, well organized and well-equipped German soldiers appeared in the streets when they left their barracks in town. The streets were empty very soon and only a few incidents occurred. The soldiers controlled the strategic points: station, post, radio. The City Hall remained aside their interest much to the great relief of the badly armed defenders. In the late afternoon, the German soldiers returned back to their barracks.[15]

At 4 p.m., Dr. Krepinsky returned to the Kommandatur with two other delegates of the National Committee, Dr. Hrbek and Capt. Sasek, for another round of negotiations with Generalmajor von Majewski. These negotiations produced a fragile truce. Generalmajor von Majewski still refused to surrender his forces to the Czechs or to transfer control of the city to them. Furthermore, he wanted safety guarantees for his soldiers and free passage to the Sudetenland for all German civilians. The Czechs bluffed that they were in contact with the Allied High Command and that more partisans would be arriving in the city.[16]

The night of 5–6 May was a very anxious time for the residents of Pilsen. Years later, Jaroslav Peklo recalled that tense night:

> The whole night my father guarded with stolen rifle on the tracks and the main railway station. During that night my mother and I prayed and listened to our radio, especially broadcasts calling for help from Prague and Pilsen in English, Russian, and French. Radio also informed us about approaching SS troops and regular German Army, especially Panzer Divisions that were moving on us. The whole night we were listening to these unhappy news.[17]

Overnight, the Germans strengthened their positions and recaptured some of the areas that had fallen to the partisans. With the Germans unwilling to surrender to the Czechs and the Czechs too weak to subdue the Germans, an uneasy standoff gripped the city. Both sides eagerly awaited for the American Army to arrive, albeit for far different reasons. For the Germans, the arrival of the Americans meant protection against Czech retributions and deliverance from Soviet captivity. For the Czechs, it meant that their long nightmare of Nazi occupation would be over.[18]

10

The Liberation of Pilsen

Gen. George S. Patton, Jr., was now in command of the largest field army ever assembled by the United States. On the morning of 6 May 1945, Patton's Third U.S. Army boasted four corps, including six armored divisions and over 540,000 soldiers. Nearly one half of this massive force was sent forward that Sunday morning to liberate western Czechoslovakia.

Early on the morning of 6 May, V and XII Corps of Third U.S. Army renewed their drives into western Czechoslovakia with their armored divisions rushing through the forward positions of the infantry divisions. In the north, Combat Command A of 9th Armored Division pushed down the road to Karlsbad with the 1st Infantry Division following behind. In the center, V Corps was sending the 16th Armored Division through the 2nd and 97th Infantry Divisions towards Pilsen. In XII Corps' area, the 4th Armored Division pushed northeastward through the mountain passes held by the 5th and 90th Infantry Divisions and headed for Prague. Further south, the 26th Infantry Division attacked to the northeast in the direction of Budweis. Meanwhile the 11th Armored Division continued its drive in Austria. By the end of the day, numerous towns had been liberated, tens of thousands of German troops and civilians had surrendered and Eisenhower's Karlsbad–Pilsen–Budweis restraining line had been reached in many places.[1]

Task Force A Advances on Pilsen

At 0430, Troop B, 23rd Cavalry Squadron began Combat Command B's advance on Pilsen down Highway 14 with 1st Platoon in the lead. They passed through the 97th Infantry Division's positions at Stribro without incident. CCB's Advance Guard followed Troop B forty-five minutes later.

10. The Liberation of Pilsen

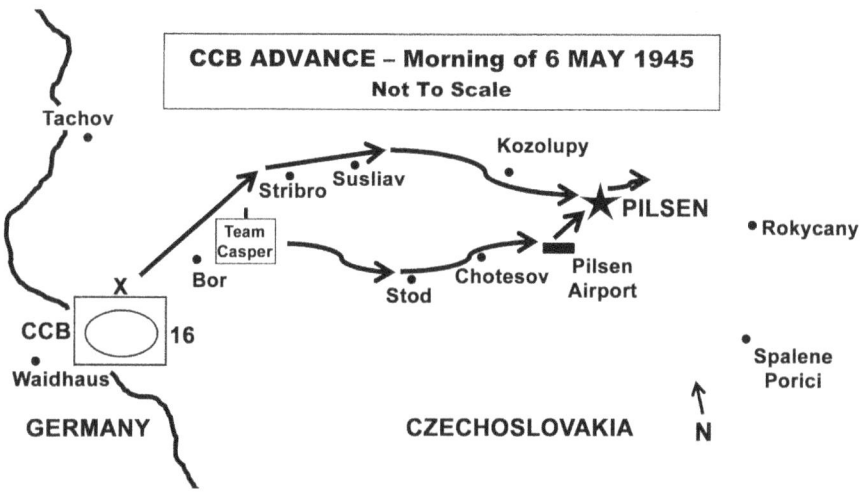

Combat Command B Advances 6 May 1945

By 0600, a major portion of CCB was heading east. Following Troop B was the rest of Task Force A with the 396th Armored Field Artillery Battalion at the end of the column. The command's other two task forces followed behind them.[2]

Soon after beginning their advance, the cavalrymen began to encounter surrendering German troops. Not stopping to take them prisoner, the Americans directed them to the rear and kept pushing forward. "It was a cakewalk at first with very little opposition," Mark Steece of Troop B later recalled. "German soldiers were giving up."[3]

1st Lt. John C. Patterson, commander of Troop B, later described entering Czechoslovakia. "The Lord was with us," he wrote. "It was still dark and it was raining so hard you couldn't see the side of the road. We moved through a line of pill box gun emplacements. We didn't know they were there and they couldn't see us."[4]

To provide flank security, Maj. Pickett grouped 1st Lt. Bernard N. Brown's platoon of armored infantry from his own battalion's Company A, with 1st Lt. Gilbert Casper's platoon of M4 Sherman medium tanks from the 16th Tank Battalion, into a team under the command of Casper. Team Casper advanced along a parallel road to the south of the main CCB columns, and subdued several roadblocks. At 0645, Team Casper captured 350 Germans at the town of Stod outside Pilsen. The team pressed on and at 0710, they overcame a roadblock at Chotesov, capturing two German officers in the process.[5]

The first resistance encountered that morning by Task Force A occurred at the town of Sulislav. As Troop B was entering the town, German soldiers opened fire with small arms. Troop B pushed through the town and continued on. The American tanks and armored infantrymen following Troop B subsequently cleared out the town, taking a number of prisoners.[6]

In the town of Kozolney, Troop B encountered a column of German vehicles hastily evacuating the town. One truck of German soldiers pulled into Troop B's column and was promptly shot to pieces with fifty-caliber machine guns on the American M8 armored cars. Seven German vehicles were destroyed and some prisoners captured.[7]

1st Lt. John Patterson later described Troop B's advance on Pilsen. "We used all of our firepower as we advanced," he wrote. "It wasn't long until we had so many prisoners; we just had to wave them on back toward the units following us. We left a trail of burning vehicles, buildings and some dead en route."[8]

Less than two hours into the attack, Troop B of the 23rd Cavalry arrived in the outskirts of the city. At this point, Col. Noble made a momentous decision. "My orders were to 'seize and hold' the high ground west of the city of Pilsen, which meant to halt west of Pilsen, but the knowledge that the other Combat Commands would soon follow gave me added confidence," Col. Noble later wrote. "I, therefore, decided to continue the advance and attempt to take the city, which would serve as a fortress against enemy armor and infantry." It was an audacious decision

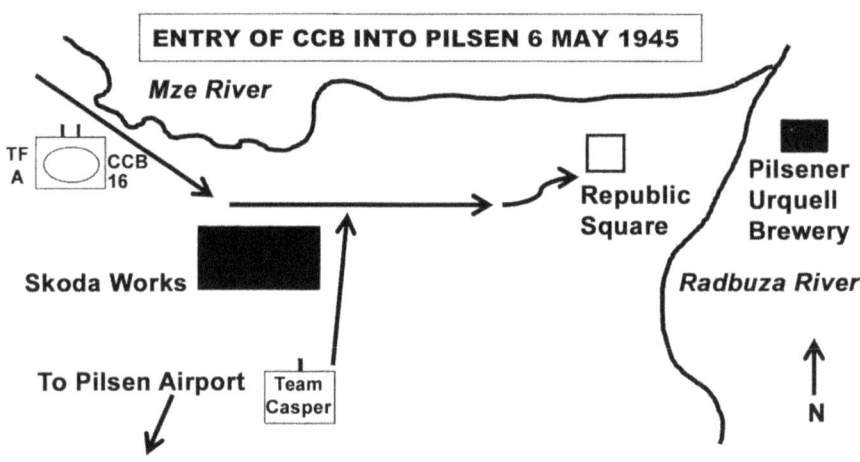

Entry into Pilsen, 6 May 1945

for Noble had only 2,500 men and the German garrison was estimated at over 10,000.⁹

Combat Command B was making good progress during its drive to Pilsen. "Resistance was slight until we approached Pilsen, and the huge Skoda Munitions Works on the outskirts of the city," Col. Noble later wrote. The Skoda Works was one of the largest armaments manufacturing facilities in Europe, producing weapons ranging in size from small arms to artillery pieces and armored vehicles. As American vehicles approached Skoda Works, small arms fire erupted from a guard tower. Light tanks from the 16th Tank Battalion were brought forward to silence enemy opposition. "After the capture of the Skoda Works, a detachment was left to secure it and we moved on toward the center of the city," wrote Col. Noble.¹⁰

Capt. Lawrence J. Minghi's Company B, 216th Armored Engineer Battalion was near the front of Combat Command B's main column. Their

Part of the massive Skoda Works munitions manufacturing complex on or about VE-Day. Note the 16th Armored Division half-track in the center foreground (National Archives Photo).

role was to construct bridges, and remove any obstacles and mines that were encountered as needed. "Captain Minghi's men were ready and willing but found only minor uses for their talents," wrote Capt. Minghi's battalion commander Lt. Col. William W. Smith, Jr.[11]

After securing Stod and overcoming the roadblock at Chotesov, Team Casper proceeded to the Pilsen Airport. By 0835 the airport was secured. In doing so, Team Casper captured some 97 German aircraft including Messerschmitt Me-262 fighter jets, a battery of 88 mm guns, twenty 40

Citizens of Pilsen welcome soldiers of the 16th Armored Division with gifts of food and drink on 6 May 1945 (National Archives Photo).

mm anti-aircraft guns, eight staff cars, eight trucks, a number of other vehicles and over 650 German prisoners including 27 officers. For their leadership, 1st Lt. Gilbert Casper and 1st Lt. Bernard Brown were each later awarded the Bronze Star Medal.[12]

Col. Noble was taking a calculated risk that surprise, firepower and audacity would enable him to liberate Pilsen and subdue the much larger German force holding it. Noble's gamble worked. By 0800 Troop B, 23rd Cavalry arrived in Republic Square at the center of Pilsen. They were greeted by thousands of cheering Czechs exuberant at their liberation from the Germans. "We circled the square with our vehicles and were swarmed by people carrying fresh baked bread, wine, etc," wrote 1st Lt. John C. Patterson afterwards. The Czechs showered their American liberators with flowers, food, and their world-famed Pilsner beer. Soon other elements of Task Force A arrived in Republic Square and joined in the celebrations.[13]

Three days later, 1st Lt. Patterson sent a letter home to his parents describing his experiences in liberating Pilsen. He wrote:

> The people mobbed us when we entered Pilsen. I never saw so many people happy at one time. They covered our cars with flowers—fed us, gave us the biggest hotel in town to sleep in and treated us like kings. It made all we have gone through worthwhile. These Czechs are wonderful people.[14]

After giving orders for the cavalry to set up outposts on the roads leading into the city, Col. Noble headed to Republic Square. He ordered a Command Post be set up in the City Hall on the square. At 0825, Noble sent a message to his division commander requesting that he join him in Republic Square.[15]

As more American vehicles and soldiers arrived in the square, they, too, were greeted by the joyous crowds. "People were all waving and handing out flowers and jugs of beer," recalled Sgt. O. J. Mooney of the 396th Armored Field Artillery Battalion.[16]

Mark Steece of Troop B later described the scene in Republic Square. "The Square was deserted at first," he said. "Then people brought us food and wine and German soldiers were coming out to surrender, mostly unarmed. Soon there were so many people in the Square we were getting in each other's way. We had to move out to make room for other troops coming in." After a couple hours in Republic Square, Troop B was sent to patrol the north side of the city."[17]

Soon after American soldiers entered the outskirts, the Czech partisans sent out a radio broadcast announcing their arrival. The announcer, Dr. Sindler stated:

> This is Pilsen, the free Pilsen calling. Long live our freedom, long live our Allies! Hereby I announce to all inhabitants of the Republic of Czechoslovakia that the tanks of the 16th Division are on Republic Square in Pilsen. I am an eyewitness of their arrival from the West!

Unfortunately, Dr. Sindler then made the erroneous claim that the American armored vehicles were leaving Pilsen for Prague via the town of Rokycany.[18]

With Col. Noble accompanying CCB's advance party, Lt. Col. Percy Perkins was left in charge of the command's main body further back in the command's column. On the way to Pilsen, Perkins came across his division commander Brig. Gen. John L. Pierce. Pierce ordered him to get to Pilsen as soon as possible to reinforce Noble.[19]

An hour after the lead elements of CCB started out for Pilsen, the Division Headquarters and Headquarters Company joined in the advance. At 0700, the Headquarters Commandant, Capt. Ward, left Waidhaus, Germany with an advance party consisting of members of the staff sections and Staff Sgt. John J. Farson's squad of the Headquarters Defense Platoon. Two hours later, Ward's group was followed by the main elements of the Division Headquarters. Ward and his small group had a very eventful trip to Pilsen. Along the way, Staff Sgt. Farson's squad captured 312 German soldiers, four command cars and a Kübelwagen (a German light military vehicle similar to the U.S. jeep). The advance party arrived in Republic Square not long after the first elements of CCB.[20]

Warrant Officer Solomon Polish rode in one of the 156th Armored Signal Company's jeeps following the Division Headquarters in the column headed for Pilsen. "The march through the Sudetenland was fairly uneventful," he later wrote. "Several times we were menaced by heavy gun emplacements along the route of march, but these had been put out of action by the infantry and we proceeded until we reached the outskirts of Pilsen on May 6th." As the column entered the city, gunfire erupted but they pressed onwards.[21]

Col. Barksdale Hamlett, Jr., commander of 16th Armored Division Artillery, rode to Pilsen in a jeep with his Division Artillery Headquarters. "I had command of part of the column rolling up the road into Pilsen and I was at the head of my column as we came into the town of Pilsen, it was just like a big holiday" he recalled. "We were liberating these people. They were happy and coming to greet us."[22]

Less than an hour after the first American units arrived at Republic Square and only a few minutes after Col. Noble had sent his message requesting that he come there, the division commander Brig. Gen. John L. Pierce arrived in Republic Square as well accompanied by Col. Hamlett.

10. The Liberation of Pilsen

Pierce addressed the crowd of exuberant Czechs and the crowd responded with thunderous cheers. "A wave of cheers swept over the city as the General [Pierce] gave the city back to the people of Pilsen," reported the Division Artillery Headquarters Battery History.[23]

Malvina Zagicova, aged 16, and Vera Fiedlerova, aged 20, were two of the thousands of Pilsen residents who turned out to welcome their American liberators. "Every inhabitant tried to express his joy and gratitude," Malvina later recalled. "I remember the smiling soldiers throwing sweets, chocolates etc., among the people, especially when they saw a child or young girl," recalled Vera. "Such a day cannot be forgotten. I can say, it was one of the happiest days of my life."[24]

At 6 a.m., Jaroslav Peklo's father returned from guarding the rail station. Two hours later, Jaroslav heard on the radio that U.S. tanks were in Republic Square. Like so many other Pilsen residents, the Peklos rushed out to greet their liberators. "You should have seen all those people who had not had a good night's rest running to the down-town very eager to

Czech children gather around Pfc Benjamin Bednars of the 16th Armored Division as he hands out candy on Liberation Day 6, May 1945 (National Archives Photo).

see those giants from another world," he later recalled. "As for me I imagined the American GIs as some kind of giants in leather uniforms. I had never seen any picture of them before. But they were normal men, same as we were." Peklo got an autograph from one of the American cavalrymen in a M8 armored car.[25]

Vaclav Malek was fourteen-years-old when the Americans liberated Pilsen. "With the other kids we ran out of town to the west to meet the American troops," he later recalled. "We saw tanks and cars and jeeps and they brought us things we had never seen before in our lives, like chewing gum and chocolate."[26]

V Corps' official history *V Corps in the ETO* also described the scenes that Sunday morning in Pilsen. "The entry of American troops into PILZEN, Czechoslovakia was reminiscent of PARIS, which units of V Corps had liberated nine months before," said the V Corps history. "Crowds of jubilant people welcomed the armored columns as they passed along streets that

Citizens of Pilsen celebrate their liberation with soldiers of the 16th Armored Division 6 May 1945. Note the bottles of Pilsner Beer in the hands of the U.S. soldiers (National Archives Photo).

had felt the Nazi boot for over five years. Flowers were strewn along the paths, into the vehicles, and upon the troops themselves."²⁷

Lt. Col. Perkins and his group hurried to Pilsen with Perkins riding in a jeep at the head of his column. "As we were entering the outskirts of Pilsen, we saw signs 'Welcome Americans' and on entering Pilsen I noted a traffic jam of tanks with the girls climbing all over them, hugging and kissing the men in them," Perkins later wrote.²⁸

Despite the pandemonium of celebrations in Pilsen, there still was a war on. Amidst the exuberant celebrations occurring in Republic Square, Maj. Pickett assembled his company commanders together at 0900 and assigned them sectors of the city to clear of German resistance. In addition, Tank-Infantry Teams formed from Company A, 16th Tank Battalion and Company A, 64th Armored Infantry Battalion were dispatched to block the six main roads leading into Pilsen. One of those teams led by Lt. Schlossberg of A Company, 64th Armored Infantry Battalion engaged in a firefight with a SS unit on the road to Prague. "Much credit for successful occupation of Pilsen is due to the efforts of Maj. George B. Pickett during the early hours of occupation," recorded CCB's After Action Report.²⁹

Soldiers of the 97th Infantry Division engage German snipers during the liberation of Pilsen, 6 May 1945 (National Archives Photo).

At 1200, CCB set up its Command Post on the second floor of Pilsen's City Hall on Republic Square. A perimeter defense for the city was set up and a plan implemented to mop up pockets of German resistance. Task Force A, Task Force B and the 396th Armored Field Artillery Battalion were each assigned an area of responsibility.[30]

Several blocks into Pilsen, Perkins and his column encountered a German sniper. Perkins and several of his soldiers dismounted and went into the nearby buildings to find the sniper. One of Perkins' soldiers found him and neutralized the threat. Having dealt with the sniper, the Perkins group pressed on and soon after, arrived at Col. Noble's headquarters.[31]

After arriving in Republic Square, elements of the Headquarters Company were tasked to clear the Grand Hotel of German soldiers. In the process, they captured a high ranking Gestapo official. 1st Lt. Carl B. Massie and Master Sgt. Joseph Fitzpatrick were guarding the prisoner when Germans in nearby buildings opened fire with small arms and machine guns. Massie was wounded in the arm and hand while attempting to return fire during the brief engagement. After the hotel was cleared, Headquarters Company set up operations in it.[32]

Task Force B Advances on Pilsen

While Task Force A was advancing east, Task Force B remained in its Assembly Area awaiting orders to join the advance. At 0805, word was received to start heading east to Pilsen on Highway 14 in fifteen minutes later. Battalion commander Lt. Col. L. F. Lewis assembled his company commanders and staff and issued verbal orders to get the battalion moving. Promptly at 0820, Task Force B rolled out of its Assembly Area and joined CCB's advance on Pilsen. Ahead of them in the command's column was the 396th Armored Field Artillery Battalion.[33]

Initially, Task Force B was hindered by a traffic congestion caused by the 97th Infantry Division. On several occasions, vehicles from the 97th Infantry Division Headquarters, 97th Signal Company and the 820th Tank Destroyer Battalion interrupted Task Force B's column.[34]

Leading Task Force B was a recon team in a jeep consisting of the 16th Tank Battalion's operations officer and three soldiers. Near Kozolupy about six miles east of Pilsen, the recon team ran into a German pillbox situated atop a railroad embankment and two German 88mm guns. Fortunately for the Americans, these 88s were set up for anti-aircraft defense and could not be brought to bear on the American vehicles. Nevertheless, the Germans resisted with small arms fire. One of the recon soldiers, Pfc. Robert Ifland, attempted to outflank the pillbox but was mortally wounded. Despite being wounded, he kept the pillbox under fire and directed a patrol to capture it from the rear. Altogether, fifty Germans and eight vehicles were captured here. For his actions, PFC Ifland was later awarded the Distinguished Service Cross posthumously.[35]

Further down the highway, Task Force B ran into another pocket of German resistance just outside of Pilsen. Eight German soldiers opened up on the Americans with small arms fire and a machine gun. Apparently, these soldiers had infiltrated into a gap that had developed between the 396th Armored Field Artillery Battalion and the lead element of Task Force B. This small nuisance group of Germans was soon neutralized and Task Force B continued on.[36]

Gunfire in Republic Square

Republic Square was full of American soldiers and their vehicles and thousands of Czech civilians celebrating their liberation from German occupation. The celebration in Republic Square was short-lived, however. At around 1000, German soldiers perched high up in the steeple of St. Bartholomew's Cathedral in the center of the square opened fire on the crowd below. Other Germans opened fire from nearby houses. The crowds dispersed to find cover.[37]

American machine gun crews returned fire on the Germans. Referring to the small arms fire, Col. Noble later wrote, "This was no trouble to the tanks who just let their hatches down (buttoned up) and the armored personnel carriers, but to the commanders in open jeeps it was no fun. We had to dismount and take as much cover as was available in the sewers, gutters, or close against the ground floors of the buildings." Sgt. O. J. Mooney's M7 self-propelled gun had a fifty-caliber machine gun so he and his crew used it to return fire on the Germans. The Germans were no match for the 16th Armored soldiers and their machine guns mounted on armored vehicles. A squad of soldiers ascended St. Bartholomew's steeple and captured the Germans holed up there. Teams of American soldiers fanned out across the vicinity and subdued other pockets of German soldiers. One squad led by Technical Sgt. John Nicolson of Company A, 64th Armored Infantry Battalion, captured a German major general, his staff and three hundred of his soldiers. Pfc. Albert Zarback of Company C, 64th Armored Infantry Battalion led his squad into several buildings in and around the city square and captured five Germans.[38]

Both Malvina Zajicova and Vera Fiedlerova were among the crowds of Pilsen citizens in Republic Square when the Germans opened fire. They rushed to find cover from the firing. "From our shelters we observed with amazement and admiration the battle experience and courage of G.I. Joes," recalled Malvina years later. Vera also described the dramatic scenes in Republic Square:

> People are running to the shelters in nearby houses. The talk finished. Americans are shooting on the tower and in the same time shooting is heard from various parts of town.... Americans are separating but they stay calm and even with smiles. After some time and shooting the [German] riflemen are captured.[39]

Task Force B Reaches Pilsen

After overcoming the German pillbox near Kozolupy, Task Force B continued on to Pilsen. At around 1030, Company C, 16th Tank Battalion reached the city's outskirts. Elements of the 64th Armored Infantry Battalion from Task Force A cleared out German soldiers holed up in the houses lining the streets into the city. Company C deployed its tanks and assisted the infantry in subduing the enemy. The Americans did not suffer any casualties.[40]

Fifteen minutes later, Company B of the 64th Armored Infantry Battalion arrived in the outskirts of Pilsen. They pressed onto into the city and headed for Republic Square. Along the way, they encountered scattered small arms fire, which they neutralized, with machine gun and small arms fire without suffering any casualties. Eventually they arrived in Republic Square and joined the numerous other American units rapidly filling the square.[41]

At 1100, Company B of the 16th Tank Battalion arrived on the outskirts of Pilsen. With Republic Square now congested with American vehicles and celebrating Czech civilians, Task Force B was halted here. At 1300, the Battalion Headquarters section continued into the city and set up a temporary Command Post in one of the buildings near Republic Square.[42]

With Task Force B setting up in Pilsen, the Intelligence and Reconnaissance (I&R) Platoon of the 16th Tank Battalion was sent to conduct a reconnaissance east of the city towards the airport. Under the command of Lt. Ray Kitchener, the I&R Platoon had four peeps, a half-track and twenty-four soldiers. Outside of the city, Lt. Kitchener's platoon came upon a German battalion numbering around 700 soldiers and some Czech partisans. They had surrendered to the Czech partisans with the understanding that they would be turned over to the Americans. Lt. Kitchener radioed headquarters for instructions, and then locked the Germans in a schoolhouse. Later, rear echelon soldiers from the division arrived to transport the Germans to prisoner enclosures in the rear.[43]

Surrender of the Pilsen Garrison

While the Americans were spreading out to secure the city and its environs, the commander of the German garrison in Pilsen, Gen. George von Majewski, his deputy Generalmajor Gerhard Müller, a German admiral, von Majewski's staff, von Majewski's wife and two other wives were gathered in his headquarters. Altogether there were about forty-eight Germans present. Telephone lines to the headquarters had been cut by the Czech partisans so von Majewski was out of direct communications with both his own troops and higher headquarters. After the Americans arrived in Pilsen, von Majewski sent a former Czechoslovak Army officer to locate their commander and inform him that the German garrison commander desired to negotiate a surrender of the city.[44]

Meanwhile, Lt. Col. Perkins had arrived at CCB's headquarters on Republic Square. Col. Noble informed his deputy that the German garrison commander had sent word of his desire to surrender the city. At the moment, Noble was busily engaged directing his troops to subdue pockets of German resistance and setting up a defense of the city. In addition, Noble was dubious of the German commander's sincerity. When Perkins offered to head over to the German Headquarters to clarify the situation, Noble authorized him to do so. Gathering together a 1st lieutenant, a squad of soldiers, a half-track and two tanks, Perkins headed over to the German Headquarters.[45]

Before Lt. Col. Perkins arrived at the German Headquarters, however, Generalmajor von Majewski and his staff received an unexpected guest: 2nd Lt. Charles Schaeffer, Adjutant of the 216th Armored Engineers Battalion. Schaeffer was not even supposed to be in Pilsen. "I was supposed to be going in the opposite direction to turn in some reports," Schaeffer later recalled. "But I saw the whole column going out and I just couldn't resist going with them. So that's what I did." The column which included Schaeffer's jeep just happened to stop at the end of the street that von Majewski's headquarters was located. A Czech civilian came up to him and pointed at the German headquarters building, saying "Bosch down there."[46]

At that moment, no other American soldiers were down that street. "I'm a brand new hero so I decided to go down there and see what I could do," recalled Schaeffer. He then dismounted from his jeep and armed with only a carbine ran down the street. He entered von Majewski's headquarters, knowing only that Germans were in the building. He had no idea what he'd find inside. In the lobby of the building, Schaeffer was surprised to meet a German general coming down a flight of stairs. The general motioned for him to follow him upstairs.[47]

Schaeffer followed the German general up the stairs to the third floor and then suddenly found himself in the presence of Generalmajor von Majewski and his staff. "I was alone and very surprised to find about 35 officers and some wives," he later recalled. "What in the hell was I going to do with them? It was quite a thing." Schaeffer had the Germans remove their weapons, place them on the floor in the corners of the room and then sit down along the wall. Next he called down the stairwell for any U.S. soldiers in the vicinity. A soldier quickly responded and came up the stairs. Schaeffer immediately sent him to find another U.S. officer. The soldier disappeared and soon after, another second lieutenant appeared. Schaeffer explained the situation to him and then sent him to find a senior U.S. officer.[48]

In the meantime, Lt. Col. Perkins and his party had arrived outside the German Headquarters. Perkins placed his two tanks directly in front of the building as a show of force. At some point, the lieutenant that Schaeffer had dispatched met up with Perkins. "I took the lead and walked into the Headquarters," recalled Perkins. "No guard was on duty. We went up 3 stories to the office of the Commanding General. I pushed the door open and a very large German Captain came to the door. He could speak English, and said he formerly lived in New York." Perkins informed the German captain that he had come to accept the surrender of the German forces and the city of Pilsen.[49]

The German captain relayed Perkins' announcement in German to von Majewski. In reply, von Majewski said "I will only surrender to the Commanding Officer of all troops in the Pilsen area." The German captain translated von Majewski's reply into English for Perkins. "I said, 'Tell the General that I am 2nd in command of all troops in the Pilsen area, and was representing Col. Noble who was in command,'" Perkins later wrote. After Perkins' statement was translated into German, von Majewski had him let into the room.[50]

In the room, Perkins found 2nd Lt. Schaeffer guarding the German officers and staff. Schaeffer updated Perkins on the situation. Schaeffer was then sent to investigate a report of SS troops shooting civilians nearby.[51]

Generalmajor von Majewski did in fact speak English, as Lt. Col. Perkins soon found out. A short discussion ensued over the terms of the surrender with Perkins insisting that von Majewski surrender unconditionally. Perkins wrote out a surrender note that read: "I agree to unconditional surrender of the city and all the troops and arms therein to the American Army." Von Majewski read the note, then signed it. Perkins signed the note as well.[52]

Having completed the formalities of the German surrender, Perkins asked if von Majewski had any weapons in his office. "He said no," Perkins later wrote. "I didn't search [him], and that was my mistake." Von Majewski led Perkins into his nearby Day Room. He retrieved an over-and-under shotgun and gave it to Perkins. Then they returned to his office.[53]

According to Lt. Col. Perkins, international law stipulated that only one captured general could ride in each vehicle. Since he had three German flag officers and only one half-track to transport them and the other thirty-something captured Germans, Perkins went downstairs to his half-track and radioed for more vehicles to be sent to the German Headquarters.[54]

Having done that, Perkins next returned to von Majewski's headquarters. Generalmajor von Majewski asked Perkins what was going to happen to him. Perkins later described what happened next:

> I said "General, you know International Law better than I do but you will very likely go to prison camp." He then reached into his desk, pulled out an American Army 45 [M1911 45 caliber pistol] and put it to his right temple and shot himself. His wife walked over and held him in her arms while he died.[55]

Having determined that the rumors of SS troops shooting civilians were just that—rumors, 2nd Lt. Schaeffer returned to von Majewski's office just before the general committed suicide. As he recalled years later, "When I returned to report, Gen. von Majewski was seated at his desk and he pulled out a pistol and killed himself. His wife was present."[56]

Quite taken by surprise by von Majewski's rash decision, Perkins nevertheless had all of the other Germans present including the women searched for weapons. A further search of the premises turned up a Panzerfaust anti-tank rocket. The Germans were then taken in custody and transported from the headquarters building.[57]

The surviving German officers were separated from their wives and interrogated by their American captors. The wives were interned at a camp for German civilians for about a month and then returned to Germany.

The German officers were also relocated back to Germany and spent varying amounts of time in prisoners of war camps before being released. Generalmajor Müller would later be interviewed by U.S. Army historians and would prepare an account of the final days of the German occupation of Pilsen.[58]

Each of the several accounts about the surrender of the German garrison in Pilsen differs in minor ways. Of these accounts, only 2nd Lt. Schaeffer, Lt. Col. Perkins and Generalmajor Müller actually participated in the surrender event. In his account, Perkins did not mention 2nd Lt. Schaeffer, which is not surprising given that Schaeffer belonged to a unit that was not part of Perkins' combat command. Despite the minor differences in the accounts, the most important facts coincide. Generalmajor von Majewski sent a messenger to inform the American commander of his desire to the surrender of the city and his forces. Noble sent Perkins to the German headquarters to investigate von Majewski's communication. Schaeffer stumbled onto the German headquarters. Von Majewski surrendered the Pilsen Garrison to Perkins and then he committed suicide.

Clearing Out German Resistance

Whether through lack of communication with their superiors or outright defiance, many German soldiers chose to resist the Americans. Even as the exuberant Czechs poured out into Pilsen's streets, U.S. soldiers were fanning out throughout the city to clear out German resistance. Technical Sgt. Mickey R. Seeley led his rifle platoon from Company A, 64th Armored Infantry Battalion in clearing out several houses of German soldiers. Encountering heavy small arms fire from a large garrison building, Seeley led a rifle squad in an attack on the building that captured five German officers and 800 soldiers. Having already captured five Germans with his squad, Pfc. Albert Zarback of Company C, 64th Armored Infantry Battalion entered another building in Pilsen and convinced a German officer and his fourteen soldiers to surrender. Both soldiers were later awarded the Bronze Star Medal for their actions.[59]

3rd Platoon, Troop C, 23rd Cavalry Squadron was sent to check out a report of German soldiers in the woods near the village of Spalene Porici. At 1300, 3rd Platoon came under fire from three directions. The U.S. cavalrymen responded with all of the weapons at their disposal including heavy machine guns. Quickly three German vehicles were destroyed and a German captain emerged from the woods with an offer to surrender the German force which was the remnants of a regiment. Approximately 600 Germans were taken prisoner.[60]

But not all of the enemy soldiers in the woods near Spalene Porici were eager to surrender. These recalcitrant soldiers opened fire again on the Americans. Again, the Americans responded with overwhelming firepower, then charged into the woods and captured up another 400 Germans and a number of vehicles. 3rd Platoon was now faced with the task of guarding over 1,000 German prisoners of war—a very difficult task for such a small unit. Fortunately, an infantry unit of the 2nd Infantry Division was nearby so the cavalrymen turned their prisoners over to them for safekeeping. Afterwards, the grateful residents of Spalene Porici hailed the 3rd Platoon members as their liberators.[61]

Though halted on the outskirts of Pilsen, Task Force B came under enemy fire several times that afternoon. At around 1300, Headquarters Company, 16th Tank Battalion was fired upon by a German machine gun. An assault gun maneuvered into position and neutralized the threat with several rounds of high explosive ordnance. Around 1700, Company B of the 16th Tank Battalion came under machine gun fire. The lead tanks knocked out the machine gun with high explosive fire and killed eight Germans. By day's end, the Task Force B had taken 791 prisoners at a cost of one soldier killed.[62]

Though most of the German garrison simply surrendered, scattered pockets of diehard German soldiers continued to fire on the Americans from numerous places in the city. For the remainder of the day, the 16th Armored soldiers fought to subdue these pockets. That afternoon, they were joined by elements of the 97th Infantry Division. Defensive positions were set up around the city. U.S. soldiers cleared out pockets of German soldiers holed up in several churches, the Jewish synagogue, the Opera House and the Gestapo headquarters.[63]

PFC Charles Lemmons of the Division MP Platoon was one of the many 16th Armored Division soldiers who encountered Germans refusing to surrender that day. He and another MP were on patrol in Pilsen. "There was a lot of sniping going on as we were walking up this street," he wrote to his wife a few days later. Nearby the crew of a M24 light tank dropped down into their tank and closed the hatches to escape from the small arms fire. So Lemmons jumped up onto the tank, took over its M2 fifty-caliber machine gun and returned fire. "We had plenty of excitement and I don't mind telling you that my knees were knocking when it first started," he wrote to his wife later. "Later on, you don't seem to notice much or think about being hit by anything."[64]

A Czech brother and sister who owned a photo shop in the city witnessed Lemmons' actions and took a photograph of him. A few days later, they tracked him down and gave him a print of the photo.[65]

That afternoon, Task Force B moved into the southern section of Pilsen and secured billeting in a school. Throughout the remainder of the day and overnight, Task Force soldiers conducted patrols and guarded important installations in their area.[66]

The Military Police Platoon had arrived in Pilsen at 1330 and set up its Provost Marshall Office in Room 34 in the Grand Hotel. Its personnel set up a Prisoner of War enclosure, which ultimately received a total of 2,467 prisoners by the end of the day.[67]

Lt. Col. James E. Norvell's 396th Armored Field Artillery Battalion fired no artillery missions in support of CCB's liberation of Pilsen. However, a number of its soldiers did assist in clearing out pockets of German hold-outs using fifty-caliber machine gun fire. By day's end, the battalion had captured or accepted the surrender of 39 German officers and 574 enlisted soldiers.[68]

Combat Command B's drive to liberate Pilsen was the main effort of the 16th Armored Division on 6 May 1945. The original plan had called for the division's commands to occupy assault positions around Pilsen then drive into the city. However, CCB's commander Col. Charles B. Noble quickly responded to the fluid situation and lack of determined German resistance by sending his command directly into Pilsen. His bold initiative liberated the city. While doing so, CCB's soldiers captured some 4,700 German soldiers and killed another fifteen of the enemy at a cost of one killed and six wounded. Two of the wounded soldiers were from the 64th Armored Infantry Battalion. By virtue of having successfully engaged the enemy in ground combat, some thirty-five officers and nearly 900 soldiers of the 64th Armored Infantry Battalion were subsequently awarded the Combat Infantry Badge.[69]

The 16th Armored Division's other two combat commands played important supporting roles in the liberation of Pilsen as shall be detailed in the next two chapters.

11

The Liberation of Pilsen Part 2

The 16th Armored Division's original plan for liberating Pilsen had Combat Command B leading the division and securing critical terrain outside the city as a preliminary for the drive by the division into the city itself. Combat Commands A and R would follow in support. Col. Charles Noble's decision on the fly to drive straight into Pilsen dramatically changed the division plan. While Combat Command B played the predominate role in liberating Pilsen on 6 May 1945, Combat Commands A and R also participated in the liberation as well as elements of the 97th and 2nd Infantry Divisions.

Combat Command R

To Combat Command B's south, Combat Command R's mission was to provide flank security for the 16th Armored Division's advance on Pilsen and seize the high ground east of the city in preparation for an assault on the city itself. CCR's commander, Lt. Col. Thoss Beck, had a third of the division's combat power at his disposal to accomplish his mission. Like Col. Noble, he had organized his command into three Task Forces named for each of their respective commanders: Horrocks, Baker and Beck.

The bulk of CCR's armored infantry were with Task Force Horrocks while the majority of its tanks were with Task Force Baker. Task Force Horrocks had most of the 69th Armored Infantry Battalion, Company B of the 26th Tank Battalion and a platoon each of armored engineers and anti-aircraft artillery half-tracks. Riding in one of Task Force Horrocks' half-tracks was Private Edward Krusheski. Task Force Baker had most of Lt. Col. William O. Baker's 26th Tank Battalion, Company B of the 69th Armored Infantry Battalion and a platoon each of armored engineers and anti-aircraft artillery half-tracks. Task Force Beck consisted of the 397th Armored Field Artillery Battalion, Company C of the 26th Tank Battalion and the bulk of Capt. Philip Raneuf's Company C, 216th Armored Engineer Battalion, and Battery C of the 571st Anti-Aircraft Artillery Battalion.[1]

CCR was ready for the Pilsen operation well before dawn on the morning of 6 May. At 0600, the command moved out from its assembly area near Waidhaus along an unimproved road to the south of Highway 14. Task Force Horrocks led CCR's advance followed by Task Force Baker at 0800. Scattered pockets of light resistance were encountered but that did not stop the American advance. The poor condition of the roads did, however, slow the American advance.[2]

Simultaneously with Task Force Horrocks, Task Force Beck advanced on a parallel route to the south. Near the town of Pavlovice, a defended roadblock was encountered by Task Force Beck. The task force bypassed this roadblock and continued east.[3]

At 1000, Task Force Horrocks reached the town of Stankov Ves. Brig. Gen. Pierce ordered the command to divert onto Highway 14 and advance into Pilsen behind CCB. Task Force Horrocks was the first CCR unit to enter the city, doing so around 1600. The Americans soon came under German fire and responded accordingly to neutralize the opposition.[4]

Meanwhile, Task Force Baker had also been diverted from its original route. Lt. Col. Baker led his column into Pilsen via Highway 20. They, too, quickly came under German small arms fire.

The American soldiers responded with liberal use of tank and machine gun fire. Eight Germans were killed and another 515 were captured or surrendered. 1st Lt. Albert Chiles and Sgt. Albert Rothacker were the only two Americans wounded and none were killed. After passing through the city, Task Force Baker advanced five miles eastward down Highway 14 and took up defensive positions for the night.[5]

Troop C, 23rd Cavalry Squadron had a minimal role in Reserve Command's drive into Czechoslovakia. 2nd and 3rd Platoons conducted some route reconnaissance prior to the command's advance but Troop C did not have a role afterwards. Troop C travelled from Rosshaupt to Bel-a-Robb then to Pilsen and finally ended for the night at Letkov. Technician 5 Makse was left as a road guide. Soon after sunset, he came under small arms fire. Returning fire with a submachine gun and the thirty-caliber machine gun mounted on his peep, Makse killed two German soldiers.[6]

By the end of 6 May 1945, Combat Command R had charged into Czechoslovakia and followed Combat Command B into the city of Pilsen,

11. The Liberation of Pilsen Part 2

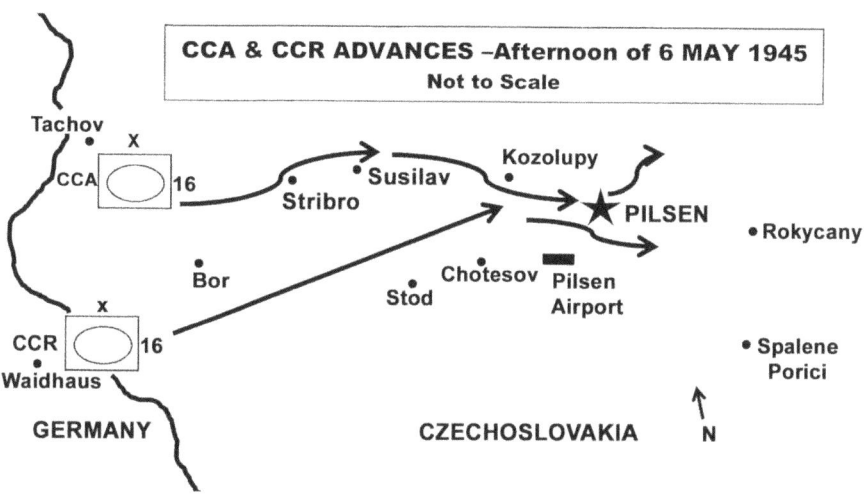

Combat Commands A & R Advance 6 May 1945

capturing hundreds of German soldiers and suffering only two casualties. As night fell, the command was poised to resume the advance the following morning. Its three Task Forces were staged east of the city awaiting the orders to attack.[7]

Combat Command A

For the advance on Pilsen, Combat Command A (CCA) was serving as the 16th Armored Division's reserve. In the plan of maneuver, CCA was to advance behind and to the north of CCB. If either CCB or CCR required reinforcement or support, CCA would be in a position to provide its firepower and forces as needed. As events developed, however, CCA was thrust into the city to assist with clearing out pockets of German resistance.

Like the other two combat commands, CCA was also split into several tank / infantry task forces. Its commander, Lt. Col. Shelby F. Williams had as his primary combat forces Maj. Lewis Adams' 5th Tank Battalion, Lt. Col. Irving K. Hendren's 18th Armored Infantry Battalion, the 393rd Armored Field Artillery Battalion, Troop A of the 23rd Cavalry Squadron, Capt. Matthew H. Rogina's Company A of the 216th Armored Engineer Battalion, Company A of the 216th Armored Medical Battalion and Battery A of the 571st Anti-aircraft Artillery [Automatic Weapons] Battalion (Self-

Propelled). The command also had Interrogation of Prisoners of War Team 231 and an Air Liaison Team to coordinate air support with the Ninth U.S. Army Air Force.[8]

The night of 5–6 May 1945 was a sleepless night as the 16th Armored Division moved its forces into position for the morning attack. Troop A / 23rd Cavalry was assigned to post road guides along the route to the assembly area. Unfortunately, a liaison officer from the Division Headquarters led the troop some distance down the wrong road before the error was discovered. While turning the troop around, six M8 armored cars got stuck in the mud and had to be winched out. By the time, Troop A was rolling again, CCA had arrived at the Assembly Area.[9]

The lead elements of CCA arrived at its assembly area in the vicinity of the town of Tachov before sunrise. Troop A caught up with CCA and were designated as the command's reserve. Having spent a couple hours near Waidhaus, the 393rd Armored Field Artillery rolled out again at 0620 heading for Tachov. Two hours later they crossed into Czechoslovakia and joined up with the rest of CCA at 1145.[10]

Originally, CCA was supposed to attack down from Plan towards Highway 95 starting at 0600. However, it was soon discovered that all of the bridges on the road to Plan had been destroyed by the Germans. So the command went into Division Reserve, refueled its vehicles and prepared to resume the offensive on two hours' notice. As CCB and CCR pushed eastward into Czechoslovakia, CCA remained in its assembly area awaiting its turn to enter the war.[11]

Finally at 1200 CCA received orders to advance and secure an assembly area to the north of Pilsen. The command promptly moved out as ordered. As CCA headed east, the 393rd Armored Field Artillery Battalion remained behind, ready to provide fire support as needed. Following the route that CCB had already taken earlier in the day, CCA received only scattered small arms fire.[12]

Staff Sgt. Gene Eike and his rifle squad from Company B, 18th Armored Infantry Battalion were riding in a half-track at the head of one CCA column heading for Pilsen. They were fully expecting to run into German opposition. Instead, oddly enough, they first encountered two Red Cross women in a jeep heading in the opposite direction. "We went down the road a little farther and we all piled out when we saw an 88 [anti-tank gun] sitting in defile," Eike later recalled. "It turned out that the Germans had heard us coming and left it but if they had ever turned the 88 loose we wouldn't be here." After this, his column had to detour around a destroyed bridge before entering Pilsen.[13]

11. The Liberation of Pilsen Part 2

Combat Command A rolled into Pilsen around 1645. Soldiers of the command soon became embroiled in numerous firefights with small pockets of German soldiers. Staff Sgt. Eike's column came under frequent small arms fire as it moved through the northern section of Pilsen. Only two CCA soldiers were wounded: Staff Sgt. Onits Dallaire and Pfc Roland Bissonnette of the 18th Armored Infantry Battalion.[14]

Though CCA did not arrive in Pilsen until late in the day, the Czechs' enthusiasm for their American liberators was undiminished. Soon the command's vehicles were adorned with flowers and Czech flags. "The Czech people were overjoyed at their liberation and celebrations were going on all over the city," recalled Harley Barrs of Company B, 18th Armored Infantry Battalion. "We were given food and drink and had a chance to enjoy real Pilsener beer from the Pilzen brewery." Years later, his company commander Capt. Howard Painter recalled, "No person will ever forget the happiness and music and street dancing exhibited by the population of Pilsen after being liberated from the Germans."[15]

Combat Command A passed through Pilsen and set up defensive positions north and east of the city in the early evening. Like the rest of the division, CCA fully expected to press on to Prague. Accordingly, reconnaissance patrols were sent out as far as 10 kilometers northeast of the Karlsbad-Pilsen-Budweis line.[16]

Capt. Howard Painter's B Company of the 18th Armored Infantry Battalion provided a number of those reconnaissance patrols. Capt. Painter ordered Staff Sgt. Eike to take six of his men and a half-track and locate Highway 19 which ran from Pilsen to the town of Rokycany on the road to Prague. "Well we took off looking for it and as we got to each little town, the people would meet us and greet us, and throw wreaths and insist we stop and make a speech and the Mayor would have to kiss me," Eike later recalled.[17]

Troop A, 23rd Cavalry entered Pilsen in late afternoon far back in the Combat Command A column. Due to a communications mix up, Troop A was unable to locate its billets and thus had to bivouac north of Pilsen along Highway 11 for the night.[18]

For most of the afternoon, the 393rd Armored Field Artillery Battalion remained in position near Tachov awaiting fire missions that never came. So at 1500, the battalion was ordered forward to Pilsen and entered the city at 2130. Their stay in Pilsen was brief. Two hours later, they set up a bivouac area about two miles east of the city.[19]

That night, soldiers of the 18th Armored Infantry Battalion remained in their bivouac area and manned check points and outposts. When morning came, many of these soldiers manning the check points discovered that the Czechs had been cooking and baking all night so that they could feed them breakfast in the morning.[20]

In its only combat operation, Combat Command A and its subordinate units encountered minimal German resistance and suffered just two soldiers wounded. Nevertheless, like so many American soldiers, they received a phenomenal outpouring of gratitude from the Czech people who had endured six long years of Nazi occupation and oppression.

The 97th and 2nd Infantry Divisions in Pilsen

Though the 16th Armored Division was the first American unit into the Pilsen, two other American divisions also participated in the liberation of the city. On 6 May and in the days that followed, both the 2nd and 97th Infantry Divisions would become involved with this important Czech city.

Prior to their advance, the 16th Armored Division had passed through the forward lines of the 97th and 2nd Infantry Divisions near the 1937 German-Czechoslovak border. The tactic of using infantry to open up routes of advance for the armor had been used with great effect by Third U.S. Army throughout the European Campaign. In the northern sector of V Corps, Combat Command A of the 9th Armored Division and the 1st Infantry Division used that tactic in its drive on Karlsbad. To V Corps' south, XII Corps sent its 4th Armored Division through the front-lines of the 5th and 90th Infantry Divisions for an advance on Prague.

After the 16th Armored Division had cleared their lines, both the 2nd and 97th Infantry divisions advanced behind the armored forces, clearing out bypassed pockets of German resistance, liberating Czech towns and receiving the adulation of the grateful Czech civilians.

The 97th Infantry Division was the third major American unit to operate on the Czechoslovak front. The division first arrived at the border in the third week of April and had liberated the border city of Cheb. Nicknamed "Trident," the division was a relative newcomer to Third U.S. Army, and had only been in Theater a few months.[21]

The 2nd Infantry Division was also a newcomer to Third U.S. Army, but not to the European Theater. Only a few days before, they had been expecting to link up with the Soviets along the Elbe River. When V Corps was transferred to Third U.S. Army, the 2nd Infantry Division was transferred as well. They conducted a lengthy road march to arrive along the

Czechoslovak border. Unlike the 97th Infantry Division and the 16th Armored Division, the 2nd Infantry Division had been fighting on the Continent since D+1, the day after D-Day. The division had fought in Brittany, the Battle of the Bulge, and the drive across Central Europe during this war and had fought in France during World War I. In World War I, the division had included the 4th Marine Brigade. Nicknamed "Indianhead" from their distinctive shoulder insignia, the 2nd Infantry Division was one of the most experienced and capable divisions in the European Theater.[22]

The first elements of the 97th Infantry Division to enter Pilsen belonged to the 303rd Infantry Regiment. Arriving in late afternoon, the Trident infantrymen set about clearing the scattered pockets of German resistance.[23]

One of the first soldiers from the 2nd Infantry Division to enter Pilsen was Pfc. George Shultz, Jr. A veteran of the Normandy Campaign who had been seriously wounded, Shultz had returned to duty and was serving as a Combat Photographer for Company I, 23rd Infantry Regiment. As he watched a column of the 16th Armored Division passing through the 2nd Infantry Division's lines, Shultz feared that he would not get into the city. So he hailed a 16th Armored jeep and caught a ride with them into the city. "The Czech populace was overjoyed as we rode into Pilsen," Shultz later recalled. "The jeep in which I was riding had no top and was pelted with lilac blooms as we rode down through the crowds into town. So many flowers and lilac blooms landed in our Jeep that I had to continually clear them out of the Jeep so the driver could see through the windshield. What a reception!" On that day and in the following days, Shultz took numerous photos, many of which are now preserved in the National Archives II, College Park, Maryland.[24]

Summation of the Liberation of Pilsen

Aside from the 23rd Cavalry Squadron, the 16th Armored Division had had no combat experience prior to its commitment in the liberation of western Czechoslovakia. By the end of the day, however, the division had liberated one of Czechoslovakia's largest city, freeing tens of thousands of grateful Czechs from Nazi German occupation and oppression. Furthermore, the division was poised to drive on the country's capital city and liberate the brave Czech partisans who were in a life and death struggle with German SS troops.

In its first day of combat operations as a division, the 16th Armored Division had demonstrated competency and flexibility. The initial plan called for Combat Command B to secure a position outside of Pilsen from which an attack into the city could be made. However, CCB's commander, Col. Charles Noble, decided on the fly to advance straight into the city itself. It was a bold gamble that proved successful.[25]

The division liberated Pilsen, one of the largest cities in Czechoslovakia. The division secured the massive war production facility in Pilsen: the Skoda Works. The division captured the Pilsen Airport, one of the last remaining air facilities of the vanquished German Luftwaffe. At the Pilsen Airport, the division captured nearly 100 German warplanes including some Messerschmitt Me-262 fighter jets. Over 8,000 German soldiers had surrendered or been captured during the day. The 16th Armored Division's own casualties were exceptionally light: one soldier killed, ten wounded and one M8 armored car knocked out. The 216th Armored Medical Battalion treated a total of eighteen patients, six of whom required evacuation.[26]

By the end of the day, American forces were firmly in control of Pilsen and its vicinity. The Division Command Post had been set up in the Grand Hotel on Republic Square. The Division Trains had arrived in the city at 2130. Combat Command A was positioned to the north and east of Pilsen. Combat Commands B and R were to the city's east. The 2nd Infantry Division and 97th Infantry Division were also nearby.

The liberation of Pilsen was a mixed experience for the 23rd Cavalry Squadron. The Squadron's subordinate units had been attached to support other commands with mixed results. Troop A found itself beset by communications problems with Combat Command A's Headquarters and was relegated to serving as the command reserve. Troop B spearheaded Combat Command B's drive on Pilsen and were the first American units into the city. Troop C initially was not assigned a mission with Reserve Command. The next day, however, Reserve Command used them to reconnoiter a report of a large force of German SS troops in Dobriv and subsequently fought a small battle against them. Troop D (Reinforced) covered the 16th Armored Division's right flank and liberated many small towns while advancing from Ronsberg through Merklin, Prestice and Stenovice to Pilsen. The remainder of the Squadron was uncommitted. Whereas Lt. Col. Adkisson had full operational control of his Squadron in the final days of their assignment to the 86th Infantry Division, most of his subordinate troops were controlled by other commands for the Pilsen operation.[27]

The exuberance of the liberated citizens of Pilsen actually had a downside to it, as Maj. George Pickett of the 64th Armored Infantry Battalion noted in his After Action Report. "A liberated city presents a difficult problem in that the people by their hilarious joy install a feeling of happiness in the men making control difficult and actually hindering operations," he wrote. "The entrance into PILSEN without opposition and the sudden outburst of firing in all directions tends to prove that hysterically joyful inhabitants cannot be taken to mean the end of tactical danger." This was a very sober assessment by a well-experienced commander who had seen fierce combat during the Battle of the Bulge.[28]

Thus by day's end, V Corps had one armored division and two infantry divisions and XII Corps also had one armored division and two infantry divisions poised for a drive to liberate Prague. With such an array of combat forces, Prague could have been liberated on 7 May ... had Gen. Eisenhower authorized Gen. Patton to do so.

12

Ike Ordered Halt!

Throughout 6 May, most American forces advancing east into Czechoslovakia encountered little or no resistance. Aware of SHAEF's restraining line at Karlsbad–Pilsen–Budweis, Maj. Gen. Huebner issued a Letter of Instruction to his corps at 1500 ordering them to halt at the aforementioned line and authorizing them to conduct reconnaissance patrols five miles beyond the line. Yet, the staffs of V Corps and its subordinate divisions continued to prepare for a drive further eastward to Prague.

Prague Cries for Help

Word of the Americans' arrival in Pilsen spread quickly through western Bohemia. To the east in the Czechoslovak capital, Czech patriots had seized a number of key places in the city but were now coming under attack from the SS troops dispatched by Field Marshall Schörner to suppress the uprising. By radio and by messenger, the Czechs in Prague cried out to the Americans to rescue them from the brutality of the SS troops. Radio broadcasts from Prague like this one conveyed the dire situation of the people in the embattled city: "Calling all Allied armies. We need urgent help. Send your planes and tanks. The Germans are advancing on Prague. For the Lord's sake, send help."[1]

Czechs all across western Bohemia listened to the cries of Prague partisans for help on the radio. Fighting raged around the radio station as German soldiers and Czech partisans struggled for control of this vital communication link. Milka Vilbova recalled hearing these radio broadcasts in her village of Stenovice. "While it was going on, it was very traumatic for those of us in western Bohemia because we could hear them being killed and being hurt, fighting with the Germans over the station," she said.[2]

In Pilsen and throughout the forward areas liberated by Third U.S. Army, Czech civilians pleaded with the U.S. soldiers to rush to the aid of their countrymen in Prague. Messengers came from Prague itself to request immediate U.S. military assistance. U.S. soldiers could hear the radio broadcasts pleading for help on their own radios. "One of the most terrible three days of my life after our war was over was hearing the Czechs in Prague crying out for help over the radio," recalled 1st Lt. Robert Gilbert, of the 38th Infantry Regiment, 2nd Infantry Division. Soldiers in the 4th Armored Division, the 16th Armored Division, 2nd Infantry Division and other Third U.S. Army units in Czechoslovakia received Prague's cries for help and sympathetically passed them up the chain of command.[3]

Throughout 6 May and the following day, reports flowed into the 16th Armored Division of German atrocities in Prague and desperate cries for help from the embattled Czech partisans. Maj. George B. Pickett, Jr.'s, Task Force A, received numerous reports of the Czech partisans fighting in Prague to free their city and relayed this up his chain of command. "All day reports came in from Prague requesting help. These messages forwarded to Division [Headquarters]" recorded the After Action Report for Combat Command B. "All day long on 7 May 1945 Czech Partisans reported enemy activities in the city of Prague and details in connection with the alleged atrocities against civilians in Prague," reported the Division G-2 (Intelligence) Section.

According to Czech partisans, the Germans had seven batteries of 105mm howitzers, seven batteries of 88mm guns and 70 tanks in Prague. They also reported that the routes from Pilsen to Prague were clear and three of Prague's five major bridges were still intact. Division Headquarters sent the reports about Prague up to V Corps Headquarters who in turn forwarded them to Third U.S. Army Headquarters. The Czechs in Prague were clearly in need of help and only the soldiers of Third Army could provide it.[4]

Even as American soldiers were clearing out diehard German soldiers in Pilsen, efforts to continue the drive eastward on Prague were underway. An Office of Strategic Services team led by Capt. Eugene Fodor had already met with leaders of the Prague uprising the day before. He reported back to Gen. George S. Patton that the Germans refused to surrender to the Czechs but were willing to surrender to the Americans instead. On the afternoon of 6 May, advance elements of the 16th Armored Division and the 4th Armored Division were heading for Prague. As Gen. Patton would later write in his memoirs, "...reconnaissance elements of the Third Army were in the vicinity of Prague, and by that act marked the furthest progress to the east of any western army."[5]

At 1000 on 7 May, CCB Headquarters received a message alerting them to be ready to advance on Prague on one-hour notice. If so ordered, CCB would utilize the southern route via Pribram and Routes 19 and 4. The Reconnaissance Platoons of the 64th Armored Infantry Battalion and the 16th Tank Battalion were sent separately to conduct a reconnaissance of the combat command's possible route of advance. The two platoons got as far as Pribram, or approximately halfway to Prague, before being recalled. Along the way, they encountered elements of the 2nd Infantry Division in the area south of Pilsen.[6]

Maj. Pickett wrote about sending his Recon Platoon to reconnoiter the route to Prague in his postwar article "The Pilsen Story." Several other soldiers of the 16th Armored Division also recalled heading towards Prague before being halted and brought back to the vicinity of Pilsen. "We were 17 miles from Prague on the 6th and they turned us around and brought us back," said Sgt. Jack Gallagher, a tank commander with D Company, 5th Tank Battalion, Combat Command A. "They were afraid we were going to meet the Russians and they wouldn't recognize us. So they brought us back and we stopped in Pilsen."[7]

Edward Krusheski of A Company, 69th Armored Infantry Battalion, Combat Command R later recalled that his company was ordered to seize one of the bridges over the Vltava River for follow on forces to use in reaching Prague. "We got to about 11 miles southwest of Prague," he later recalled. "But we were ordered to return 75 miles back to Pilsen."[8]

Halted Before Prague

"In view of the radio reports that the Czechoslovakian citizens had taken Prague, I was very anxious to go on and assist them, and asked Bradley for authority to do so, but this was denied," Patton wrote in *War As I Knew It*. Patton pleaded his case with his superior, Twelfth U.S. Army Group commander Gen. Omar Bradley. While sympathetic, Bradley could not authorize Patton to go beyond Eisenhower's restraining line and so he relayed Patton's request to Eisenhower. The Supreme Commander refused Patton's request and ordered Bradley to stop Patton at the Karlsbad–Pilsen–Budweis line. Late on the morning of 6 May, Bradley relayed Eisenhower's orders to Patton, informing him that "Ike does not want any international complications at this late date." Undeterred, Patton continued to press his case, offering to go incommunicado for several hours and then call Bradley from a phone booth in Prague. Not surprisingly, Bradley rejected his suggestion.[9]

Unable to convince his superiors, Patton began reining in his advancing divisions. Doing so proved difficult. As a result, a number of units, including CCA of the 9th Armored Division, and units of the 1st, 2nd and 5th Infantry Divisions were still advancing on the morning of 7 May 1945.[10]

After entering into the center of Pilsen, the 156th Armored Signal Company set up the Division Message Center near the Division Headquarters and began transacting communications. At 1600 on 6 May, a radio operator in the Message Center received an Urgent Top Secret message from V Corps Headquarters in cypher. After the message was deciphered, Warrant Officer Solomon Polish read the text. He was shocked to learn that the message was an order halting the 16th Armored Division and directing it not to advance any further than five miles from Pilsen. He later wrote:

> I was amazed to learn that General Patton would hold a complete Armored division in limbo while Prague was still German held. My first instinct was to tear that message up and let the division continue on to Prague, but after a second thought, I scrubbed that plan. I had no desire to spend the rest of my years in Leavenworth. There was a record of my receiving the message at V Corps.[11]

Immediately recognizing the importance of the message, Warrant Officer Polish skipped normal protocol and delivered the message directly to Brig. Gen. Pierce, instead of passing it to the Division G-3 (Operations) Officer, Lt. Col. James M. Worthington. At first, Pierce was angry at Polish for not following proper channels but after reading the message, his anger abated. Pierce then issued the order, which halted his division's drive on Prague and recalled those units which were still heading east.[12]

Third U.S. Army could easily have liberated the city of Prague and rescued thousands of Czech patriots from the brutality of the German SS troops still fighting in the city. With the exception of these SS troops, the German soldiers and civilians in Prague had had enough of the war and were making their way west to surrender to the Americans. In fact, the German commander in Prague Gen. Toussaint decided to evacuate the city on 7 May but the SS troops continued to fight on regardless of his orders. By the afternoon of 6 May, the 4th and 16th Armored Divisions were heading towards Prague with the 2nd, 97th, 5th and 90th Infantry Divisions following them to consolidate their gains. In the north, CCA 9th Armored Division and the 1st Infantry Division were heading towards Karlsbad on a route that ultimately led to Prague. In addition, Combat Command B and Reserve Command of the 9th Armored Division still had not been committed to the offensive. Unlike the Soviets who were encountering fanatical German resistance on their own drive on Prague, the Americans were encountering little or no opposition. Most Germans opposing the Americans were content to be taken prisoner, secure in the knowledge that capture by the Americans meant escaping indefinite Soviet captivity. As Gen. Bradley later wrote in his memoirs, "Indeed had SHAEF remanded its order, he [Patton] could probably have been in Wenzel Square [Wenceslaus Square in Prague] within 24 hours."[13]

Writing after the war, Lt. Col. George Pickett and Capt. Edgar Millington of the 64th Armored Infantry Battalion summarized the significance of Third U.S. Army not being allowed to liberate Prague. "Prague is the Paris of Czechoslovakia," they wrote in an April 1951 article for *Combat Forces Journal*. "All roads—political, cultural, historical—lead to Prague. Our failure to go into Prague was a defeat for our side."[14]

Col. Barksdale Hamlett, Jr., was also critical of the decision not to liberate Prague. During the 1976 interview for his Oral History, Hamlett spoke of the controversial decision:

> Unfortunately, we were held up in Pilsen. Of course, this was all part of the big picture that we did not know anything about, and neither did the Czechs. But it was a very, very upsetting thing to me because we could have gone right into the capital of Czechoslovakia. We could have rolled right on into Prague the next day. No trouble. The German Army was between Prague and our column but these people had had it. They didn't want to fight anybody, but they wanted to get away from the Russians.[15]

One of the American outposts outside of Pilsen on the road to Prague fell under Col. Hamlett's responsibility. Around this time, a German force approached the outpost. The German commander offered to let the Americans pass through him and head to Prague where the garrison there would surrender to them.[16]

Word of the German commander's offer was communicated up the Chain of Command from the outpost to Col. Hamlett at his Headquarters in the Grand Hotel in Pilsen. A retired Czechoslovak Army major general happened to be there at the time. Through an interpreter, the major general urged the Americans to accept the German offer. As Hamlett later recalled, the Czechoslovak major general predicted that Communists would take over the country if the Soviets got to Prague. This could be avoided if the Americans went into Prague and the Czechs were able to set up a democratic government.[17]

In 1958, President Benes' secretary Edward Taborsky wrote about the significance of Eisenhower halting Third Army east of Pilsen. In a biographical article about Benes published in *Foreign Affairs* magazine, Taborsky wrote:

> Had Patton continued to advance he could have liberated not only Prague but the whole of Bohemia and a substantial portion of Moravia. The Communists would have been denied the advantage conferred by the presence and active support of the Red Army and the N.K.V.D. [Soviet Communist Secret Police—BD] in entrenching themselves in the most populous and most strategic areas of Czechoslovakia. It was from these positions of strength, in the police, army, central and local administration, workers militias, and the communications system, that they were able to so successfully sabotage Benes' efforts to restore democracy in Czechoslovakia.[18]

So why did Eisenhower halt Patton and allow the Soviets to capture Prague? The answer lies in the re-emergence of pre-war political hostilities between the Soviet Union, and the U.S. and Great Britain. On 4 May 1945, Eisenhower had broached the idea of advancing to the Vltava River in a message to the Soviet High Command. Replying for the Soviet High Command the following day, Gen. Aleksei Antonov reminded Eisenhower that the Soviets had halted their forces short of the lower Elbe River at Eisenhower's request and he expected him to return the favor in Czechoslovakia to avoid a confusion of their respective forces. "The fine hand of the Soviet Foreign Office could be seen in Antonov's attitude—Czechoslovakia was to be in the orbit of the Soviet Union and Czech gratitude to America for the liberation of their capital was not part of the program," Gen. John Deane, Head of the U.S. Military Mission, Moscow, later wrote in his memoirs.[19]

There were two problems with Gen. Antonov's reply. The first deals with the lower Elbe River. In the opening days of May, the Soviet armies were driving in northern Germany towards the Baltic Sea near Lübeck; a combined British and American force under Field Marshall Sir Bernard Montgomery's command was also driving towards Lübeck with the intention of preventing the Soviets from gaining access to Denmark. The Soviets had not halted their forces at Eisenhower's request—Montgomery's troops had gotten to Lübeck first. The second problem deals with Antonov's concerns over the juncture of American and Soviet forces. Eisenhower and Bradley, too, were greatly concerned that U.S. and Soviet forces might crash into each other and cause unnecessary "friendly fire" casualties. If the Soviet intention was to avoid such collisions, then a well-defined geographical feature such as the Vltava River was a much better halt line than an arbitrary line drawn on a map from Karlsbad south to Pilsen and then onto Budweis. Indeed, to the north, the Elbe River had been used for this exact same reason only two weeks before. No, the Soviet reply to Eisenhower's proposed advance to the Vltava River was a purely political move designed to grab Prague for the Soviets, aid the Czechoslovak Communists, and prevent postwar American influence with the new Czechoslovak government which was then in the process of being formed.[20]

13

The End of the War in Europe

In a schoolhouse in Reims, France, representatives of the Third Reich surrendered to the Allied Powers in the early morning hours of 7 May 1945. All hostilities were to cease at 0001 local time on 9 May 1945. Gen. Eisenhower immediately ordered all of his forces to halt in place and not advance any further. As part of the surrender protocols, all German forces not within American lines prior to midnight 8 May 1945 belonged to the Soviets. Thus, hundreds of thousands of German soldiers and civilians became engaged in a literal race of life and death to reach American lines before the surrender deadline.

Word was passed down the chains of command to halt Third Army units. At 0800, Maj. Gen. Huebner received word of the German surrender and Eisenhower's order to halt all eastward advances. Immediately, he sent orders out to his corps to halt in place. The 1st, 2nd and 97th Infantry Divisions and CCA 9th Armored Division had already resumed their attacks early on 7 May 1945. CCA's two task forces were only a few miles short of Karlsbad when they received the halt order. The 303rd Infantry Regiment of 97th Infantry Division reached its morning objective by 0900 and then halted after receiving the order to do so. The 2nd Infantry Division halted only after reaching the southern and eastern outskirts of Pilsen.[1]

Once the halt orders had been received, the units of XII Corps and V Corps consolidated their positions, participated in liberation festivities with the Czechs and processed the huge mass of German soldiers and civilians flooding into American lines.

With the German surrender, the war in Europe now entered into a transition period. In anticipation of the shift from offensive operations to occupation duties, Maj. Gen. Huebner had issued a Letter of Instruction at 1500 on the afternoon of 6 May. This instruction dealt with how to handle the massive flood of displaced persons, and surrendering German soldiers and civilians. For security reasons, all Germans were to be screened by Counter-Intelligence Corps (CIC) personnel to segregate out members of the Nazi Party, the German Secret Service and the German General Staff. Surrendering units were permitted to retain a specified number of rifles with ten bullets per rifle for security purposes. Huebner's instruction also included detailed protocols for contact with the Soviet Army which would likely occur in the next few days.[2]

Soon American forces in western Czechoslovakia were inundated with tens of thousands of Germans and refugees seeking to escape from the Soviets. "They [the Germans] were coming in everything that would move," recalled Col. William Smith, Jr., commander of the 216th Armored Engineer Battalion. "We had all kinds of vehicles and all kinds of animal-drawn equipment. They were just coming in in tremendous numbers." Staff Sgt. Gene Eike also was involved with processing the flood of Germans surrendering to the Americans. "The Germans just poured through our lines running from the Russians," he later recalled. "They were coming in from all directions. We didn't have enough men to guard them."[3]

Task Force B of CCB spent the duration of 7 May 1945 patrolling, rounding up German prisoners and guarding key installations. At 1830, Czech civilians reported to the Task Force that German soldiers were firing at civilians in the nearby town of Ujejd. The Battalion Executive Officer led a composite force of 3rd Platoon, Company D, and a platoon of anti-tank and machine gun soldiers from Company B, 64th Armored Infantry Battalion to investigate. There they discovered evidence to verify the Czechs' report but darkness prevented them from taking any action. The team returned to their billeting area and prepared to clear out the Germans in the morning.[4]

Combat Command B was still expecting to resume its advance on Prague. At 1330, Lt. Kitchen of the 16th Tank Battalion's Recon Platoon and Lt. Clark of the 64th Armored Infantry Battalion's Recon Platoon were ordered to make a joint road reconnaissance with their platoons from Pilsen to Pribram to ascertain road conditions and the locations of enemy forces. The Kitchen / Clark Team headed for Pribram but were diverted to the town of Spalena Porici investigate reports that a German general desired to surrendered his force of some 5,000 soldiers. By the time they arrived there, a unit of the 2nd Infantry Division had already accepted the general's surrender and was processing his soldiers.[5]

The two recon platoons continued eastward on their mission. Along the way, Czech civilians reported that SS troops were holding Rezmital and several other nearby villages. They proceeded to the village of Veltus from which the Americans observed a column of German vehicles emerging from Rezmital. Lieutenants Kitchen and Clark realized that their small force was outnumbered, and having been previously ordered to avoid combat, they decided to withdraw to the village of Hvezdazy five miles to the west.[6]

At a road junction on the way back to Hvezdazy, the American recon team suddenly discovered that the German column had come by a different route and were now approaching that same road junction. The Americans quickly halted and took up fighting positions. The commander of the German force displayed a white flag and promptly surrendered his men. His force included eight officers, 61 soldiers and eight vehicles. Like so many other German soldiers in Bohemia that day, these Germans were in no mood for fighting and were eager to escape Soviet captivity. Accordingly the Germans were sent back to Pilsen under the guard of just two American soldiers.[7]

Again, the American recon platoons pushed forward. When they finally arrived in Pribram, they discovered two Russian paratroopers. The Americans and the two Russians conversed as best they could for a short time. Then the two lieutenants decided to return to Pilsen after having accomplished their mission. Altogether they had reconnoitered 43 miles of roads and located several German forces, one of which surrendered en masse to them.[8]

The return to Pilsen soon became essentially an impromptu victory parade. A Czech motorcycle sped off in advance of the American column, alerting all of the villagers and townspeople ahead of them of their imminent arrival. "Seemingly the entire population lined the streets, each offering cakes, cookies, wine and beer," wrote Maj. Pickett in his After Action Report for the 64th Armored Infantry Battalion.[9]

Combat Command R had been alerted to advance on Prague at a moment's notice with the 26th Tank Battalion in the lead. CCR would lead the entire division in the drive on Prague. The command spent most of 7 May expecting orders that never came. Instead at 1600, word was received from higher headquarters that the German High Command had surrendered. All further advances were cancelled.[10]

That evening, however, CCR formed a task force to investigate a report of German panzer units advancing from the east. Company C of the 216th Armored Medical Battalion provided a detachment of three officers, 20 enlisted men and five ambulances for the ad hoc task force. After driving twenty miles to the east and finding no sign of the rumored panzers, the task force returned to American lines.[11]

Combat Command A too had been alerted for the advance on Prague. Like CCR, the command waited all morning for orders that never came. Instead, they were told at 1300 that the attack had been called off.[12]

Having finally been re-united with their armored vehicles, the soldiers of the 633rd Tank Destroyer Battalion (SP) finally began working with their new parent division. At 1100 on 7 May, the battalion (minus Reconnaissance Company) motor-marched into Czechoslovakia. About two miles east of Kozuluky, they met up with contact parties from the three Combat Commands and reverted to their control. From there, the three tank destroyer companies proceeded to join up with their respective combat command while the Battalion Command Group and Headquarters Company headed for Pilsen. For the next three days, the separated units of the battalion would be engaged in processing and guarding German prisoners of wars and civilians. Aside from receiving some sporadic small arms fire in Germany and Czechoslovakia, the battalion did not see any combat action.[13]

For much of the day, the 23rd Cavalry Squadron continued to operate as dispersed units. Troop A was relieved of its assignment to Combat Command A at 0800. Subsequently they were tasked with manning outposts on Highway 95 northeast of Pilsen. Upon arriving at their assigned location, Troop A discovered that elements of the 97th Infantry Division had already set up outposts here. So Troop A moved to the Squadron's Assembly Area near Doubrauka. Troop B conducted reconnaissance patrols for most of the day and then returned to Pilsen in the evening. Troop D patrolled the road between Pilsen and Gihana then rejoined the Squadron at Doubrauka. Troop E performed vehicle maintenance. In the afternoon, the Squadron occupied billets in the city of Pilsen. The Squadron Rear Echelon and Company F travelled from Ronsburg and rejoined the main body in Pilsen that evening. All along the way, they were greeted by cheering Czech civilians. A team from Troop B was tasked for a special mission deep behind the German lines which is the subject of the next chapter.[14]

14

The Pratt Mission

Though representatives of the German High Command had surrendered at Reims early on the morning of 7 May, there were still many German forces continuing the war either through ignorance of the surrender or outright refusal to obey it. Most of these forces were under the command of Generalfeldmarschall Ferdinand Schörner, a fanatical Nazi and personal favorite of Adolf Hitler. In order to affect the surrender of Schörner's forces, elements of the 16th Armored Division became involved in one of the more unusual special missions of the war in Europe.

Getting the word of the German High Command's surrender out to its scattered remaining forces was most problematic. Allied forces had occupied all of Germany but still sizeable forces remained in western Czechoslovakia and parts of Austria. Other German garrisons were still holding out in the Channel ports and Norway. With German communications in a poor state, and Schörner's well-known opposition to surrendering, Eisenhower sent a representative of the new German government and its leader Grossadmiral Karl Dönitz to deliver news of the surrender to Schörner. Col. Wilhelm Meyer-Detring, head of the Wehrmacht High Command Planning Section, was selected to deliver this highly important message on their behalf.[1]

V Corps was ordered to provide an escort for Meyer-Detring and his interpreter Lt. Otto Verber from its 16th Armored Division. The escort consisted of Lt. Col. Robert H. Pratt—Assistant V Corps G-3 (Operations) Officer, the Executive Officer of the division's 23rd Cavalry Squadron Maj. Carl O'Dowd, a small force from Troop B led by Lt. Gerard Dalton, the Squadron medical officer Capt. Stewart Kephart, two U.S. Army newspaper correspondents, a correspondent from Reuters News Agency, and a Czechoslovak Army officer. Altogether Pratt's team consisted of over 40 men, a staff car, five M8 armored cars, three jeeps, and an ambulance.[2]

Lt. Col. Robert H. Pratt was the Assistant Chief of Staff (G-3) Operations for V Corps. Born on 12 February 1908 and raised in Wisconsin, Pratt was a 1929 graduate of the University of Wisconsin and a former member of the Wisconsin National Guard. When President Roosevelt had called the National Guard into Federal service in 1940, Pratt became part of the U.S. Army. As part of V Corps, he helped plan the Normandy Invasion and landed on Omaha Beach on D–Day.[3]

Col. Meyer-Detring was flown under guard on a Royal Air Force C-47 cargo plane to Pilsen airport, arriving there in the early evening of 7 May. Speed was essential. The escort party was immediately assembled. A half hour after Meyer-Detring landed in Pilsen, the Troop B team headed off for Prague traveling at 40 miles per hour with headlights blazing and white flags of truce flying. Czech resistance fighters began notifying the towns and villages ahead on their route that they were coming. As a result, the Americans found their progress delayed by crowds of Czech citizens who gathered to greet them as they passed through these towns and villages. "In spite of darkness, each town had its own welcoming

Col. Wilhelm Meyer-Detring of the German High Command (center) arrives at the Pilsen Airport, 7 May 1945 (National Archives Photo).

committee out with red, white and blue flags and more flowers," stated the V Corps history.[4]

Inside Prague the Czechs were still battling the Germans. Around 2330, Pratt's team entered the city and met up with the partisan leaders. "The Czechs in Prague knew we were coming but they were expecting an armored division and were disappointed when they saw our small group pull into the city," Pratt recalled soon after. Pratt explained to them that they were there to arrange the surrender of the German forces. "The Prague civilians were so overjoyed at seeing us, and so rabid in their hatred for the Germans, that I felt very concerned about the safety of the German colonel riding with me."[5]

The Chief of Police for Prague offered to guide Pratt and his team through the city. Around midnight, they arrived at the city's center and soon after, passed through the forward most barricades erected by the partisans. From there, the Americans and their German dignitaries were on their own.[6]

Pratt, Maj. O'Dowd, Lt. Verber and Col. Meyer-Detring dismounted from their vehicles and proceeded ahead on foot through the barricades. "When I stepped through that barrier, it was the worst feeling I ever had in my life," said Pratt later. "We walked down the long street with our flashlights on the white flag and talked nonsense to keep from showing our nervousness."[7]

At last they encountered a German soldier. Col. Meyer-Detring explained his mission to the soldier and requested that he be brought to the German Command Post. After considerable arguing, he obtained permission for two of the American vehicles to pass through the barricade. A German guide led them down a street lined with some sixty tanks and assault guns.[8]

At last, the group came to the German Command Post for Prague. Meyer-Detring was led inside while Lt. Col. Pratt and the others awaited outside. Eventually a German lieutenant emerged and invited the Americans inside to wait in an officers' lounge. He also provided them with cognac and some food. Before they ate, the lieutenant proposed a toast to their fallen comrades.[9]

When Meyer-Detring rejoined his American escorts, he brought some disturbing news. Schörner was not in Prague; rather he had set up a headquarters at Welchov (Velichovky in Czech)—some 120 kilometers further east, near the Polish border. To deliver their highly important surrender message, the Pratt Mission would have to push farther to find Schörner.[10]

Col. Meyer-Detring (second from left) and Lt. Col. Robert Pratt (far right) attempt unsuccessfully to locate Feldmarschall Schörner in Prague on the night of 7–8 May 1945 (National Archives Photo).

The Americans soon discovered that alcohol was freely flowing amongst the German troops in Prague. "When we got into our cars it was evident that many of the German troops here had been drinking heavily," Lt. Verber later explained. "They felt that they were living their last night because they were to attack in the morning, and they knew they could not succeed."[11]

Lt. Col. Pratt and his group now headed east to locate Schörner's headquarters. Almost immediately they ran into insurmountable obstacles. "We started off for Welchau on a road that was supposed to be entirely in German hands," stated Lt. Col. Pratt afterwards, "and the first thing we ran into was a Czech partisan street blockade made up of streetcars filled with cobblestones, trucks, wagons, parts of airplanes, and everything else imaginable."[12]

Unable to get past the barricade, the Pratt Mission returned to German lines. They requested a German escort to guide them to Schörner's headquarters. At first, the Germans refused and a heated argument ensued.

14. The Pratt Mission

Finally, the Germans relented and provided Pratt and Meyer-Detring with a motorcyclist to guide them. With Lt. Col. Pratt and Lt. Verber riding on the outside of the sedan carrying the German colonel, the group pressed on. Soon after leaving Prague, two of the jeeps suffered tire damage from spikes placed in the road by Czech partisans and were forced to drop out of the column. Continually Pratt and the remaining vehicles were slowed by crowds of Czechs. Eventually they reached the main road to Koniggratz. Their guide left them. The Americans were now on their own to find their way to Welchau.[13]

Pratt and the remaining vehicles and members of his group continued eastward. Czech roadblocks continued to thwart their progress. Lt. Col. Pratt later explained:

> The Czech partisans had done a good job of breaking up German supply routes, and about dawn we ran into another roadblock, this one of felled trees. We tried to go around it by taking a side road, but ran into another block. We got through this one but after 15 minutes of riding we hit another. From then on they were all over the road.[14]

About 15 kilometers from Welchau, Pratt and his group were suddenly fired upon. The Americans halted and dove for cover in roadside ditches. A man wearing a blue pants, red shirt and red cap emerged with a rifle. "Comrades! Me Russky!" he called out. The Americans had stumbled upon a group of Russian guerrilla forces operating in the German rear area. These guerrillas had cut all communications lines to Schörner's headquarters and incited a riot in Welchau the previous night. After explaining their mission to the Russians, Pratt's men re-mounted their vehicles and proceeded on with their mission.[15]

At around 1000 on the morning of 8 May, the Pratt Mission reached Schörner's headquarters. While Meyer-Detring met with the recalcitrant field marshal and delivered news of the German surrender, the Germans fed the Americans a breakfast of fresh eggs, fresh butter, bread, sausage and coffee. Among their hosts were two German colonels, a major and two captains.[16]

After some time spent in discussions with Schörner, Col. Meyer-Detring re-joined his American escorts. But now the Americans had another problem to overcome. Having driven far beyond Prague, the Pratt Mission vehicles were running low on fuel. At first, the Germans declined to provide them with any of their meager supplies, claiming that they needed that fuel for their own vehicles so they could escape the Soviets. "They told us that the gasoline had been issued to the troops for their trip to the American lines, and that if we took it away from them we would be denying their right to life," Lt. Verber later stated. "The German colonel said he could not be responsible for their actions if the gasoline were taken."[17]

Pratt was equally adamant in securing fuel for his vehicles. He pressed his case with the German colonel until the latter relented and two fifty-gallon drums of gasoline were provided to the Americans. It was not certain whether these two drums would be sufficient for Pratt and his men to complete the trip back to Pilsen. Nevertheless, the fuel offered was better than nothing and so the Pratt Mission departed from Schörner's headquarters in early afternoon of 8 May.[18]

From Welchov until Königgrätz (Hradec Králové), the trip was uneventful. Czech partisans had cleared the roads and no obstacles were encountered. In Hradec Kralove, however, the Americans became caught up in an impromptu liberation celebration held by the people of the town. "It was like seeing a moving picture," said Pratt afterwards. "The Czechs

U.S. soldiers of the 23rd Cavalry Squadron celebrate the end of the war with the citizens of Welchow, Czechoslovakia on 8 May 1945. Staff Sgt. Meyer Rodelle is holding a baby and standing on the M8 armored car. The M8 armored car is armed with a 37mm gun, a co-axial .30 cal. machine gun and a turret-mounted M2 50 cal. machine gun (National Archives Photo).

milled around us waving flags, singing, shouting, shooting their guns, and asking us to sign their ration books."[19]

In the midst of the raucous celebrations, some Czechs were able to obtain additional fuel for the Americans' vehicles. The refueling was accomplished but the Americans found it difficult to leave the city and its exuberant residents. Finally, around 1630, Pratt and his group departed Hradec Kralove and pushed westward.[20]

Next the Pratt Mission encountered a group SS soldiers in the town of Cesky Brod who were holding more than fifty Czechs as hostages. The Americans freed the hostages and prevented the SS troops from executing them.[21]

Expecting difficulties in passing through Prague, Pratt decided to bypass the city to the north. Around midnight, they encountered unmistakable signs of battle in the Czechoslovak capital. They could hear small arms fire and see numerous fires off in the distance.[22]

All along the route west, the Pratt Mission passed by large groups of liberated peoples trying to return home and truck loads of retreating Germans trying to escape the Soviets. The Americans were also hailed as liberators at many of the towns and villages through which they passed.[23]

At around 4 am on the morning of 9 May, Lt. Col. Pratt, Col. Meyer-Detring and Pratt's soldiers returned to Pilsen. Despite the early hour, the city was a bustle. Lt. Col. Pratt later reported:

> Even at that hour there were streams and streams of German soldiers coming into American lines. They were riding in horse drawn vehicles, in trucks, in wagons, in anything that would roll. And they weren't coming in alone. Right along with them were their wives, sweethearts, mistresses, children and dogs. I guess word of the purpose of our visit got around fast.[24]

Pratt and his group had safely returned to Pilsen but not all of the Pratt Mission members had done so. The two jeeps and their crews that had dropped out due to tire damage returned to American lines several days later after having had a wild experience of their own. First they were captured by a group of German soldiers who intended to use them as escorts into the American lines. Then, a Czech/Russian guerrilla force overtook the Germans and rescued the several Americans. After celebrating the war's end and the Allied victory with the guerrillas, the Americans finally managed to return to American lines.[25]

Despite Grossadmiral Dönitz's orders, Schörner himself never surrendered. He was captured in eastern Austria two weeks later and handed over to the Soviets. The Soviets in turn sentenced him to 10 years in prison for war crimes. After returning to West Germany, the new government

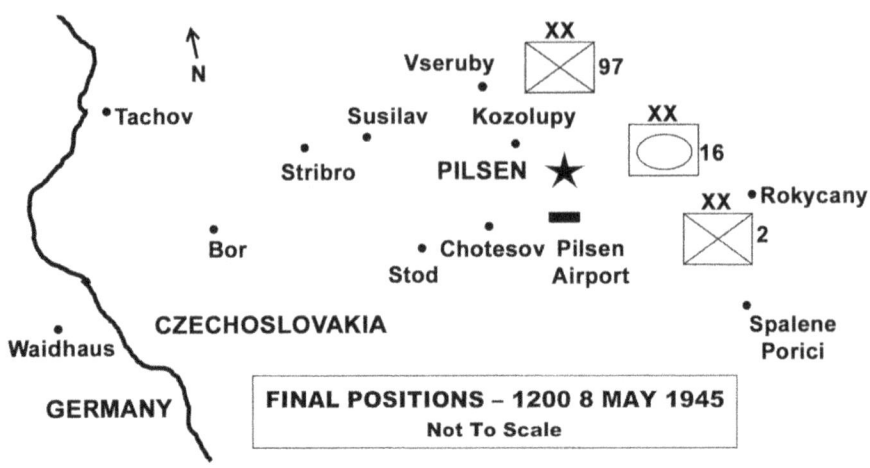

Final Positions 8 May 1945

tried and convicted him of killing German soldiers in the closing days of the war. He served another four years in prison.²⁶

For their extraordinary mission, the members of the Pratt Mission received unit and individual awards. Lt. Col. Pratt, Maj. O'Dowd and several other officers and soldiers who participated in the mission were awarded the Bronze Star Medal. Everyone else received the U.S. Army Certificate of Merit. In part, Maj. O'Dowd's medal citation read: "The coolness, leadership, energy, courage, and daring disregard for personal danger demonstrated by Maj. O'Dowd were factors that contributed in great degree to the successful completion of the mission." The 23rd Cavalry Squadron received a Letter of Commendation from V Corps commanding general Maj. Gen. Clarence Huebner. In praising the team members, Maj. Gen. Huebner wrote,

> Their ability to keep going under the most trying conditions was proof of their stamina and willingness. The leadership demonstrated by the officers and non-commissioned officers of the detachment was of the highest order. I wish to extend my personal congratulations to the individuals of this Detachment and to thank them for the valuable service which they rendered to the Allied cause."²⁷

In making their journey to Welchov (Velichovky) which is near the Czechoslovak-Polish border, Pratt and his team earned the distinction of having advanced the farthest east of any unit of the western Allies. The Pratt Mission was a unique way for the newly arrived 16th Armored Division to conclude not only its only combat operation but also to conclude the Second World War in Europe.

15

V-E Day and Occupation Duties

Tuesday, 8 May 1945 was declared "Victory in Europe" Day. While the world rejoiced at the end of the Second World War in Europe, V-E Day was the start of occupation duties for American soldiers in western Czechoslovakia. In many ways, the occupation period was far more complicated than the combat operations. Previously, the mission had been to defeat and destroy the remaining German forces. Now, the American soldiers were expected to process and guard German prisoners, repatriate freed Allied prisoners of war, assist displaced persons from numerous nations in getting to their homes, assist the Czechs in re-establishing their local governments and government services, help the Czechs rebuild areas damaged or destroyed during the war, apprehend Nazi war criminals, maintain law and order especially by protecting the surrendered German soldiers and the Sudeten Germans from retribution by angry Czechs, and maintain cordial relations with the soon to arrive Soviet Army, who oftentimes would be hostile and belligerent. All of this had to be done in the midst of a power struggle between pro-democracy Czechs and Soviet-supported Czech Communists.

Throughout the summer of 1945, soldiers of the 16th Armored Division and other Third U.S. Army units would perform these tasks with great professionalism and effectiveness, thereby winning the heartfelt appreciation of the Czech people In addition, the summer of 1945 was also a time for fraternization with the Czech people and the forging of lifelong bonds of friendship.

Victory in Europe Day—8 May 1945

When many people think of V-E Day, they imagine a worldwide celebration of the end of Nazi tyranny and a disastrous war that devastated

Soldiers of the 5th Tank Battalion, 16th Armored Division process German prisoners of war for discharge to their homes in June 1945 (National Archives Photo).

large swaths of Europe. To some extent that is true. But in western Czechoslovakia, reactions amongst U.S. soldiers were mixed. For some, this was a day of great rejoicing. For those who had fought through hardest fighting, there was the relief that they had survived but also the sadness that many of their friends had not. For others, V-E Day was a day of apprehension, especially those who were slated to redeploy to the Pacific Theater for the invasion of the Japanese Home Islands. For many, V-E Day was anti-climactic. For most soldiers of V Corps, VE-Day was a busy day of transition from combat to occupation.

On V-E Day, V Corps Headquarters relocated and took over a German Luftwaffe training camp in Pilsen. The new corps command post was established at 1300 that afternoon. Four hours later at 1700, Maj. Gen.

Huebner issued his final Letter of Instruction of the war in Europe. The war in Europe was now over but a war was still to be won in the Pacific. Accordingly, troop redeployments for the Pacific were to begin almost immediately. Thus Huebner's Letter of Instruction dealt primarily with the movements and dispositions of his corps. The 102nd Cavalry Group was directed to be prepared to move to Pilsen on or about 11 May. The 1st Infantry Division and its attached CCA 9th Armored were to remain in northwestern Czechoslovakia processing the tens of thousands of German soldiers and civilians being held there. 9th Armored Division's other commands remained in their assembly areas just over the border in Germany.

Upon oral orders from V Corps Headquarters, 2nd Infantry Division was to relieve the 16th Armored Division in Pilsen. Pilsen was declared "Off Limits" to all troops except for 2nd Infantry Division, and V Corps Headquarters and support troops. After relief by 2nd Infantry Division, the 16th Armored Division was to relieve the 97th Infantry Division north and northwest of Pilsen and maintain contact with 1st Infantry Division. Lastly, after being relieved by the 16th Armored Division, the 97th Infantry Division was to move into an assembly area in the vicinity of Tachov and to be prepared for further movements back into Germany. Some of these reliefs and movements started to occur on VE-Day.[1]

The 97th Infantry Division had been designated as one of the Americans units which would redeploy to the Pacific Theater for the upcoming invasion of the Japanese Home Islands. This was an interesting turn of events for the Trident Division. Originally they had been designated to serve in the Pacific and had even undergone amphibious training in California. But instead they were deployed to Europe as a result of the heavy casualties that the U.S. Army had suffered during the Battle of the Bulge. Now, they were heading to the Pacific as had originally been intended. Needless to say, VE-Day for the soldiers of the 97th Infantry Division was the conclusion of one war with another war still to be finished.[2]

PFC George Shultz, Jr., of 23rd Infantry Regiment, 2nd Infantry Division was in Pilsen on V-E Day and he later described the celebrations that occurred there. "People were bestowing drinks, food, ice cream, on any GI walking the streets," he later wrote. "People had their Czech flags flying. Young ladies were wearing the traditional Czech costume and dress. I photographed a Czech cavalry unit coming into town and being greeted by the people. Folks were dancing in the streets, hugging us, crying and cheering."[3]

U.S. soldiers in western Czechoslovakia had some time to celebrate the end of the war with the newly liberated Czech people but other tasks took precedence as Third U.S. Army had to almost instantaneously switch from combat operations to occupation duties. This transition included shuffling units around and re-positioning to better administer the occupation areas. For example, CCB's Task Force B was relieved of its assignment in south Pilsen at 1300 by elements of the 18th Armored Infantry Battalion, Combat Command A. Two hours later, they relocated to an area about four miles north of Pilsen. Here they established roadblocks and patrolled the northeast outskirts of Pilsen. To their south, the 26th Tank Battalion and other units of Combat Command R were astride Highway 14 manning roadblocks and processing German soldiers and civilians and displaced persons heading west ahead of the advancing Soviet Army.[4]

Either through a breakdown of communications or outright obstinacy, some German soldiers refused to surrender. At 0600 on the morning of 8 May, the composite team of 16th Tank and 64th Armored Infantry Battalions returned to the village of Ujejd to deal with the Germans harassing the Czech civilians there. The team captured twenty-eight SS soldiers.[5]

At 0001 local time on 9 May 1945, the Second World War in Europe officially ended. V Corps was holding a 115 mile line that stretched from west of Karlsbad to southeast of Pilsen and XII Corps was holding a similarly long line that stretched from southeast of Pilsen to the Austrian border.

The Disintegration of the German Army

V-E Day was a time for widespread celebrations throughout Europe and America but in western Czechoslovakia, other vital tasks took precedence over celebrating the end of the war in Europe. Even before the war had officially ended, large waves of German soldiers and civilians had been streaming towards the American lines to escape from the oncoming Soviet armies. After the German surrender at Reims, these waves quickly became a veritable flood of humanity.

Mark Steece of B Troop, 23rd Cavalry Squadron, later related his impressions of the captured German soldiers. "At one time, the Germans were pretty good soldiers," he said. "Most of them were pretty demoralized. They gave up pretty easily. We captured a lot of them."[6]

The ethnic complexities of the region soon became a formidable problem for the American soldiers now in western Czechoslovakia. On one hand, they were liberators who had freed the Czechs from German occupation. On the other hand, they were conquerors who had defeated the German Army and were now their captors. Lt. Col. William W. Smith, Jr., of the 216th Armored Engineers Battalion later recalled the difficulties experienced by U.S. soldiers in this volatile situation between Czechs and Germans:

> Now this is the Sudeten-German lands. There were Czechs and there were Sudeten German Czechs and the Czechs were really perturbed with the German soldiers. We really needed to protect these German soldiers, and the Sudeten Germans also needed to be protected because the Czechs really went after them. There was no question about that. We really didn't understand what the big problem was but we knew we had a problem when these people started shooting at each other.[7]

Other soldiers of the 16th Armored also wrote of the animosity between the newly liberated Czechs and the German soldiers and civilians. "At last they [the Czechs] gave vent to their pent-up feelings and openly sought out and attacked all German civilians and unarmed uniformed members of the German military. They beat them with any kind of weapon available," wrote Lt. Col. Frank Houlihan. "We could not blame the Czechs for seeking revenge, but it had to be stopped by our troops to prevent bloodshed and possible attacks on non-guilty persons," wrote Col. Charles Noble.[8]

At 0300 one morning soon after the German surrender, Col. Noble was awakened because Gen. Andrei Vlasov and his staff had come into American lines. Having been rebuffed by the Czech partisans in Prague, Vlasov had brought his troops west to surrender to the Americans and thus escape Soviet captivity. Col. Noble's men provided Gen. Vlasov and his staff with breakfast then took them to see the Commanding General of V Corps, Maj. Gen. Clarence Huebner. Faced with this tricky political situation, Huebner consulted with his Chain of Command for guidance on how to proceed. Ultimately, Vlasov and his soldiers were detained by the Americans. Senior American leaders well above Huebner and Patton had Vlasov and his men turned over to the Soviets so as not to offend their increasingly belligerent ally. Vlasov and a great many of his men were later executed or died in harsh Soviet captivity.[9]

In the days that followed the German surrender, the 216th Armored Engineer Battalion was busily engaged in a variety of missions. The battalion's soldiers investigated suspected German booby traps and mines, and established water points for the division's soldiers. Places were needed to contain the huge numbers of German soldiers and civilians flooding into the 16th Armored Division's area, so the 216th Armored Engineers constructed barbed-wire enclosures and sanitary facilities for these prisoners. The battalion's soldiers also manned check-points and conducted patrols to round up Germans and displaced persons wandering the countryside.[10]

Several days after the war ended, Company B, 18th Armored Infantry Battalion was relocated to Theusing, Czechoslovakia. Because the Division Prisoner of War Camp had become full of surrendering Germans, Company B was tasked to set up a temporary POW enclosure in an alfalfa field. A perimeter of machine guns was established to enclose the ten-acre field. "The German soldiers were then organized under the leadership of German officers," Capt. Painter later wrote. "Doctors and nurses (German) organized sick call and set up a treatment tent. In a short while the Germans were organized and caring largely for themselves." Harley Barrs of Company B later wrote about processing the surrendering Germans: "We had to take any weapons the Germans carried, then placed the prisoners in compounds and try to get food and protection for the displaced persons." After about eleven days, Company B was pulled back to Marienbad. There the Americans were assigned to military government duties in the nearby villages. Soon after, Capt. Painter was reassigned to another unit.[11]

Company A, 18th Armored Infantry Battalion was also tasked with processing the surrendering German soldiers and the displaced persons. "The Germans just poured through our lines running from the Russians," recalled Staff Sgt. Gene Eike. "They were coming in from all directions. We didn't have enough men to guard them. We were few and far between. So we just disarmed them and sent them to the rear. We had a field full of everything you can imagine—motorcycles, trucks, cars. Everyone in our unit got a motorcycle until the higher ups took them away because so many guys were getting injured."[12]

After 633rd Tank Battalion finally caught up with the 16th Armored Division on 7 May, its companies were attached to the division's three combat commands. With the war at an end, the battalion's separated units were tasked with processing and guarding German prisoners of wars and civilians. This lasted until 9 May when the companies were detached from the combat commands, and re-assembled under the battalion commander Lt. Col. Brisack's control. Thus re-assembled, the battalion relocated to the vicinity of Krelovice. There they established camps for the Prisoners of War and Displaced Civilians and manned outposts to control the movement of people in their area. This mission lasted about five days until they were relieved of assignment to the 16th Armored Division and placed directly under the control of V Corps Headquarters.[13]

On 9 May 1945, 23rd Cavalry Squadron was conducting patrols east of Pilsen and manning roadblocks. Very early in the morning, the troopers of 2nd Platoon, Troop C received a report from Czech civilians that a German Panzer Division was coming from Prague. At 0300, a German column of soldiers and civilians arrived at the platoon's positions. The column was led by the Commanding General of Wehrkreis Prague, Gen. Rudolf Toussaint. Seeing no further need for bloodshed, Toussaint had made an agreement with Czech partisans in Prague to leave the city with his troops and many German civilians. Now arriving at the American lines, Gen. Toussaint then surrendered his force to the platoon leader, Lt. Smith. The rest of the day was then spent processing in this very large assemblage of German soldiers and civilians. "As the long endless motorized column passed our lines we took over their armored and motor vehicles," Col. Noble wrote. The German soldiers were disarmed and segregated from the civilians, a great many of whom were women, and housed in separate prisoner of war camps[14]

The American soldiers of V Corps quickly became overwhelmed with the massive flood of German soldiers and civilians. On 10 May alone, V Corps accepted the surrender of 55,087 soldiers and a number of general officers. Soon the 1st Infantry Division was holding 63,000 Germans in several camps with the 2nd Infantry Division holding another 44,000 and the 16th Armored Division holding 18,000. The 16th Armored Division Military Police Platoon received 5,408 German prisoners for processing and holding in just three days![15]

For weeks following VE-Day, V Corps and its divisions guarded tens of thousands of German prisoners of war in temporary camps set up throughout the occupation zone. The 16th Armored Division was responsible for many of these PW camps and accordingly, numerous 16th Armored Division soldiers found themselves guarding their former enemies. In the camps, the German prisoners were screened for possible war criminals and other high value persons. The war criminals and high value persons were transferred to more secure confinement facilities. The ordinary German soldiers and civilians were processed for discharge and return to their homes. In addition, German prisoners were often used to perform labor and work on reconstruction projects.

Sgt. O. J. Mooney of the 396th Armored Field Artillery Battalion was one American soldier who supervised German soldiers on a work detail following VE-Day. After leaving Pilsen, his battalion had been sent to Stribro to assume occupation duties in the town and its environs. One day, Sgt. O. J. Mooney and the crew of his M7 self-propelled gun were assigned the task of disposing of ordnance in an ammunition factory. To assist in this endeavor, Sgt. Mooney was given twenty German prisoners. While carrying crates of "potato masher" grenades, two of the Germans dropped a crate. The resulting explosion killed ten of them and seriously wounded nine more. "It was real unfortunate—I don't know how long those Germans had been in the Wehrmacht," recalled Mooney years later. "The war had just ended and they get blown to smithereens."[16]

The Flood of Humanity

The collapse of the Third Reich and the liberation of its numerous concentration camps unleashed a veritable flood of humanity upon the western Allies. All across Germany, Austria and Czechoslovakia, hundreds of thousands of released prisoners from dozens of ethnic groups were suddenly now roaming about trying to get home. Coupled with the hundreds of thousands of displaced Germans and surrendered German soldiers, this flood threatened to overwhelm the western Allies.

Having liberated Pilsen and its environs, the 16th Armored Division was now confronted with the full force of this human flood. Lt. Col. Houlihan of the 137th Armored Ordnance Battalion later described the situation facing the division's soldiers:

> We were simply not equipped to handle the food, water and other supplies needed daily by the surrendering German forces and not only were these forces in need, but in addition, hundreds of fleeing Polish, Italian, French and other refugees added to the problem. Lines of displaced persons, consisting of shattered humanity, stretched for mile upon mile around us.

To help provide for the basic needs of these people, many of the battalion's trucks were unloaded of military equipment and supplies and used to transport food and water to the holding areas for the German prisoners and the displaced persons.[17]

Another unit that found itself overwhelmed by the enormous numbers of displaced persons was the 18th Armored Infantry Battalion. Already processing thousands of surrendered German soldiers, the battalion had to establish several camps to house the displaced persons. As the battalion's Unit History recorded:

> Providing for these displaced persons of all nationalities presented a much greater problem than handling prisoners of war, as the latter were evacuated to enclosures as quickly as possible. The displaced persons, however, were obliged to remain in the battalion area, and it was necessary to provide food, water and medical supplies

for them. This was accomplished by taxing the facilities of the nearby towns to a maximum.[18]

For a week, the 18th Armored Infantry Battalion operated the displaced persons camps. Deaths were a daily occurrence as were births with U.S. soldiers serving as mid-wives on several occasions. Finally on 20 May, the battalion was relieved by the 69th Armored Infantry Battalion and relocated to Marienbad. They would stay in Marienbad for most of the summer guarding displaced persons camps and performing other occupational duties.[19]

Changes in the American Occupation Forces

Almost immediately after the official end of the war in Europe, Third U.S. Army undertook major changes in the dispositions of its many divisions serving in western Czechoslovakia. The 97th Infantry Division left western Czechoslovakia and returned to Germany a couple days after VE-Day. At 1200 on 9 May 1945, the 2nd Infantry Division officially relieved the 16th Armored Division in Pilsen. Having liberated the important city only three days earlier, the 16th Armored Division now took over responsibility for the sector formerly occupied by the departing 97th Infantry Division. By 1800, soldiers of the 18th Armored Infantry Battalion had assumed responsibility for all of the posts formerly held by the 303rd Infantry Regiment, 97th Infantry Division. Not long after, the 1st Infantry Division and Combat Command A of the 9th Armored Division also left Czechoslovakia. With the notable exception of the 26th Infantry Division and several supporting units, XII Corps completely withdrew from western Czechoslovakia within a couple weeks of V-E Day.[20]

Other changes took place within the 16th Armored Division as its units relocated and the task forces employed for the liberation of Pilsen were broken apart and their component parts re-assembled into their parent units. For example, Company B, 64th Armored Infantry Battalion was relieved from its temporary assignment with 16th Tank Battalion and rejoined its parent battalion. Meanwhile the 16th Tank Battalion regained its Company A which it had loaned to 64th Armored Infantry Battalion. The 216th Armored Medical Battalion and the 216th Armored Engineers Battalion regained the companies that they had loaned out to the division's combat commands for the Pilsen drive.[21]

Meeting the Soviets

Around 9 May, the first Soviet troops arrived in the vicinity of Pilsen. Over the course of the next several days, more and more American troops encountered the Soviets. On 10 May, patrols from the 16th Tank Battalion contacted elements of the 134th Field Artillery Regiment, 172nd Infantry Division of the 13th Russian Army near Kaznejon. On 13 May, patrols of the 18th Armored Infantry Battalion first contacted Russian troops.[22]

For Col. Noble, initial meetings with the Soviet troops were cordial. "Before the Russian Party Commissars arrived, we were on very friendly terms with the Russians," Noble later wrote. His Soviet counterpart invited him to a lavish banquet and Noble soon after returned the Soviet hospitality by hosting a dinner of his own for the Soviet colonel and his wife.[23]

This atmosphere abruptly changed after the Communist Party Political Commissars who accompanied the army began to assert themselves. The Soviet colonel was relieved and relations became hostile. "The Russians were continuously forcing our forward contact sentries back, sometimes with the excuse that they were straightening their lines," Noble wrote. "Finally, General Harmon [XXII Corps Commanding General] gave orders to dig in the tanks along our front and not give another inch or we would be back in the Atlantic Ocean, treaty or no treaty."[24]

Col. Barksdale Hamlett's reactions to the Soviets were decidedly negative as well. One day, Brig. Gen. Pierce, Col. Hamlett, and their staffs hosted a large group of Soviet officers in Pilsen. Before leaving the city, the Soviets stole all the gas cans off the nearby U.S. jeeps. Another time, a group of Czechoslovak Communists from Prague barged into a town under Hamlett's military government and demanded that the battery commander in charge evacuate the town immediately. Hamlett and his German speaking secretary Hilda drove over to the town to ascertain the situation. After learning of their intentions, Hamlett ordered them through Hilda to clear out of the town in one hour or he'd have them shot. The Communists hastily left the town.[25]

The 23rd Cavalry Squadron operated near the U.S. / Soviet demarcation line for much of the summer of 1945. At night, they ran patrols. "We had some interaction with the Russians," Mark Steece of Troop B later recalled. "We didn't have high regard for them."[26]

The freed Russian civilians also caused problems for the American soldiers serving in Czechoslovakia. These Russians had been forcibly brought west to work as slave labor by the Germans. Unable for the moment to return home, many of them terrorized the Germans and

Czechs alike. "Yesterday as another MP and I were patrolling, we heard a terrible scream," PFC Charles Lemmons wrote to his wife on 26 May. "We went into the house and a Russian had a young German girl by the throat. He had been drinking and was going to get even for what the Germans had done to the Russians. It's going to be terrible after the American troops leave these places."[27]

Unfortunately, the 16th Armored Division's experiences with belligerent, hostile Soviet soldiers and officers were not isolated incidents. Throughout the U.S. zone of occupation, American soldiers had hostile encounters. "The Russians were so mad at us that at times we were ready to shoot it out with them because we had so many thousands of Germans surrender to us," recalled PFC Carmine Caiazzo of the 2nd Infantry Division's 9th Infantry Regiment. Around VE-Day, a Soviet column tried to force its way through one of the 2nd Infantry Division's forward outposts and into Pilsen. After learning of the situation, the division's commanding general, Maj. Gen. Walter Robertson, headed to the outpost and turned the Soviets back by threatening to unleash his tanks and artillery on them.[28]

Problems with the Soviets continued throughout the occupation period. On 9 September, a group of twenty armed Soviet soldiers crossed into the U.S. occupation zone and looted the village of Jaronin in the 301st Infantry Regiment / 94th Infantry Division's area of responsibility. To protect the Czech civilians and prevent further raids by Soviet troops, the 301st Infantry began sending regular armed patrols into the village.[29]

XXII Corps Assumes Responsibility for Western Czechoslovakia

The next major change in Third U.S. Army occurred at the corps level. In the second week of June 1945, V Corps Headquarters was relieved by Lt. Gen. Ernest Harmon's XXII Corps. The 2nd Infantry Division left with V Corps and was replaced by the 79th and 94th Infantry Divisions. For the remainder of the American occupation of western Czechoslovakia, Lt. Gen. Harmon and XXII Corps would be in charge of all American units in the country which included as many as five divisions and over 175,000 soldiers at its peak strength. XXII Corps assumed responsibility for the occupation of some 3,400 square miles of western Czechoslovakia.[30]

Ernest N. Harmon was one of the outstanding divisional commanders in World War II. He was born on 26 February 1894 in Lowell, Massachusetts. In 1917, he graduated from the U.S. Military Academy at West Point and received a commission in the cavalry. During World War I, he fought in the St. Mihiel and Meuse-Argonne Offensives. After the war, he transferred to the new armored force. In the 1930s, he completed courses at the Army Command and General Staff School at Fort Leavenworth, Kansas and the Army War College at Carlisle Barracks, Pennsylvania.[31]

It was during World War II that Harmon achieved his greatest military successes. When the U.S. entered the war, Brig. Gen. Harmon was the Chief of Staff for the Armored Forces Headquarters. Promoted to major general in July 1942, Harmon commanded the 2nd Armored Division in North Africa. As a II Corps staff officer, Barksdale Hamlett worked with him during this time. Next, he commanded the 1st Armored Division in Italy during combat operations at Salerno in 1943 and Anzio in 1944. In the summer of 1944, Harmon briefly commanded VIII Corps in the U.S. In September, he was sent to Belgium and placed back in command of the 2nd Armored Division. In the Battle of the Bulge, his division mauled the 2nd Panzer Division and halted the tip of the German advance before the Meuse River. The 2nd Panzer Division never recovered from this crushing defeat. Following the Bulge, Harmon was placed in command of XXII Corps. When the war in Europe ended, Harmon and his XXII Corps were occupying an area in the Ruhr Industrial region along the Rhine River.[32]

Relations with the Czechs

The Czechs repeatedly showed their gratitude to their American liberators in both small ways and large public displays. In June, Czechoslovak President Eduard Benes hosted an awards ceremony in Pilsen during which time he decorated Gen. Patton, his Chief of Staff Maj. Gen. Hobart Gay, Brig. Gen. John Pierce, several corps and division commanders and Col. Noble with Czechoslovakia's highest military honor—the Order of the White Lion. Several other American officers including Brig. Gen. Pierce and Col. A. Worrell Roffe received the Czechoslovak Military Cross. Following the awards presentation, a grand parade of American and Czechoslovak military units was held.[33]

During the combat operations in Germany, American troops were prohibited from fraternizing with the Germans. However, Czechoslovakia was an Allied nation and therefore, fraternization was freely permitted. Many friendships and even romances quickly developed between the

15. V-E Day and Occupation Duties 159

Three of the senior U.S. Army commanders in Czechoslovakia: (L-R) Gen. George S. Patton, commanding Third U.S. Army; Maj. Gen. Ernest Harmon commanding XXII Corps; and Brig. Gen. John L. Pierce commanding the 16th Armored Division. Photo taken in Cheb on 7 September 1945 (National Archives Photo).

American soldiers and the Czech civilians. The local opera in Pilsen offered nightly performances. Despite being accidentally bombed by the 8th U.S. Army Air Force in late April, the famed Pilsner Brewery would recover to the enjoyment of many American servicemen.[34]

Helping the Czechs Re-build

In the weeks following the end of the war in Europe, the 16th Armored Division's G-5 (Civil Affairs) Section was heavily involved in assisting the

Czechoslovak government and people in re-building their nation and reconstituting their governmental institutions. After six long years of Nazi occupation, much had to done. To assist Division G-5, Maj. McConnell and a lieutenant from Headquarters Company, 216th Armored Engineer Battalion were transferred to the G-5 Section in the middle of May. Maj. Surbey then became Battalion Executive Officer.[35]

In June, the 216th Armored Engineer Battalion engaged in a variety of engineering and construction projects to help re-build war-torn Czechoslovakia. Headquarters Company and Companies B and C repaired roads and re-built and repaired numerous bridges in the vicinity of Bor, Plan, Tachov and Konstantinbad. In the town of Plan, 2nd Platoon of Company B constructed a timber trestle bridge.[36]

After VE-Day, Sgt. George Thompson of the 137th Armored Ordnance Battalion was tasked with fixing captured German trucks and vehicles so that they could be turned over to the Czech people for their use. He later described his experiences:

> At Bory Airport, there were German vehicles lined up a mile long. The Germans had disabled them by pulling all the wiring from under the dashboards. Since I was in the ordnance and a mechanic, my assigned job was to go down the line and try to start each vehicle to make it run. We had a German Volkswagen with a giant jumper battery on the back of it. At each vehicle, we'd stop and try to jump start it…. We got many trucks, Volkswagens, and rolling stock to run and then we turned them over to the Czech government in Pilsen because the farmers and the government had no vehicles that would run. I have to say that was probably my biggest contribution to the Czech Republic after the war.[37]

Summation

Having been rushed to the front in the closing days of the war, the 16th Armored Division soldiers were thrown into a major operation to secure one of Czechoslovakia's largest cities. Then almost overnight their mission changed from combat to occupation and civil government. The 16th Armored Division soldiers guarded prisoners, assisted displaced persons, helped the Czechs rebuild civil government and infrastructure, dealt with recalcitrant often hostile Soviet "allies," and a host of other non-combat tasks that they had not been trained for. Nevertheless, these soldiers performed with a high degree of professionalism and competency. The 16th Armored Division soldiers' liberation of Pilsen and its environs won the admiration of the Czech people; their professional conduct helped to ensure that that admiration would last in the coming decades.

16

The 16th Armored Division Shuffle

Several times during its stateside training the 16th Armored Division had experienced significant transfers of personnel to other units that were deploying to war theaters. In the summer of 1945, the 16th Armored Division experienced another significant transfer of its soldiers. During this time, the division essentially became a redeployment vehicle for soldiers returning to the United States. Here's what happened.

When the war in Europe ended on 8 May 1945, the 16th Armored Division had only been in the European Theater for three months and had only engaged in combat as a division for three days. Many other U.S. divisions in the European Theater had served far longer and experienced much more combat. Landing on Omaha Beach on D-Day, the 1st Infantry Division fought a total of 292 days in combat during the European Campaign, suffering 29,005 casualties and a 205.9 percent turnover of its personnel. Including its service in North Africa and in Sicily, the 1st Infantry Division experienced 443 days in combat during World War II. The 2nd Infantry Division came ashore the day after D-Day and fought a total of 303 days in combat. That division suffered 25,884 casualties and had a 183.7 percent turnover in personnel. The 4th Armored Division first entered combat on 28 July 1944 in Normandy and fought 230 days in combat. The 4th Armored suffered 10,496 casualties and a 98.4 percent turnover in personnel. Numerous other U.S. Army divisions in Europe had similar experiences. Despite such high turnovers in personnel, there were many soldiers in each of these divisions that had served throughout their divisions' service in Europe.[1]

As the war in Europe came to a close, the U.S. Army in Europe had a two-fold mission for the future employment of its forces. This affected both individual soldiers and entire units. To ensure fairness in redeployment and discharge of soldiers in Europe, the U.S. Army adopted the

Adjusted Service Rating. This system prioritized solders for discharge based upon the length of their service, combat experience and dependent children at home. The Army also categorized its units for future employment as well. The Army needed to retain forces in Europe for occupation and to redeploy units to the Pacific Theater for future invasions of the Japanese Home Islands.[2]

To ensure fairness in rotating troops home, the U.S. Army established the Adjusted Service Rating that prioritized soldiers for rotation home and discharge based upon time overseas and family obligations back home. A point system was developed whereby soldiers received points based upon the months that they had served in uniform since September 1940, the number of months that they had served overseas, their combat awards and the number of dependent children under 18 that they had. Under this system, a soldier received one point for every month of service since September 1940, a point for every month served overseas since September 1940 and five points for each combat decoration or battle star received. A soldier could also receive twelve points for each dependent child under 18 years of age with points allotted for a maximum of three such children. An enlisted male soldier with 85 points or more was entitled for immediate return to the United States and discharge from service. A female enlisted soldier required 44 points for an immediate return home and discharge. Those soldiers with less than 85 points would either remain in Europe on occupation duties or be sent to the Pacific Theater. Soldiers returning to the U.S. or redeploying to the Pacific would not do so as individuals. Rather, they would go as part of complete units.[3]

U.S. Army units serving in Europe at the end of the war were categorized based upon how they would be used. Category I units would stay in Europe for occupation duties. This included the 1st Infantry Division, the 79th Infantry Division and the 4th Armored Division. Category II units would be sent to the Pacific. Category II units included the 97th Infantry Division and the 2nd Infantry Division. Category III units would be re-organized and either remain in Europe or be sent to the Pacific. Soldiers with over 85 points could not be assigned to units in these three categories. Nevertheless, many soldiers and officers volunteered to serve with units redeploying to the Pacific. Category IV units would be used exclusively to redeploy soldiers with 85 points or more back to the U.S. for discharge or re-assignment stateside.[4]

At first glance, the Army's Adjusted Service Rating system and unit categorizations seemed to be a fair and relatively straightforward system of getting the troops home to the U.S. In practice, it proved to be much more complicated. On VE-Day, the U.S. Army had 61 divisions and a total of 3,077,000 soldiers in the European Theater. Of these, eight divisions would remain in Europe with the remainder redeploying to the U.S. or the Pacific Theater. "All movements were to be made by complete units, which necessitated a reshuffling of personnel throughout the theater and the classification of all units into four categories," wrote U.S. Army historian Earl F. Ziemke in his *The U.S. Army in the Occupation of Germany 1944–1945*. The Army could not just send home entire divisions as they were constituted on V-E Day because of the high turnover of personnel in many of these divisions. Even in the most experienced divisions, there were numerous soldiers who had joined only weeks or even days before V-E Day. Such soldiers thus had very low point totals and were not eligible for immediate redeployment to the United States.[5]

In early August, the U.S. dropped two atomic bombs on Japan. The subsequent surrender of Imperial Japan negated the necessity of the planned invasions of the Japanese Home Islands. The Army's redeployment and discharge plans thus became drastically changed. Army units were still needed for the occupation of Germany and some units were required for the occupation of Japan. The 97th Infantry Division, for instance, actually redeployed to the Pacific and served on occupation duties in Japan. However, the vast majority of U.S. soldiers were no longer needed. Thus intense pressures were brought to bear on Army leadership to bring these soldiers home to the U.S. and discharge them back into civilian life as quickly as possible. The Adjusted Service Rating scores for discharge were lowered and huge numbers of soldiers thus became eligible for immediate discharge.[6]

This explains what happened with the 16th Armored Division in the summer and fall of 1945. Designated as a Category IV unit, the 16th Armored Division was selected to return to the United States in the fall of 1945 with high points soldiers for discharge or re-assignment stateside. Since the division had only arrived in Theater in February, few of its members were actually eligible to return home that soon. While still performing occupation duties in Czechoslovakia, the division experienced a great shuffling of personnel. Soldiers with low points were transferred to units remaining in Germany. They were replaced by soldiers from other units who had high points. Thus the 16th Armored Division became a vehicle for returning high points soldiers back to the United States for re-assignment and/or discharge.[7]

One of those units that transferred its high point soldiers to the 16th Armored Division was the 79th Infantry Division. Nicknamed the "Cross of Lorraine" for its service in World War I, the 79th Infantry Division came ashore at Utah Beach a week after D-Day and helped liberate the port of Cherbourg. During the campaigns across western and central Europe, the division spent 248 days in combat. In April, the 79th Infantry Division helped reduce the Ruhr Pocket and was serving on occupation duties in that region when the war ended on 8 May 1945. The 79th Infantry Division was selected to remain in Europe to continue performing occupation duties. In early June, the division relieved the 1st Infantry Division of occupation duties in northwest Czechoslovakia.[8]

The 79th Infantry Division had numerous high points soldiers. Accordingly, in late June, the 79th Infantry Division was directed to transfer all of its members who had 80 or more points to the 16th Armored Division. In the 314th Infantry Regiment, both the S-2 (Intelligence) officer Maj. Hermann G. Schulze and the S-3 (Operations) officer Maj. Walter J. Jung were both transferred to the 16th Armored Division. Lt. Col. Daniel T. McFadden was transferred from the 313th Infantry Regiment to assume command of the 18th Armored Infantry Battalion.[9]

Another of the soldiers transferred to the 16th Armored Division was 1st Lt. James W. Dollar of the 315th Infantry Regiment. Originally from "the river bottoms of west Tennessee" as he described his hometown, Dollar enlisted as a private in the Tennessee National Guard's 30th Infantry Division on 1 May 1938. He volunteered for active duty when the division was activated for Federal service in September of 1940. He attended Officer Candidate School and was commissioned as a 2nd lieutenant on 24 July 1943. In June 1944, he was shipped overseas as a replacement officer. Near the end of June, he was assigned as Platoon Leader of the 3rd Platoon, 2nd Battalion, 315th Infantry Regiment, 79th Infantry Division in Normandy. He was wounded twice in combat in France and subsequently reassigned to Regimental Headquarters.[10]

"The effective date of my association with the 18th Armored Infantry Battalion of the 16th Armored Division was July 7, 1945," Dollar later recalled. "We got everything organized, people transferred, paper work done, and had a division review for Gen. Patton. We started shipping people back home." By summer's end, nearly all of the members of the battalion who had participated in the liberation of Pilsen had been transferred to the 1st and 79th Infantry Division and been replaced by high point soldiers from those two divisions.[11]

Throughout June and July, soldiers who had trained and deployed with the 16th Armored Division were reassigned to veteran combat units that were remaining in Europe, including the 1st Infantry Division and the 4th Armored Division. Staff Sgt. Gene Eike of the 18th Armored Infantry Battalion was transferred to Company B, 16th Infantry Regiment, 1st Infantry Division to replace sergeants with high points who had been sent home. Private Edward Krusheski of the 69th Armored Infantry Battalion was transferred to the 1st Infantry Division for the Nuremburg War Crimes Trials. In September 1945, Mark Steece of Troop B, 23rd Cavalry was transferred to the 4th Armored Division for occupation duties in Germany. Sgt. George Thompson of the 137th Armored Ordnance Battalion was also transferred to the 4th Armored Division. Assigned to Company C, 127th Armored Ordnance Battalion, Thompson was designated as motor sergeant and given a group of German prisoners of war to assist him with performing his duties.[12]

In July 1945, the 216th Armored Engineer Battalion began experiencing its inevitable shuffling of personnel. About half of the battalion was transferred to the 1st Engineer Combat Battalion of the 1st Infantry Division. This included battalion commander Lt. Col. William W. Smith, Jr., and 2nd Lt. Charles Schaeffer. At the time, the 1st Engineers were located in the town of Markt Bergl, to the west of Nuremberg, Germany. Other members of the 216th Armored Engineers were transferred to the 79th, 84th and 102nd Infantry Divisions and the 20th Engineer Combat Battalion. Eventually, many of these former 216th Armored Engineers members ended up with the 1st Engineer Combat Battalion serving all over southern Germany in such places as Bamberg, Regensburg, Grafenwöhr, and Munich.[13]

In mid-summer, the 23rd Cavalry Squadron was broken up and its personnel reassigned. "Tears were in a lot of eyes as they broke up my Troop and as they drove off," Capt. John Patterson later wrote. He served in a succession of posts including as S-3 (Operations) Officer for the 186th Field Artillery Battalion and commander of an engineer company.[14]

Not even high ranking 16th Armored Division officers were immune from the personnel shuffle. Col. Charles Noble was transferred to XXII Corps and served as its Assistant Chief of Staff G-4 (Logistics) for several months until all U.S. forces left Czechoslovakia in December 1945. Lt. Col. Percy Perkins assumed command of the 12th Armored Group on 13 June 1945 and brought the group back to the United States for training for redeployment to the Pacific Theater. Like many other U.S. Army units from the European Theater, the 12th Armored Group was intended for the invasion of the Japanese Home Islands and specifically designated for Operation Olympic—the amphibious landing on Honshu near Tokyo.[15]

In July, Col. Barksdale Hamlett and many of his artillerymen were transferred from the 16th Armored Division to the 190th Field Artillery Group. The 190th Field Artillery Group was a unit of the Pennsylvania National Guard that had been activated for World War II. Coming ashore on 7 June 1944 in Normandy, the 190th Field Artillery Group had fought with V Corps all across Europe and was now preparing to redeploy for the invasion of Japan. Col. Hamlett later recalled the transition:

> Most of the people in the division had no points at all, because they had only been in combat a short time. The 190th Group on the other hand had a tremendous number of points among their enlisted men and officers, too. So, they were all cleared out and sent back and I moved a great number of my Division Artillery people into the 190th Group. Actually you might say, it was a continuation of the 16th Armored Division Artillery under a different name with different types of material, with 155 howitzers and 155 guns plus an Observation Battalion in the 190th Group.[16]

Another 16th Armored Division soldier who was scheduled to redeploy to the Pacific for the invasion of Japan was Sgt. O. J. Mooney of the 396th Armored Field Artillery Battalion. One of his battalion's officers was tasked to form a group of the battalion's soldiers into a medium-range self-propelled artillery battery for the invasion of Japan. This battery was to return to the United States, train in California for six weeks and then deploy to the Pacific Theater for the invasion.[17]

Thus as a result of the U.S. Army's desire to get its longest serving soldiers home first, the 16th Armored Division was radically changed in its personnel make-up and in just a few weeks became almost an entirely new division.

17

Returning Home and Deactivation

Though divested of its original soldiers and its attached supporting units, the 16th Armored Division had one further mission to perform. That mission was to get high points soldiers home to the U.S. for discharge and return to civilian life.

The 16th Armored Division's return home was preceded by two other units formerly associated with it: the 633rd Tank Destroyer Battalion and the 1st Battalion, 5th Armored Regiment (now known as the 717th Tank Battalion.)

No longer part of the 16th Armored Division, the 633rd Tank Destroyer Battalion remained in the European Theater for less than two more months. On 22 May 1945, the battalion received orders to redeploy to the Pacific Theater via the United States. For the next three weeks, they remained in bivouac in Czechoslovakia preparing for the redeployment. On 13 June, the battalion turned in its tracked vehicles to the 463rd Ordnance Collecting Company at Bischoftneinitz, Germany and began moving to France for embarkation back to the United States. On 1 July 1945, the battalion embarked aboard *USS Sea Pike* at the port of Le Havre, France. Ten days later they arrived in New York. A few days later, they moved to Fort Bragg, North Carolina to conduct training for their redeployment to the Pacific Theater. The dropping of the two atomic bombs on Japan and Imperial Japan's subsequent surrender negated the battalion's redeployment. On 30 October 1945, the 633rd Tank Destroyer Battalion was deactivated at Fort Bragg.[1]

The 717th Tank Battalion (formerly 1st Battalion, 5th Armored Regiment, 16th Armored Division) remained in the European Theater only a few weeks after V-E Day. The battalion was designated to re-deploy to the Pacific Theater and participate in the invasion of the Japanese Home Islands. Accordingly, the battalion went by ship back to the U.S. and arrived there in early July 1945. The Japanese surrender negated that mission.[2]

The shuffling and re-shuffling of the division's personnel continued through the summer. By the end of the summer, the 16th Armored Division was a very different division that the one which had disembarked in France the previous February. Gone were most of the soldiers and officers who had deployed with the division and liberated Pilsen. The division now consisted primarily of seasoned combat veterans and high points soldiers from a wide range of units including the 79th Infantry Division. The mission of the 16th Armored Division was now to get these soldiers home for demobilization and return to civilian life.[3]

In mid-September 1945, the various units of the 16th Armored Division left Czechoslovakia for France. On 16 September, the 18th Armored Infantry Battalion left Loket, Czechoslovakia aboard trains bound for Camp Lucky Strike in western France. The journey took five days. After arriving at Camp Lucky Strike, the battalion's members completed preparations for the voyage home.[4]

In early October 1945, the 16th Armored Division embarked in ships for the crossing back to the United States. The voyage home was much different from the one taken earlier that year. Most importantly, there were no German U-Boats to contend with. In addition, most of the division's equipment and vehicles had been left behind in Europe.[5]

Having accomplished its purpose in war and in the peace that followed, the mission of the 16th Armored Division and its necessity to national defense had come to an end. Units of the division assembled at Camp Kilmer, a sprawling U.S. Army facility in Middlesex County, New Jersey. On 15 October 1945, Brig. Gen. John L. Pierce presided over the deactivation of the 16th Armored Division at Camp Kilmer, New Jersey. Those soldiers still with the division were then transferred to other Army units and either discharged or retained on Active Duty. The 16th Armored Division had been in existence for a total of 27 months and had served in combat for three days.[6]

18

The Postwar Lives of the 16th Veterans

The post–Czechoslovakia and postwar lives of the 16th Armored Division veterans were as varied and diverse as their lives before the war. Some chose to make the U.S. Army a career. Most returned to civilian life to return to pre-war jobs, start new careers or use the GI Bill education benefits to attend college or trade school. Some chose a combination of the two by serving in the National Guard or Army Reserve.

Following the war, Maj. Gen. Douglass T. Greene retired from the Army and returned to the Drexel Institute of Technology. He became Executive Assistant to the President of DIT. His son Lt. Col. Thomas Patrick Greene was killed during the Korean War. From 1952 to 1961, Greene served as Athletics Director and Business Manager for DIT. He died at the age of 73 and was inducted into Drexel University's Hall of Fame in 1985.[1]

After returning to the United States and overseeing the deactivation of his division, Brig. Gen. John L. Pierce became President of the Secretary of War's Discharge Review Board. In 1946, he retired from the Army after nearly thirty years of service and returned home to Brownsville, Texas. He suffered a series of strokes and died in San Antonio on 12 February 1959 at the age of 63. He was buried at Fort Sam Houston National Cemetery in San Antonio.[2]

Col. Richard A. Gordon commanded Reserve Command of the 12th Armored Division throughout the division's campaigns in central Europe in 1945. He led his command in the drive across central Germany and into Austria before the war ended. Towards the end of the war, he was wounded in action. The following September, he was elected President of the newly 12th Armored Division Association and was active in the association for many years.[3]

Col. Noble was transferred to XXII Corps and served as its Assistant

Chief of Staff G-4 (Logistics) for several months until it left Czechoslovakia in December 1945. He was awarded the Legion of Merit for his service as XXII Corps G-4. While XXII Corps G-4, Col. Noble became friends with Czechoslovakia's Foreign Minister Jan Masaryk. Noble next served as G-4 for Third U.S. Army in Germany. As G-4, Col. Noble was responsible for Third Army's logistics including transportation, supply, vehicle maintenance, and food and housing for the troops. He was also responsible for several Displaced Persons camps and POW camps. After returning home, Noble remained in the Army until retiring on 30 June 1949. He helped found the 16th Armored Division Association and served as its first president from 1951–1953. He likewise helped found the West Point Society of South Texas, serving as the first president of the latter. He served as Executive Secretary of the Printing Industry Association of San Antonio and owned his own investment and property management business. He died on 12 August 1979.[4]

Col. Barksdale Hamlett, Jr., Commander of 16th Armored Division Artillery, had an extraordinary post–Czechoslovakia career. In August, he took his 190th Field Artillery Group to Hoenfelds, Germany, for artillery training preparatory for redeployment to the Pacific Theater. After the dropping of two atomic bombs on Japan and the subsequent Japanese surrender negated the necessity of the invasion of the Japanese Home Islands, Col. Hamlett was transferred to the Fifteenth U.S. Army which was then compiling and writing the history of the U.S. Army in the European Campaigns. Having been relieved of his command of Third U.S. Army due to some inflammatory comments about ex–Nazis working in the postwar occupation of Germany, Gen. George S. Patton, Jr., was now in command of Fifteen U.S. Army. While serving with Fifteen U.S. Army, Col. Hamlett travelled extensively across France and Germany, conducting interviews and gathering source material. Hamlett also spent time as a student at the Ecole Militaire in Paris. Returning to the United States, Hamlett became Director of the Battery Officers Course at the U.S. Army Artillery School at Fort Sill, Oklahoma. Then he studied at the National War College. In December 1949, he joined Gen. Douglas MacArthur's staff in Japan and was the G-4 Chief of Planning when the Korean War broke out. He coordinated logistics planning for the Inchon invasion. In December 1951, he became Division Artillery Commander for the 24th Infantry Division. In 1955, he served as Artillery Commander for VII Corps in West Germany. Following this assignment, he was promoted to major general and assumed command of the 10th Infantry Division. A year later, he became commander of U.S. forces in Berlin and Deputy

Chief of the U.S. Mission. He served in these capacities during the 1958–59 Berlin Crisis. His firm and decisive leadership played a key role in the Soviets' backing down. Returning to Washington in January 1960, Maj. Gen. Hamlett served in senior staff positions until being promoted to lieutenant general and being appointed as Vice Chief of Staff of the Army. Following a massive heart attack in 1964, he retired as a general. From 1965 to 1972, he served as President of Norwich University in Northfield, Vermont. Then he retired to Charleston, South Carolina. In 1979, he died of a heart attack at Walter Reed Army Medical Center and was buried at West Point.[5]

Lt. Col. Raymond C. Adkisson was transferred from the 16th Armored Division and remained in Germany. He died in Bamberg, Germany on 14 July 1946 at the age of 36 and was buried in Columbia, Tennessee.[6]

Capt. Howard Painter left B Company, 18th Armored Infantry Battalion in June 1945. He stayed in the Army and eventually retired as a lieutenant colonel.[7]

Harley Barrs stayed with the 16th Armored Division for part of the summer, then was sent home for further training and eventual redeployment to the Pacific Theater for the invasion of Japan. Given a thirty day furlough, Barrs returned home to visit his wife, family and friends. While having dinner at a restaurant in mid–August, he heard news of the Japanese surrender over the radio. Several months later, Barrs was discharged from the Army. He was active in the 16th Armored Division Association until his death on 27 January 2003.[8]

Capt. Howard P. Schaudt completed the U.S. Army Infantry School's Advanced Officers Course at Fort Benning, Georgia in 1946–1947. As part of the course, he wrote a paper critiquing the 23rd Cavalry Squadron's pursuit operations with the 86th Infantry Division. He retired from the U.S. Army as a lieutenant colonel. He died 17 January 1981 and was buried at Fort Sam Houston National Cemetery in Texas.[9]

After serving for several months on Occupation duties with the 1st Infantry Division in Germany, Staff Sgt. Gene Eike returned home in April 1946 and was discharged. He attended Washington University in St. Louis under the GI Bill and graduated with a Bachelors of Science in Chemical Engineering in 1950. He married while in college. After graduation, Eike had a long and successful career with Upjohn. When Upjohn sold its chemical division to Dow Chemicals in 1985, Eike began working for Dow. He retired a year later. He had four children and eight grandchildren. After his first wife passed away, he re-married and lived in New

Braunfels, Texas for many years. He went back to Pilsen several times for the Liberation Anniversary celebrations. On 6 August 2008, Eike passed away at the age of 83. He was buried in Fort Sam Houston National Cemetery in San Antonio.[10]

During the fall of 1945, Private Edward Krusheski served with the 1st Infantry Division and participated in the Nuremburg War Crimes Trials. One day he came across Nazi Reichsmarschall and Luftwaffe commander Hermann Goering, who was out for a walk escorted by two military policemen. Krusheski returned to the United States on 25 December 1945 and was discharged shortly thereafter. He got married in 1947 to his first wife Almeda and worked for Whippany Paper Board for 32 years as a machinist. They had three children and four grandchildren. After Almeda died in 1984, he re-married. His second wife Anna also predeceased him. He lived in Manahawkin, New Jersey until his death on 22 June 2014.[11]

Verne Lewellen of the 137th Armored Ordnance Battalion left the Army after the war and worked for a time in the Post Office. Acting on the advice of his high school coaches, Lewellen attended college and played football. He earned a Bachelor's degree from Chadron State College in Nebraska and a Masters degree from Colorado State University. He was a teacher and a coach for nine years, then served as a school administrator for 26 years.[12]

2nd Lt. Charles T. Schaeffer of the 216th Armored Engineers Battalion served in Czechoslovakia until the complete U.S. withdrawal in early December 1945. Then, he was transferred to the 1st Engineer Combat Battalion of the 1st Infantry Division and was re-united with his previous commander Col. William Smith from the 216th Armored Engineers. Schaeffer remained in Germany until 1948 and brought his wife over to live with him. He served a total of 23½ years in the Army in such locations as Japan, Korea, Germany, Missouri, California, and Washington State. From 1958 to 1960, Maj. Schaeffer served with the Military Advisory Group in Pakistan. During this time, he was at the air base that Francis Gary Powers took off from on his fateful U-2 flight that ended up with him being shot down, captured and imprisoned by the Soviets. Schaeffer retired from the Army in 1965 as a lieutenant colonel. He then worked for Catepillar as a manager in their engine department and sold engines all across the Pacific. His wife Joyce passed away in 1999. He resided in Hawaii for many years until passing away on 1 September 2011. He was buried at the National Memorial Cemetery of the Pacific in Honolulu, Hawaii.[13]

George Thompson remained in Germany with the 127th Armored

18. The Postwar Lives of the 16th Veterans   173

Ordnance Battalion, 4th Armored Division until April 1946. After returning home to the U.S. and being discharged from the Army, he completed mechanics training under the GI Bill. He worked as a mechanic for his entire life, eventually serving as an automotive technician for the State of California. As such he was responsible for repairing everything from boats to fire trucks. Thompson served several terms as President of the 16th Armored Division Association. He has traveled to Pilsen for the annual Liberation Anniversary celebrations nearly every year since 1990. He lives in Oregon.[14]

Mark Steece of Troop B / 23rd Cavalry Squadron was transferred to Troop B / 25th Cavalry Squadron of the 4th Armored Division and remained with them in Germany until January 1946. He then was transferred to the 327th Engineer Combat Battalion of the 102 Infantry (Ozark) Division. The 327th Engineers had the duty to operate a Prisoner of War Camp near Auerbach, Germany that held some 40,000 German Prisoners of War. Steece was assigned to supervise the Camp's Tool Room and daily give out to the prisoners thousands of shovels, axes and other construction tools used to repair roads, bridges, buildings. In April 1946, he was assigned to an anti-aircraft battalion and returned to the United States via a Victory Ship. After landing at Camp Kilmer, N J he was soon sent by train to Camp McCoy, Wisconsin and discharged on 4 May 1946, having served for three years in the Army. He returned home to Sioux Falls, South Dakota. He attended Augustana College on the G I Bill and graduated with a Bachelor's of Arts degree in Economics. He and his brother John started a hobby business, which operated a retail store and sold mail order. After he sold the business to his brother, he moved to California and got married. He and his wife Alida raised three children. Their son Tom is a lawyer, daughter Kathy is a Doctor and their youngest daughter Theresa is a stockbroker. Happily, he also has 7 grandchildren (4 boys and 3 girls). His wife Alida died after 25 years of marriage. In California he went to work for several Insurance Companies as a Safety Engineer and spent 30 years with The Transamerica Insurance Co before retiring in 1968. After many Company transfers he was finally sent to Schaumburg, Illinois where he met his present wife Jan and they were married in 1988. He now keeps busy collecting stamps and post cards and writing his life's history. A book about his three years in the Army is ready to publish. He first joined the 16th Armored Division Association in 1968 and has been active since then.[15]

Lt. Col. Robert H. Pratt returned to Wisconsin after the war. He eventually retired from the Army as a colonel. In 1953, he formed the Pratt

Manufacturing Corporation which made packaging machinery and printing, textile and surgical equipment. He and his wife Dorothy had two daughters. An avid stamp collector, Pratt also wrote two books on the subject. He died on 19 October 1995 and was buried in Forest Home Cemetery in Milwaukee.[16]

Solomon Polish, the Division Message Center Officer for the 16th Armored Division, volunteered for a transfer to one of the units scheduled for the invasion of Japan. He left the division with a group of other volunteers. The dropping of the atomic bombs cancelled their transfer to the Far East and so they were reassigned to other duties in Europe. Polish was reassigned to the Delta Base Headquarters in Marseilles, France where he worked as a signal center officer and was billeted in the Signal Officers Club. "This was a better deal than facing grave dangers storming the mainland of Japan," he later wrote. Polish eventually returned to New York and later became a columnist for *Harbor Watch*, a military affairs newspaper printed in New York City.[17]

Charles R. Lemmons served with the 4th Armored Division performing security duties in Germany until March of 1946. On 18 March 1946, he left Germany for home. He arrived back in the United States on 26 March 1946; five days later, he was discharged at Camp Atterbury, Indiana. Soon after, he rejoined the Covington Police Department and worked his way up through the ranks. After the war, he and his wife Pauline added daughters Kathy and Carol to their family. Pauline passed away in 1966. Sometime in the 1960s, he joined the 16th Armored Division Association and was an active member. In 1996, he, his daughter Kathy and her husband hosted the Association's annual reunion in Kentucky. Lemmons served on the force until retiring in 1979 as a Detective Lieutenant. He never missed a day of work in 35 years of being a police officer. On 14 September 2001, Lemmons died at the age of 87. "His highest rank was Pfc. which was a source of irritation to him," his daughter Kathy wrote in 2014. "He was very proud of his service and in later years would laugh and say that he would do it again as long as the outcome was the same."[18]

John C. Patterson learned via telegram that his son John Jr. had been born back in Oklahoma on 24 May. Also that month, Patterson was promoted to captain and awarded the Bronze Star for the Pilsen operation. After Troop B was disbanded, Capt. Patterson was made S-3 (Operations) Officer for the 186th Field Artillery Battalion and then commander of an Engineer company. He returned home to the United States in late November 1945. He was re-united with his wife Dora and daughter in Okmulgee, Oklahoma in early December and met his son John for the first time.

In January 1946, he was assigned as commander of the Reconnaissance Detachment of the Infantry, Engineering and Reconnaissance Detachment of the "School Troops" at Fort Knox, Kentucky. From the summer of 1946 until the spring of 1949, he served as Division Athletic Officer for the 1st Cavalry Division in Japan. His next assignment was as Special Services Officer for Fifth Army Headquarters at Fort Sheridan, Illinois and also attended the Special Services School at Fort Monmouth, New Jersey. In 1950, he was promoted to major and his son Douglas was born. He and his wife ultimately had four children. In 1951, he served at Fort McCoy, Wisconsin and Fort Leonard Wood, Missouri. In November 1952, he returned to Japan and was assigned to the 24th Infantry Division. The following summer, the 24th Infantry Division returned to South Korea and was about to be sent into combat when the peace armistice was signed at Panmunjon on 27 July 1953. Later that year, he was released from the Army as part of a Reduction in Forces (RIF). Given the option as re-enlisting as a master sergeant, Patterson re-joined the Army in early 1954 and was assigned to Fort Bliss, Texas as a Brigade Athletic NCO. The following year, Patterson was accepted into fire control school to learn how to maintain the electronics of missile radars and fire control computers. Graduating second in his class, he was promoted to Warrant Officer W-1 and assigned to air defense missiles Fairchild Air Force Base near Spokane, Washington. Next he was assigned to an anti-aircraft battalion near Mineral Wells, Texas. He attended Nike Hercules missile control (atomic weapons) school at Fort Bliss. After graduating first in his class, Patterson was promoted to Chief Warrant Officer. In 1962, he retired from the Army at the Army Reserve rank of lieutenant colonel. Next he went to work for General Electric and ended up working in support of NASA's Apollo space program. After ten years of working for GE, Patterson took a course in air conditioning equipment and then started his own repair business. In 1973, he was hired as an air conditioning instructor by San Jacinto College and did that for several years until retiring. He and Dora traveled extensively until she was diagnosed with Alzheimers disease in 1986. She died in September 1991. He died on 6 June 2011 in Aledo, Texas. His son Clay is a Professional Genealogist and author.[19]

Lt. Col. James E. Norvell was transferred to Division Artillery Headquarters on 28 May 1945. He was relieved by Lt. Col. John R. Hector. His second son David Carter was born in August 1945 followed by a daughter Sarah in August 1951. Norvell remained in Germany as part of the U.S. Constabulary until 1948. His next assignment was as Assistant Chief of Staff (G-3) at the Ground General School at Fort Riley, Kansas. In 1949–

50, he completed the Army Command and General Staff School at Fort Leavenworth, Kansas. From 1950 to 1953, he served as a staff officer in the Pentagon. From 1953 to 1955, he was Assistant Chief of Staff (G-3) for Headquarters, Eighth U.S. Army in South Korea and earned the Legion of Merit. He next served as secretary of the U.S. Army Artillery School at Fort Sill, Oklahoma. Col. Norvell commanded the 17th Field Artillery Group from February 1956 to February 1957, then served as Deputy Director of the Department of Tactics and Combined Arms and Director of the Department of Communications and Electronics at the U.S. Army Artillery and Missile School. From 1959 to early 1961, Col. Norvell was in command of the 8th Infantry Division Artillery. His next assignment was as commander, U.S. Army Garrison, Piotiers, France. Later that year, he was appointed as Chief of Staff of First Logistical Command. For the remainder of his career, Col. Norvell served with the U.S. Army Artillery Board, first as Deputy President and then as President. He retired in 1967 and spent his remaining years living with his wife in Oklahoma. He died in June 1984. He was survived by his wife, three children, three grandchildren and two brothers.[20]

Lt. Col. Herbert W. Semmelmeyer remained with the 16th Armored Division and served as Executive Officer of Combat Command A. After the war, he returned to the insurance business and his family in California. He died on 10 November 1967, leaving behind his wife Marian, and a son and a daughter. He was interred at Golden Gate National Cemetery, San Bruno, California.[21]

Maj. George B. Pickett, Jr., was awarded the Silver Star for his service with the 11th Armored Division in March 1945. He was subsequently promoted to lieutenant colonel and remained in command of a battalion in the postwar occupation forces in Germany until 1947. From 1947–1950, he served as an instructor in armor tactics at the Infantry School in Fort Benning, Georgia. After the outbreak of the Korean War, Lt. Col. Pickett deployed to South Korea and served as the Chief of the Armor Section for IX Corps Headquarters until November 1951. He earned a Legion of Merit for his service there. Following this assignment, Pickett served as the first senior adviser to the Japanese Military and Naval Academy in Tokyo. From 1953–56, Lt. Col. Pickett served as Assistant G-3 (Operations) Officer for Fourth Army at Fort Sam Houston, Texas. In 1956, he was promoted to colonel. He attended the Armed Forces Staff College in 1956 and became an instructor in the Research and Development Division following graduation. He next attended and graduated from the National War College in Washington, D.C. Then he assumed command of the 2nd Armored Cavalry Regiment in Nuremberg, Germany and oversaw its vital mission of deterrence and border surveillance opposite Communist East Germany and Czechoslovakia. In 1963, he was promoted to brigadier general and in July of that year, was appointed Chief of Staff of Combat Developments Command in Fort Belvoir, Virginia. Three years later, Pickett was promoted to major general and placed in command of the 2nd Infantry Division in South Korea. In May 1967, Maj. Gen. Pickett became Vice Director for Operations (J-3) for the Joint Chiefs of Staff. Then he served as Chief of the Joint U.S. Military Advisory Group to the Republic of the Philippines. His last assignment was as Deputy Commanding General of the Third Army. In March 1973, he retired and settled in his native Alabama. He remained active in retirement with the National Rifle Association, Sons of the American Revolution and the West Point Society of Alabama, among other organizations. His wife Beryl died of cancer and he married Rachel Copeland Peeples. Pickett died on 4 January 2003 and was interred in Greenwood Cemetery in Montgomery, Alabama. During his career, Pickett was a prolific writer, publishing articles on leadership, tactics and military topics in such journals as *Military Review* and *Armor* magazine. In May 1951, he and Capt. Edgar Millington co-wrote "The Pilsen Story" about the liberation of Pilsen for *Combat Forces Journal*.[22]

Lt. Col. Percy H. Perkins, Jr., was at Camp Gruber, Oklahoma when the dropping of the atomic bombs eliminated the need of the invasion of Japan. No longer needed for the invasion of Japan, the 12th Armored Group was inactivated on 20 October. Perkins was promoted to colonel on 21 December 1945 and discharged from Active Duty on 23 January 1946. Returning to Georgia, Perkins served for fifteen years in the Army Reserve. His assignments included command of the 301st Armored Group, the 305th Replacement Depot, and the 3282nd Army Reserve Corps. He retired at the rank of colonel in 1961. Concurrent with his Army Reserve service, Perkins practiced as an architect, and was active in several civic organizations. A noted gemologist, he published *Gemstones of the Bible* in 1964. Perkins died on 16 January 1998 at the age of 92 and was buried in Flemington, Georgia.[23]

After leaving the 16th Armored Division in August 1944, Lt. Col. Mont Hubbard deployed to the European Theater. In 1945, he assumed command of the 54th Armored Field Artillery Battalion of the 3rd Armored Division and led it through its operations in Germany. In 1946, he was discharged from the Army as a colonel. He returned to Virginia and became the President of Altavista Concrete Products. He died on

16 April 1968 at the age of 58 and is buried at Green Hill Cemetery in Altavista.[24]

After leaving the 16th Armored Division in July 1944, Lt. Col. William H. G. Fuller led the 38th Armored Infantry Battalion of the 7th Armored Division during its campaigns in France. During the Battle of the Bulge in December 1944, Lt. Col. Fuller was responsible for the eastern defenses of the vital road junction of St. Vith until being relieved at his own request due to combat exhaustion.[25]

After completing Command and General Staff College, Lt. Col. Charles A. Symroski served as Assistant Chief of Staff G-2 (Intelligence) with the 12th Armored Division in the European Campaigns. In 1946–48, he served as a member of the U.S. Army Equestrian Team. For the next five years, he served in France in a succession of posts that included attending the Ecole Superieure de Guerre (French Senior War College), and serving with Supreme Headquarters Allied Powers Europe (SHAPE). He later attended the Armed Forces Staff College and the Army War College. In 1958–60, he served in South Vietnam with the Military Assistance Advisors Group. Promoted to brigadier general, Symroski served as U.S. Defense Attache at the U.S. Embassy in Paris. In the mid–1960s, he commanded I Field Force Artillery in South Vietnam. His final assignment was with the Army's Training and Doctrine Command. He retired from the Army in January 1970. After retirement, he and his wife settled in Williamsburg, Virginia. He lived there until suffering a fatal heart attack in April 2001. He was interred at Arlington National Cemetery. He and his wife had two daughters and five grandchildren.[26]

Lt. Col. William W. Smith, Jr., served in the Army Corps of Engineers until retiring in 1968 at the rank of colonel. After retiring from the Army, Smith went to work for the Department of County Development of Fairfax County, Virginia. He was active in the 16th Armored Division Association. He retired from the County in 1986 and lived in McLean, Virginia until his death on 27 October 2013. He was interred at the U.S. Military Academy Cemetery, West Point, New York.[27]

Sgt. O. J. Mooney, Jr., was in California training for the invasion of Japan when the two atomic bombs were dropped on Hiroshima and Nagasaki in early August. The subsequent Japanese surrender cancelled the invasion of Japan and Sgt. Mooney's planned participation in it. After being discharged from the Army, Mooney returned home to Weogufka, Alabama. He worked for the Kimberly Clark Corporation for eighteen years, then went into farming the family farm full-time. On 21 July 1950, he married Jeannette Rodgers and together they had a son and a daughter.

O. J. Mooney passed away on 6 December 2015 at home and was interred in the Mooney Family Cemetery.[28]

1st Lt. James W. Dollar returned to the United States in November 1945 and was discharged from the Army at Fort Leavenworth, Kansas. Nine months later, he rejoined the Army and went back to Europe as part of the U.S. Constabulary that performed the occupation of Germany. In 1952–53 he served in the Korean War. Altogether he served 33 months in combat in two wars. He retired from the Army as a lieutenant colonel on 1 September 1962. His wife Jane had a distinguished career in the Women's Auxiliary Army Corps and Army Nurse Corps. He lived in Apple Valley, California until his death.[29]

At a dance held in her village of Stenovice, Milka Vildova met 1st Lt. Richard Ferguson, an observation aircraft pilot with the 2nd Infantry Division. Though Milka did not speak English and Richard did not speak Czech, they were able to talk to each other in German. They fell in love and were married in Stenovice the following year. Milka moved to the United States and was happily married until Richard's death in the late 1980s. In May 1990, she attended the Pilsen Liberation Anniversary Celebrations and met 97th Infantry Division veteran Harold Yeglin. Like Milka, Harold had lost his spouse. Milka and Harold were married in Roanoke, Virginia in 1991. Milka died in February 2010.[30]

Malvina Zajicova and Joseph Zajic were married after the war. They lived in Prague for many years.

Vera Fiedlerova became friends with Carl Sosna of the 23rd Infantry Regiment, 2nd Infantry Division. After the war, Vera married Georg Fiedler. Despite the postwar Communist rule, Vera and Georg maintained a friendship with Carl and his wife, periodically visiting each other's homes in the succeeding decades.

Jaroslav Peklo earned a college degree and became an architect. After the fall of Communism, he worked for many years in various projects commemorating the U.S. Army and the liberation. In 2000, he was one of several persons who put together a commemorative book entitled *Americans in West Bohemia 1945—Exclusive Pictures* that was published in both Czech and English. He was a friend to many U.S. veterans. He died in 2012 or 2013.

19

The Legacy of the 16th Armored Division

The 16th Armored Division left Czechoslovakia in late August 1945 but it never left the hearts and minds of the Czech people whom they liberated from Nazi oppression. Despite four decades of Communist attempts to eradicate all recognition and memory of the U.S. Army and the 16th Armored Division in liberating the western sections of Czechoslovakia, the Czech people never forgot their liberators and have been celebrating their liberation every May since the Communists were ousted in 1989.

The Cold War

The United States Army remained in western Czechoslovakia only three more months after the 16th Armored Division went home. Skillful diplomacy by President Benes and President Truman convinced Soviet Premier Stalin to agree to a mutual withdrawal of all U.S. and Soviet forces from Czechoslovakia in December 1945.

For a time, it seemed as if Czechoslovakia might be able to exist as a democratic, independent nation. That dream came to a violent and abrupt end in February 1948 when Soviet-supported Czechoslovak Communists orchestrated a coup. The Communists ousted the pro-democracy members of the government and forced President Benes to resign. Democratic Foreign Minister Jan Masyrk was murdered by Soviet intelligence agents. Czechoslovakia became firmly in the Soviet orbit for the next forty years.[1]

After taking over Czechoslovakia in February 1948, the Communists immediately undertook a systematic campaign to re-write the U.S. Army out of the history of World War II in Czechoslovakia. Monuments that had been erected by the Czechs in honor of the U.S. Army and specifically the 16th Armored Division were torn down. Children were taught in school that Pilsen and western Czechoslovak towns and villages had actually been liberated by Soviet soldiers dressed like Americans. Public ceremonies of remembrance of the U.S. liberation were banned. Persons acknowledging the U.S. Army's liberation risked severe punishment by the Communists. "They tried to erase history and create new history," Pilsen lawyer Vaclav Zeman told the New York Times in April 1990. "Teachers taught children that it was Russian soldiers in American uniforms who liberated us."[2]

Despite six long years of Nazi tyranny and four even longer decades of Soviet/Communist oppression, the flame of freedom and democracy was never extinguished among the Czech people. That flame was kept alive by such courageous leaders as Alexander Dubcek and Vaclav Havel. In 1968, Czechs and Slovaks attempted to liberalize their country and create "Socialism with a Human Face" in what became known as the Prague Spring. With all the grace of Hitler's seizure of Czechoslovakia in 1938–39, the Soviet Army led a massive invasion force of Warsaw Pact troops that crushed the Prague Spring and re-imposed the Soviet puppet dictatorship. Unlike 1945, however, the Soviet Army did not leave Czechoslovakia.[3]

Czechoslovakia remained firmly in the Soviet Union's Communist grasp until 1989. Reforms within the Soviet Union rapidly grew out of the control of the Communist leaders. In the fall of 1989 and early 1990, an irresistible wave of democracy and freedom swept across Eastern Europe as the long suppressed peoples of these Soviet-occupied nations rose up in public demonstrations. Communist Parties in Czechoslovakia, East Germany, Poland and other Eastern European nations fell out of power and were replaced by democratic, popular governments. In Czechoslovakia, the peaceful transition from Communism to democracy led by Vaclav Havel and other pro-democracy liberals became known as the "Velvet Revolution." In June 1990, the Czechs and Slovaks held their first democratic elections since 1946. A year later, the last of the Soviet Army's 75,000 troops left Czechoslovakia for good. Six months later, the Soviet Union ceased to exist, having been replaced by the Commonwealth of Independent States centered upon Russia. In January 1993, the Czechs and Slovaks went their separate ways, peacefully dissolving Czechoslovakia into the new nations of the Czech Republic and Slovakia respectively. This peaceful separation became known as "the Velvet Divorce."

The course of history oftentimes takes unusual twists and turns. Relations between the United States, the Czech Republic, Germany and Russia/Soviet Union are no different. In 1999, the Czech Republic became a member of NATO—a military alliance that Czechoslovakia had opposed, albeit under Soviet coercion, for forty years as part of the Soviet-led Warsaw Pact. Today, the United States and the Czech Republic are once again Allies. As a member of NATO, the Czech Republic is also allied with Germany. The Soviet Union no longer exists but in many ways, the its repressive, anti-democratic, belligerent legacy lives on in the leadership of Russia, thus necessitating the continuance of the NATO defensive alliance.

Liberation Remembered 1990 and Afterwards

The Communists did all within their power to eradicate the truth of the U.S. Army's liberation of western Czechoslovakia. They literally rewrote history in attempt to erase all memory and acknowledgment of the U.S. Army's heroic deeds. Yet, the people of Pilsen and western Bohemia never forgot their liberators. In 1990 after the Communists had been ousted, the Czechs undertook a major effort to re-claim their history and correct the Communist lies about their past. One of the key components of this effort was the resumption of the annual liberation anniversary ceremonies that had been curtailed by the Communists after their seizure of power in 1948. The Czechs invited their American liberators to participate in these historic celebrations.

Barely six months after the Communists had been ousted from power, the Czechs held their first liberation anniversary celebrations since 1947. In Pilsen and many other west Bohemian towns, returning U.S. Army veterans from the 1st, 2nd, and 97th Infantry Division and the 16th Armored Division were greeted by exuberant Czechs welcoming them back to the country that they had liberated forty-five years before. "A sea of American flags floated above Pilsen's Republic Square and a U.S. Air Force band struck up 'The Star Spangled Banner' in an emotion-packed tribute by West Bohemians for the American GIs who liberated the region at the end of World War II," wrote correspondent Peter S. Green of United Press International.[4]

Many American veterans returned to western Czechoslovakia for the liberation anniversary celebrations. "To me it was May 1945 all over again—a feeling that 45 years had not intervened," recalled Robert H. Carlson, a former 1st lieutenant with the 2nd Infantry Division. "The people here, they treated us swell," said former 1st Sgt. Steve Chylinski of the 16th Armored Division. "Out in the town square, I couldn't move through the crowd, they were kissing me and giving me beer and flowers." Milka Vildova was also there visiting her homeland.[5]

Among those participating in the Pilsen ceremonies was Czechoslovak President Vaclav Havel. "It is not true that Czechoslovakia was liberated only by the Red Army," said Havel in a speech in Republic Square. "The southwestern part of our country was liberated by the American Army. We'd like to remember this fact after years of silence."[6]

The Pilsen ceremonies were two days of festivities reminiscent of the 1945 liberation itself. A parade of several dozen restored U.S. Army vehicles was held through the city. These vehicles had been given to the Czechs by the U.S. Army in 1945, hidden by them during the Communist years and brought back out of hiding in the preceding months. A monument was dedicated to the 2nd Infantry Division and the cornerstone was laid for a monument to all American soldiers. A new plaque was dedicated on the Pilsen City Hall to replace the original one removed by the Communists in 1951. President Havel and U.S. Ambassador to Czechoslovakia Shirley Temple Black participated in these ceremonies.[7]

Every year since 1990, the people of western Bohemia and Pilsen in particular have held festivities to mark the anniversary of their liberation from Nazi tyranny by the U.S. Army. Every year since 1990, U.S. Army veterans of the liberation, including those from the 16th Armored Division, have made the journey back to Bohemia to participate in those celebrations. George Thompson has made the journey numerous times. Many of the U.S. veterans have brought their families along and other family members have made the trip after their loved ones have passed away. Kathy Hoffman and her husband Mickey have visited Pilsen several times and visited the places where her father, Pfc Charles Lemmons of the Division Military Police, had served during 1945. Though the passage of time is steadily reducing the numbers of those who experienced the liberation, the Czechs' enthusiasm for their liberators remains unabated.

Czech Republic, May 2000

At the invitation of George Thompson, I traveled to Germany and the Czech Republic for the 55th Anniversary of the Liberation ceremonies held in Pilsen and nearby towns and villages. The trip was an unforgettable experience to visit the sites associated with the liberation with the men who had liberated the Czechs from Nazi oppression nearly thirty years before I was born.

George Thompson and his group of 16th Armored Division veterans and family members were just one of several groups of U.S. Army veterans converging on the Czech Republic. I decided to travel independently and visit some historic sites in Germany as well. In the first days of May 2000, I flew to Frankfurt, Germany, rented a car and retraced Third U.S. Army's route across central Germany from the Rhine River to the Czech Republic. On 5 May, I visited Cheb and the area where the 9th Armored Division and 1st and 97th Infantry Divisions operated in northwestern Czech Republic. After this, I returned to Germany and drove southeasterly parallel to the Czech border. Picking up the route of the 16th Armored Division near Waidhaus, I then drove east back into the Czech Republic along route E50. Spring was in full bloom in west Bohemia and the fields and forests adjacent to the highway were inundated with color. In late afternoon, I arrived in Pilsen and checked into my hotel on Republic Square (namesti Republiky). The 55th Anniversary celebrations in Pilsen had already begun that day but I arrived too late to attend any of them. Nevertheless, I was able to meet up with Carl Sosna from the 2nd Infantry Division, his wife Ginny and their Czech friends, Vera Fiedlerova and her husband Georg Fiedler that night.

The next day, Saturday 6 May, was one of the most extraordinary days of my life as the Czechs went all out to honor their American liberators. Everywhere they went, the American veterans were treated like heroes and celebrities. Czechs asked them for autographs, to pose for photos and to shake hands. Some had fifty-five year old photos of American soldiers that they hoped to locate amongst the returning veterans.

The day began with the unveiling of the new memorial to the 16th Armored Division. I attended this ceremony with the Sosnas and Georg Fiedler. Hundreds of American vets, their families, dignitaries and citizens of Pilsen gathered for the dedication of the glass pyramid etched with the logos of the division that had liberated the city 55 years ago that day. As President of the 16th Armored Division Association, George Thompson spoke on behalf of his division's veterans. Brig. Gen. Stephen Speakes, Chief of Staff of the U.S. Army's V Corps, was one of the guest speakers. Music was provided by a Czech Army band. After speeches by various other dignitaries, the new memorial was unveiled. The memorial was a glass pyramid resting on steel supports. Etched into the glass were the 16th Armored Division's insignia and words of remembrance.

The next ceremony was held at the 2nd Infantry Division Memorial located at Chodske Square. The Sosnas, Georg Fiedler and I headed over to that monument and met Jaroslav Peklo there. Though the 16th Armored

19. The Legacy of the 16th Armored Division 185

Division had actually liberated Pilsen, the people of Pilsen are also quite fond of the 2nd Infantry Division veterans for their time spent here during the postwar occupation period.

The most spectacular of all the anniversary celebrations was the Liberation Parade held in late morning through the heart of Pilsen. A special viewing area was set up outside a theater for the families of the American vets. Thousands of people representing various community organizations marched in honor of the Americans. Contingents of the Czech and American armed forces also participated, including a group of combat engineers from the Oregon National Guard who were performing their Annual Training in Germany. The centerpiece of the parade was the American veterans. Each one rode in a restored U.S. Army vehicle from World War II provided by the Czechs' Military Vehicle Club. With an estimated 200,000 Czech people lining the streets and cheering the vets riding in jeeps, command cars and trucks, the parade was as close to the actual liberation event as I could ever get.

The most astonishing indication of just how far the Czechs had come since 1989 occurred about halfway through the parade. As I watched the parade, the air and ground suddenly shook violently. Seconds later a flight

The 16th Armored Division Monument in Pilsen after its dedication on 6 May 2000 (author's photograph).

of three massive Soviet-made Hind D helicopter gunships flew over in tribute to the U.S. veterans. Though the Czechs were now part of NATO, they still had much of their Warsaw Pact / Soviet-made military equipment. Only ten years before it would have been completely unthinkable that the newest NATO members, the Czechs, would be flying Soviet gunships in a tribute to the U.S. Army liberators of their country from World War II!

Following the parade, we headed over to Bory Park where the Czechs had re-created a U.S. Army encampment from May 1945. The encampment featured the restored U.S. Army vehicles, tents, displays and Czechs dressed in U.S. Army uniforms from World War II. Refreshments were provided by the world-renown Pilsener Urquell Brewery.

In mid-afternoon was a ceremony at the "Thank You America" Memorial. Dedicated on 6 May 1995, the Memorial is appropriately located at the intersection of Klatovska Boulevard and Americka Street. This memorial features two pillars with those words inscribed in both English and Czech (Diky Ameriko!). A small marble stone dedicated on the 45th anniversary of the liberation bears the inscription "To the Men of the Sixteenth Armored Division—We'll Never Forget." Unlike the two previous

George Thompson, 137th Armored Ordnance Battalion, signs an autograph for a Czech citizen in Pilsen on 6 May 2000 (author's photograph).

19. *The Legacy of the 16th Armored Division* 187

Gene Eike (left) of the 18th Armored Infantry Battalion, Harold Yeglin of the 97th Infantry Division and Miloslava Vildova Yeglin in Epjovice, Czech Republic on 7 May 2000 (author's photograph).

ceremonies that featured specific divisions, this third ceremony was to honor all of the American units which had participated in the liberation of western Bohemia. Veterans from the 2nd and 97th Infantry Divisions and the 16th Armored Division were in attendance as well as several Belgian Army veterans who had served in the postwar occupation.

In late afternoon, an ecumenical memorial service was held at St. Bartholomew's Cathedral on Republic Square. In the evening there was a free concert in Republic Square performed by a band from the U.S. Air Force, Europe. The square was packed with festive Czechs celebrating the anniversary and American veterans reliving their past. The day concluded with a fireworks display late that night.

Compared with Saturday's celebrations, Sunday was more subdued but still very poignant. Like so many of the Catholic soldiers who had served in Pilsen, I attended Mass at St. Bartholomew's Cathedral. Even though the Mass was said in Czech, I was able to follow along. Catholic Masses follow the same basic format regardless of the language or country, and I had previously attended Masses in French, Polish and German with no trouble following along.

After Mass, I joined up with George Thompson and his group from the 16th Armored Division Association to attend ceremonies that were being held east of Pilsen in the towns of Epjovice and Rokycany. In Epjovice, I met Harold and Milka Yeglin and renewed my acquaintance with Gene Eike whom I had met previously at the 16th Armored Division Reunion in 1998. The town of Rokycany had been liberated by the 9th Infantry Regiment of the 2nd Infantry Division and American forces were officially halted to the east of the town. Here U.S. and Soviet soldiers had linked up following V-E Day. A convoy of restored U.S. military vehicles participated in both ceremonies and a restored Soviet T-34 tank was at the Rokycany ceremony. In Rokycany, I met O. J. Mooney and Lt. Col. Charles Schaeffer of the 16th Armored. Col. Schaeffer shared with me his personal experiences in witnessing the surrender and suicide of Pilsen's German commander Gen. von Majewski.

That night the city of Pilsen held a special dinner in honor of the American veterans and their families at the Pilsener Urquell Brewery

Lt. Col. Charles Schaeffer, 216th Armored Engineers Battalion, poses for a photo with two Czech World War II re-enactors dressed in U.S. Army uniforms in Rokycany on 7 May 2000. The re-enactor on the right is wearing the shoulder patch of the U.S. 2nd Infantry Division, the Parachute Badge and the Combat Infantry Badge (author's photograph).

(Plzeňský Prazdroj)'s Na Spilce Restaurant. First brewed in 1842 by Josef Groll, the Pilsener beer is the world's first blond lager and arguably one of the world's greatest beers. I attended with Carl and Ginny Sosna and met Charlie Savage and Vern Lewellyn of the 16th Armored Division and John Shobey of the 2nd Ranger Battalion. Like so many of those American soldiers who liberated and served in Pilsen back in 1945, I savored the brewing craftsmanship of the Pilsner Urquell Brewery.

I left Pilsen on the morning of 8 May and returned to Germany for some rather random wandering unrelated to the liberation of western Czechoslovakia. For the next two days, I visited Rothenburg ob der Tauber—a meticulously restored medieval walled town in Bavaria, drove much of the Romantische Strasse (Romantic Road) and toured Aschaffenburg. I returned home to the United States on 10 May 2000.

To truly understand history, especially military history, one must visit where that history occurred. One gains a perspective and an insight into events that cannot be obtained from photos or maps or written descriptions. My four days in the Czech Republic in May 2000 enabled me to see the liberation in a whole new light, especially since my visit was during the 55th Anniversary celebrations. It was a tremendous blessing from God for which I am most appreciative.

Epilogue

The 16th Armored Division was only in existence for 27 months, two-thirds of which was spent in the United States, and was in combat as a division for only three days. Other U.S. Army divisions were in existence for many more years and spent far more time in combat. Yet the 16th Armored Division in its one and only combat operation liberated the most important city in western Czechoslovakia and forever earned a place in the hearts of the Czech people. Neither the passage of time nor the decades of systematic Communist anti–American propaganda have diminished the Czech people's appreciation for their American liberators.

Most of the 16th Armored Division soldiers who participated in the 1945 liberation have passed away. Hopefully this book will help to ensure that their heroism and their deeds do not pass away from historical memory.

Chapter Notes

Chapter 1

1. Robert S. Cameron, *Mobility, Shock, and Firepower: The Emergence of the U.S. Army's Armor Branch, 1917–1945* (Washington, D.C.: Center of Military History, 2008), 253–55. During the 1930s, there was no Armor Force or Branch. The U.S. Army's armored vehicles, such as they were, were split between the Cavalry and the Infantry Branches; John B. Wilson, *Maneuver and Firepower: The Evolution of Divisions and Separate Brigades*. In the Army Lineage Series (Washington, D.C.: Center of Military History, 1998), 147–52; Shelby L. Stanton, *Order of Battle, U.S. Army, World War II*. Novato, CA: Presidio, 1984; Several of the German panzer divisions were formed late in the war and existed only on paper.

2. *Ibid.*; Robert R. Palmer, "Reorganization of Ground Troops for Combat." Found on pages 261–384 of Kent Roberts Greenfield, Robert R. Palmer and Bell I. Wiley's *The Army Ground Forces: The Organization of Ground Combat Troops*. In the series *The United States Army in World War II* (Washington, D.C.: Center of Military History, 1987). See Part V specifically for the armored forces reorganization; Mary Lee Stubbs and Stanley Russell Connor. *Army Lineage Series Armor-Cavalry Part 1* (Washington, D.C.: Office of the Chief of Military History, 1969), 58–63; George Forty, *United States Tanks of World War II in Action* (New York: Blandford P, 1983), 22–28. [Hereafter cited by title]; George Forty, *U.S. Army Handbook 1939–1945* (New York: Barnes & Noble Books, 1995), 79–86. [Hereafter cited by title.] U.S. Army. Army Ground Forces. Historical Section. *Reorganization of Ground Troops for Combat*. Army Ground Forces Study No. 8 (1946). Accessed online on 23 January 2014 at http://www.history. army.mil/books/agf/AGF08/index.htm. See Chapter III-7; Stanton, Chapter 3 "Armored Divisions."

3. *Ibid.*; Cameron, 373–5.
4. *Ibid.*; Wilson, 184–187.
5. *Ibid.*
6. *Ibid.*; Cameron, 383–385.
7. *Ibid.*
8. John W. Wilson. *Maneuver and Firepower: The Evolution of Divisions and Brigades*. In the *Army Lineage Series* (Washington, D.C.: Center of Military History, 1998), 169–70; Bell I. Wiley, "The Building and Training of Infantry Divisions." found on pp. 429–498 of Robert R. Palmer, Bell I. Wiley, and William R. Keast. *The Procurement and Training of Ground Combat Troops*. In the series *United States Army in World War II: The Army Ground Forces* (Washington, D.C.: Center of Military History, 1991). The armored divisions followed a similar activation and training procedure as the infantry divisions.

9. Record Group 407. National Archives and Records Administration. Archives II. College Park, MD. [Hereafter cited as RG407. NARA.]

10. Stanton, 598.

11. "Major General Douglas T. Greene." Hall of Fame Listing, Drexel University. Accessed online on 24 January 2014 at http:// www.drexeldragons.com/hof.aspx?hof= 548&path=&kiosk= [Hereafter cited as Greene biography.]

12. Dale Weaver, editor. *16th Armored Division History. Patton's Third Army, WWII*. Privately published by the 16th Armored Division Association in 1986.

13. *Ibid.*

14. William G. Smith. Col. Battalion Commander. 216th Armored Engineers Battalion / 16th Armored Division. Interview by author

at 16th Armored Reunion, 16 Oct. 1998. Hereafter cited as Smith interview.
15. Ibid.
16. Ibid.; "Division Hq," II-1, II-2.
17. Wilson, 192. The 10th Division later was re-organized as the U.S. Army's only Mountain Division and the 71st Light Division subsequently became a regular infantry division.
18. Gontrum, III-2.
19. Stubbs, 436; Cameron, 373-5; Stanton, 262, 287, 288, 321-2, 410, 573; Capt. John Buckheit, "16th AD Was the Last U.S. Armored Division Formed During WWII, and the Last Deployed." *Armor* (July-August 1993), 38-39. [Hereafter cited as Buckheit 16AD]. Buckheit wrote several articles about U.S. armored divisions for *Armor* magazine in honor of the 50th Anniversary of World War Two; "Division Headquarters & Headquarters Co." Weaver, II-1 to II-9. [Hereafter cited as "Division Hq."]
20. Lt. Col. Symroski assumed command of the battalion on 16 July 1943.
21. Gontrum, III-2.
22. U.S. Army. 16th Armored Division. Combat Command A. 5th Tank Battalion. After Action Report. May 1945. RG407. NARA. Hereafter cited as 5th Tank AAR.
23. U.S. Army. 16th Armored Division. Combat Command B. 16th Tank Battalion, Unit History, 1945? RG407, NARA. [Hereafter cited as 16th Tank History].
24. U.S. Army. 16th Armored Division. 18th Armored Infantry Battalion. Unit History. October 1945. RG407. NARA. [Hereafter cited as 18th AIB Unit History.]
25. U.S. Army. 717th Tank Battalion. History. 1 January 1945 to 31 July 1945. Camp Swift, Texas. August 1945. Accessed online at http://cgsc.cdmhost.com/cdm/singleitem/collection/p4013coll8/id/3459/rec/15 on 19 February 2014 from the U.S. Army Combined Arms Research Library; U.S. Army. 717th Tank Battalion. *717th Tank Battalion Record.* Privately published by the battalion in October 1945. Accessed online at http://digicom.bpl.lib.me.us/ww_reg_his/25/ on 19 February 2014; U.S. Army. Headquarters. Army Ground Forces. Memorandum for the Adjutant General. 322/5 (16th Armd Div) (R) Subject: Reorganization of 16th Armored Division. 1 September 1943. RG407, NARA. [Hereafter cited as 16AD Re-Organization Memo.]
26. *717th Tank Battalion Records*; U.S. Army. 16th Armored Division. 23rd Cavalry Reconnaissance Squadron [Mechanized]. Unit History. 1 January 1945. RG407, Archives II, NARA. [Hereafter cited as 23rd CAV Unit History JAN 1945.]
27. *717th Tank Battalion Record.*
28. 16AD Re-Organization Memo; Stanton, 288, 302; Harry Yeide, *The Infantry's Armor: The U.S. Army's Separate Tank Battalions in World War II* (Mechanicsburg, PA: Stackpole Books, 2010), 329; The 787th Tank Battalion arrived in France in March. However, the ship carrying its equipment had a collision at sea near Bermuda and did not arrive until the following month. The battalion personnel were re-united with their equipment and vehicles in Wurzburg, Germany and hastily rushed to the front. On 6 May 1945, they were attached to the 86th Infantry Division and entered Austria that same day. They did not see any combat.
29. Stanton, 262; 18th AIB Unit History, 1; 16AD Re-Organization Memo.
30. Stanton, 287-8, 321-2; 16AD Re-Organization Memo.
31. 16AD Re-Organization Memo; Col. William W. Smith, Jr., USA. "A Brief History of the 216th Armored Engineer Battalion, 16th Armored Division 1943-1945." Weaver, XII-1 to XII-28. [Hereafter cited as 216AEB History.] See p. XII-16; In his history, Col. Smith was uncertain of the date of these TOE changes but given the re-organizations of other armored divisions, it most likely took place that fall.
32. Stanton, 410, 573; 16AD Re-Organization Memo.
33. *Ibid.*
34. *Ibid.*
35. *Ibid.*; U.S. Army. U.S. Army European Theater of Operations. History Section. *Order of Battle of the United States Army. World War II. European Theater of Operations. Divisions* (Paris, France: December 1945), 546-551, 559. Hereafter cited as U.S. Army Order of Battle.
36. *Ibid.*; *U.S. Army Handbook 1939-1945*, 79-81.
37. "Division Headquarters," II-1, II-2.
38. *U.S. Army Handbook 1939-1945*, 79-80.
39. U.S. Army. 8th Armored Division. 80th Armored Regiment. "Meet the Chief." *Turret Topics* (Newspaper of the 80th Armored Regiment). 21 May 1943. Accessed online at http://www.8th-armored.org/pics/papers/80th-regt-paper.pdf [Hereafter cited as Noble biogra-

phy.] Additional details provided by the Brians Journey (Brian LaViolette Scholarship Foundation) website http://www.briansjourney.com/soh/pilsen-noble accessed 14 January 2014. A 2013 Scholarship of Honor was given in Col. Noble's name.

40. *U.S. Army Handbook 1939–1945*, 80.

41. *U.S. Army Handbook 1939–1945*, 85; U.S. Department of War. U.S. Army. Field Manual 17–42. *Armored Force Field Manual: Armored Infantry Battalion*. 10 November 1944.

42. "History of the 18th AIB." Weaver, XIII–1 to XIII–5; 18th AIB Unit History, 1–4.

43. Lt. Col. Howard Painter, USA (Ret.). Company Commander. Company B. 18th Armored Infantry Battalion. Combat Command A. 16th Armored Division. "Recollections." Weaver, XIII–20 to XIII–22.

44. Harley Barrs, Armored Infantryman, Anti-tankPlatoon / B Company / 18th Armored Infantry Battalion / Combat Command A / 16th Armored Division. "Recollections." in *16th Armored History*, XIII–18.

45. Edward Krusheski, Rifleman, A Company / 69th Armored Infantry Battalion / Combat Command R / 16th Armored Division. Phone interviews by the author, 20 June 1998 and 17 January 2000. I also had the pleasure of meeting him at the 16th Armored Division Reunion in Baltimore, MD, on 16 October 1998.

46. *U.S. Army Handbook 1939–1945*, 85.

47. U.S. Army. 16th Armored Division. 393rd Armored Field Artillery Battalion. After Action Report. May 1945. Reprinted in Dale Weaver's *16th Armored History*, XVII–1 to XVIII–4. Hereafter cited as 393rd AFAB AAR; Semmelmeyer's biography is from his Legacy page written by classmate Donald H. Nelson on the West Point Association website http://apps.westpointaog.org/Memorials/Article/6306/ accessed on 30 October 2015. Hereafter cited as Semmelmeyer Tribute.

48. U.S. Army. 16th Armored Division. 396th Armored Field Artillery Battalion. After Action Report. May 1945. RG407, NARA. Also reprinted in Dale Weaver's *16th Armored History*. Hereafter cited as 396th AFAB AAR; Hubbard's biographical details are drawn from the Register of his Personal Papers at Virginia Military Institute Archives http://www.vmi.edu/Archives/Manuscripts/Military_History_Manuscripts/; his obituary. *Danville Register* (Danville VA) (17 April 1968); and Murray H. Fowler's *Spearhead in the West, 1941–45: The Third Armored Division* (Frankfurt, Germany: Privately published for the 3rd Armored Division by F. J. Heinrich, 1945), 25; U.S. Army. 16th Armored Division. 396th Armored Field Artillery Battalion. Unit History. 15 July 1943–31 July 1943. RG407. NARA.

49. Oscar Jackson Mooney, Jr. (Dec.). Sgt. Battery C / 396th Armored Field Artillery Battalion / Combat Command B / 16th Armored Division. Interview by the author. Pilsen, Czech Republic, 7 May 2000. Hereafter cited as Mooney interview. This was one of several interviews that I conducted while attending the 55th Anniversary of Liberation ceremonies in the Czech Republic in May 2000.

50. U.S. Army. 16th Armored Division. 397th Armored Field Artillery Battalion. Unit History. 1945. RG407. NARA. [Hereafter cited as 397th AFAB Unit History.]

51. Charles A. Symroski, Brig. Gen., USA (dec.). His biographical information is taken from the tribute to him written by his wife and daughters on the West Point Association website http://apps.westpointaog.org/Memorials/Article/10226/, accessed on 19 November 2015. Hereafter cited as Symroski biography; Mandy Malone and Norman Tippens. "Obituary, Charles Albert Symroski." *Daily Press* (April 14, 2001). Accessed online at http://articles.dailypress.com/2001-04-15/news/0104150120_1_west-point-fort-riley-headquarters on 20 November 2015. [Hereafter cited as Symroski obituary.]

52. U.S. Army. 16th Armored Division. Division Artillery. Headquarters Battery. Battery History. Camp Chaffee, Arkansas. 1944. RG407. NARA.

53. *U.S. Army Handbook 1939–1945*, 79, 82; "Headquarters Company, 16th Armored Division Trains," Weaver, IV–1.

54. *U.S. Army Handbook 1939–1945*, 84; George Thompson. Sgt. C Company. 137th Armored Ordnance Maintenance Battalion. 16th Armored Division. Phone interview by author 18 January 2000. And email to the author, 11 February 2013. George is also past president of the 16th Armored Division Association. I have him to thank for most of my 16th Armored contacts; Buckheit 16AD, 38; Frank J. Houlihan. Lt. Col. 137th Armored Ordnance Maintenance Battalion. 16th Armored Division. "History and Records, 137th Armored Ordnance Maintainance [Sic] Battalion 16th AD 1942–1953," Weaver, VIII–1 to VIII–21. [Hereafter cited by author's name.]

55. Houlihan, VIII–1 to VIII–6.

56. *Ibid.*
57. Verne Lewellyn, Parts Clerk, 137th Armored Ordnance Battalion / 16th Armored Division, letter to the author, 31 May 2000. I met Verne in Pilsen earlier that month.
58. *U.S. Army Handbook 1939-1945*, 83. "216th Armored Medical Battalion." Weaver, VII-1.
59. U.S. Department of War. U.S. Army. Field Manual 17-45. *Armored Force Field Manual: Armored Engineer Battalion.* 13 November 1942. Accessed online at U.S. Army Combined Arms Research Library on 21 January 2014 at http://cgsc.contentdm.oclc.org/utils/getfile/collection/p4013coll9/id/792/filename/793.pdf
60. 216AEB History.
61. *Ibid.*, XII-3.
62. *Ibid.*; Charles Schaeffer, Lt. Col., USA (Dec.), 2nd Lt. Adjutant, 216th Armored Engineers Battalion / 16th Armored Division. Phone interview by author, 6 January 2003.
63. 216AEB History, XII-3.
64. *U.S. Army Handbook 1939-1945*, 81; Solomon Polish, "History of 156th Signal Company." Weaver, IX-1 to IX-8.
65. *Ibid.*
66. Polish, IX-1 to IX-2.
67. *U.S. Army Handbook 1939-1945*, 82; 23rd CAV Unit History JAN 1945; Schaudt, Howard P. Capt., USA. *The Operations of 23rd Cavalry Reconnaissance Squadron (Mecz) in Pursuit Action with the 86th Infantry Division from Ingolstadt to Wasserburg, Germany.* Advanced Infantry Officers Course 1946-1947. The Infantry School. Fort Benning, Georgia. Posted online by the U.S. Army Maneuver Center for Excellence. Fort Benning Georgia. Accessed online on 5 February 2014 at http://www.benning.army.mil/library/content/Virtual/Donovanpapers/wwii/STUP2/SchaudtHowardP%20CPT.pdf
68. Schaudt, 24.
69. Adkisson, Raymond C. 1st Lt., USA. *Night Marches: Action of Australian and Indian Units Battle of Sari Bair (Gallipoli) 6-7 August 1915.* Regular Course. The Infantry School. Fort Benning, Georgia. Posted online by the U.S. Army Maneuver Center for Excellence. Fort Benning Georgia. Accessed online on 5 February 2014 at http://www.benning.army.mil/library/content/Virtual/Donovanpapers/wwi/STUP1/AdkissonRaymond%20C.%201LT.pdf; Thomas R. Buecker, *Fort Robinson and the American Century 1900-1948* (Norman, OK: U of Oklahoma P, 2002), 53.

70. Mark Steece, Armorer. B Troop / 23rd Cavalry Reconnaissance Squadron [Mechanized] / 16th Armored Division. Phone interview by author. 22 February 2014. Hereafter cited as Steece interview.
71. "M. P. Platoon," Weaver, VI-1 to VI-2.
72. Betsy Stakauskas. "Charles R. Lemmons, Covington Police Officer." Obituary. *The Cincinnati Enquirer* (17 September 2001); Kathy Lemmons Hoffman. "Charles Robert Lemmons." March 2014. This is a biography written by Charles Lemmons's daughter. Hereafter cited as Lemmons biography; My thanks to Kathy for providing me with copies of both documents.

Chapter 2

1. 16th Tank History.
2. 18th AIB Unit History.
3. *Ibid.*
4. "History of the 18th AIB"; Painter, XIII-20; 18th AIB Unit History.
5. Barrs, XIII-16.
6. 216AEB History, XII-5.
7. *Ibid.*
8. *Ibid.*; Symroski obituary.
9. Houlihan, VIII-6 to VIII-7.
10. Information on Lt. Bowlby's death provided by Edward Krusheski; 216AEB History, XII-12; "Name Landing Strip Iwan Field." *The Armodier* (23 September 1944). Found in U.S. Army. 16th Armored Division. 393rd Armored Field Artillery Battalion. Unit History. 1945. RG407, NARA.
11. Houlihan, VIII-7.
12. Stanton, 4; Buckheit 16AD, 38; 216AEB History, XII-4.

Chapter 3

1. For an in-depth discussion of Hitler's annexation of Austria and Czechoslovakia, see William L. Shirer's masterpiece, *The Rise and Fall of the Third Reich: A History of Nazi Germany* (New York: Simon & Schuster, 1959). I specifically refer you to "Chapter 11: Anschluss: The Rape of Austria," and "Chapter 12: The Road to Munich." Shirer, a reporter, was an eyewitness to many of the events in Nazi Germany.
2. Chamberlain and Churchill, quoted in Shirer, 417 and 423.
3. George F. Kennan, *Memoirs 1925-1950* (Boston: Little, Brown & Co., 1967), 87.

4. See Shirer's "Chapter 14: Czechoslovakia Ceases to Exist"; "The Consul General at Praha (Linnell) to the Secretary of State, 25 March 1939," U.S. State Department, *Foreign Relations of the United States 1939: Volume I General* (Washington, D.C.: GPO, 1956), 60–61. [Hereafter cited as *FRUS 1939.*] Linnell forwarded a message from Ambassador Carr reporting on additional details he had learned about the German takeover of Bohemia and Moravia.

5. *Ibid.*

6. Harold Denny, "Road To Prague Lined With Debris." *New York Times.* 11 May 1945: p. 7. Denny had been in Prague at this time and returned six years later shortly after it had been liberated.

7. Kennan, 97, 99.

8. *Ibid.*

9. Vera Fiedlerova, Citizen of Pilsen, letter to the author, 12 September 1998. [Hereafter cited as Fiedlerova letter.]

10. "The German Charge (Thomsen) to the Secretary of State, 18 March 1939," *FRUS 1939*, 51–52. The Preamble to the 16 March 1939 decree was transmitted via this message.

11. The decree is contained in the message "The German Charge (Thomsen) to the Secretary of State, 17 March 1939." *FRUS 1939*, 45–47.

12. "Wilbur John Carr." Biography. U.S. Department of State. Office of the Historian. Accessed on 27 June 2014 at http://history.state.gov/departmenthistory/people/carr-wilbur-john; "The Minister in Czechoslovakia (Carr) to the Secretary of State [Extracts], 19 March 1939," *FRUS 1939*, 54.

13. "The Acting Secretary of State to the Minister in Czechoslovakia (Carr), 17 March 1939," *FRUS 1939*, 47; "The Minister in Czechoslovakia (Carr) to the Secretary of State, 17 March 1939," *FRUS 1939*, 51.

14. "The Acting Secretary of State to the Minister in Czechoslovakia (Carr), 20 March 1939," *FRUS 1939*, 55–56. See also Footnote 90.

15. "The Acting Secretary of State to the German Charge (Thomsen), March 20, 1939," *FRUS 1939*, 56.

16. Kennan, 103.

17. For an excellent expose on the Nazi occupation of Bohemia see Gotthold Rhode, "The Protectorate of Bohemia and Moravia 1939–1945," which may be found on pp. 305–321 of Victor S. Manatey and Radomir Luza, eds. *A History of the Czechoslovak Republic 1918–1948* (Princeton, NJ: Princeton UP, 1973).

18. Jaroslav Peklo, Citizen of Pilsen, "The Last Days of War in Pilsen and Prague," from a letter to the author, 8 April 1998. [Hereafter cited as Peklo letter]; Vildova interview.

19. Malvina Zajicova, Citizen of Pilsen, letter to the author, 15 April 1998. [Hereafter cited as Zajicova letter.] Vildova interview.

20. Peklo letter; Vera Fiedlerova, Citizen of Pilsen. "My Memories on the End of the WW2," from a letter to the author, 28 June 1998. [Hereafter cited as Fiedlerova letter 2].

21. Jaroslav Peklo, "The End of the War in Pilsen, Bohemia," from a letter to the author, 10 March 1998. [Hereafter cited as Peklo letter 2].

Chapter 4

1. U.S. Army. 16th Armored Division. Unit Historical Report. Czechoslovakia: 28 June 1945. RG407. NARA. [Hereafter cited as 16th AD UHR]; Florine Pierce Faulk, and Grace Edman, "PIERCE, FRANK CUSHMAN," *Handbook of Texas Online* (http://www.tshaonline.org/handbook/online/articles/fpi09), accessed January 24, 2014. Published by the Texas State Historical Association; Kate Bodine Pierce, "PIERCE, JOHN LEONARD," *Handbook of Texas Online* (http://www.tshaonline.org/handbook/online/articles/fpi11), accessed January 24, 2014. Published by the Texas State Historical Association; Ward, Isabell Pierce. "My Father, John Leonard Pierce." Accessed on the D-Day to VE-Day website on 24 January 2014 http://dday.slavnostisvobody.cz/index.php?menu=veterans&submenu=seznam&id=17&lang=en

2. *Ibid.*

3. *Ibid.*

4. *Speed Is the Password: The Story of the 12th Armored Division*. Paris, France: Printed by Desfosses-Neogravure in 1945 for *Stars and Stripes* newspaper as part of the G.I. Stories series; United States Army, "A History of the United States Army Twelfth Armored Division, 15 September, 1942–17 December, 1945" (1947). *World War Regimental Histories*. Book 43. http://digicom.bpl.lib.me.us/ww_reg_his/43

5. Barksdale Hamlett, Jr.'s, biography is from several sources: "Hamlett, Barksdale, Jr." Biography included in Personal Papers. Manuscripts and Folklife Archives. Department of Library Special Collections. Kentucky Library and Museum. Western Kentucky University. Bowling Green, Kentucky. Accessed online on

27 January 2014 at http://digitalcommons. wku.edu/cgi/viewcontent.cgi?article=2016& context=dlsc_mss_fin_aid [Hereafter cited as Hamlett biography.] Barksdale Hamlett, Jr. Gen., USA (dec.). Oral history interview. Senior Officers Debriefing Program. Interviewed in 1976 by Col. Jack Ridgway and Lt. Col. Paul Walter. U.S. Army Military History Research Collection. Barksdale Hamlett Personal Papers. U.S. Army Heritage and Education Center, Carlisle Barracks, PA. See Sections 1 and 2. [Hereafter cited as Hamlett oral history.]

6. *Ibid*. Hamlett oral history Section 3.
7. *Ibid*.
8. *Ibid*.; Hamlett oral history, Section 3, 24–5.
9. John C. Patterson, Maj., USA (dec.) Troop Commander. Troop B. 23rd Cavalry Reconnaissance Squadron [Mechanized]. 16th Armored Division. *My Life*. Memoirs dictated to his daughter Faye Ellen Coleman in 2001 and posted online by his son Clay Patterson in 2011 at http://www.rose316.com/images/ john_my_life_-_part_i.pdf and http://www. rose316.com/images/john_my_life_-_part_ii. pdf [Hereafter cited as Patterson, My Life, Part II]. See also Chapter 7 of Clay Patterson, CPG, FSA Scot. *Patterson: A Scots-Irish Family* (Dandridge, TN: RoseCrag Publications, 2013). My thanks to Clay for a copy of his superb family history.
10. "James E. Norvell 1937." Memorial Page. West Point Alumni Organization. Accessed online on 22 January 2015 at https:// Apps.Westpointaog.Org/Memorials/Article/10 876/. Additional career details traced through back issues of *The Field Artillery Journal* accessible online at http://sill-www.army.mil/ firesbulletin/archives/.
11. "Colonel Percy Harold Perkins, Jr., Obituary." *Savannah Morning News* (17 January 1998). Accessed online at http://savannahnow. com/stories/011798/obits011798.html on 12 February 2015. [Hereafter cited as Perkins obituary.] Jack N. Averitt. *Families of Southern Georgia* (Baltimore, MD: Genealogical Publishing Company, 2007). Reprint of 1964 edition, 20–21; Percy H. Perkins, Jr., Col.,USA (dec.) Executive Officer. Combat Command B. 16th Armored Division. Personal Account. This typewritten record was prepared by Col. Perkins in 1975 for the 16th Armored Division Association. My thanks to Kathy Hoffman, Secretary of the Association, for providing an original of the document. Hereafter cited as Perkins Account.

12. 397th AFAB Unit History; Symroski biography; Symroski obituary.
13. Stanton, 4; Buckheit 16AD, 38.
14. Col. Gordon is mentioned several times in the 12th Armored Division history; United States Army, "A history of the United States Army Twelfth Armored Division, 15 September, 1942–17 December, 1945" (1947). *World War Regimental Histories*. Book 43. Accessed on 2 January 2015 at http://digicom. bpl.lib.me.us/ww_reg_his/43; U.S. Army. 16th Armored Division. 396th Armored Field Artillery Battalion. See Unit Histories for 1 August 1944–31 August 1944 and 1 September 1944–30 September 1944. RG407, NARA; Maj. Hubbard had been promoted to lieutenant colonel in October 1943.
15. 18th AIB Unit History, 4.
16. Gene Eike, Staff Sgt. Squad Leader. A Company / 18th Armored Infantry Battalion / Combat Command A / 16th Armored Division. Phone interview by author, 29 December 2002.
17. Hamlett oral history, Section 3, 25–6.
18. *Ibid*.
19. 397th AFAB Unit History.
20. Houlihan, VIII-8; 18th AIB Unit History.
21. 216AEB History, XII–17.
22. Houlihan, VIII-10.
23. 216AEB History, XII–17–18.
24. "History of the 18th AIB," Weaver, XIII-4; 18th AIB Unit History.

Chapter 5

1. 397th AFAB Unit History.
2. David Levin, "Remembering Camp Shanks," *Hudson Valley Magazine* (August 16, 2010). Accessed online at http://www.hvmag. com/hudson-valley-magazine/september-2010/remembering-camp-shanks/ on 24 January 2013.
3. Buckheit 16AD, 39; 18th AIB Unit History.
4. Polish, IX–3; 18th AIB Unit History.
5. Noble, XXIV-1; Buckheit 16AD, 39; 216AEB History, XII–18–9; 397th AFAB Unit History; For more about USS *Hermitage*, see the *Dictionary of American Naval Fighting Ships* online at http://www.history.navy.mil/ danfs/h5/hermitage-i.htm.
6. Lemmons's letter home was quoted in his daughter's 2014 biography of him; 216AEB History, XII–19; Patterson, My Life, Part 2, 6.

Notes—Chapter 5

7. *Ibid.*; Noble, XXIV-1; Buckheit 16AD, 39.
8. Steece interview; Polish, IX-3.
9. Painter, XIII-21; Barrs, XIII-16; 18th AIB Unit History.
10. *Ibid.*
11. 5th Tank AAR.
12. U.S. Army. 16th Armored Division. 64th Armored Infantry Battalion. Unit History. 1 January 1945 to 31 May 1945. RG407. NARA. [Hereafter cited as 64th AIB Unit History].
13. 397th AFAB Unit History.
14. Eike phone interview.
15. 216AEB History, XII-20 to XII-21.
16. Patterson, My Life, Part 2, 6.
17. 16AD AAR.
18. Noble, XXIV-2 to XXIV-3; U.S. Army. 16th Armored Division. 396th Armored Field Artillery Battalion. See Unit History for 1 March 1945 to 31 March 1945. RG407, NARA; 397th AFAB Unit History.
19. Perkins, 2-3; Averitt, 20-1.
20. 64th AIB Unit History.
21. *Ibid.*; see *Order of Battle of the United States Army. World War II. European Theater of Operations. Divisions*; Capt. Edgar N. Millington, USA. *The Operations of the 64th Armored Infantry Battalion (16th Armored Division) at Pilsen, Czechoslovakia, 5-7 May 1945 (Central Europe Campaign) (Personal Experience of a Machine-Gun Platoon Leader)*. Advanced Infantry Officers Course 1948-1949. The Infantry School. Fort Benning, Georgia, 6-7. Posted online by the U.S. Army Command and General Staff College, Fort Leavenworth, KS; Lt. Col. George B. Pickett, USA, and Capt. Edgar N. Millington, "The Pilsen Story." *Combat Forces Journal* (April 1951), 33-36. [Hereafter cited as "The Pilsen Story."]
22. "George B. Pickett, Jr., 1941." Memorial posted online on the West Point Association of Graduates http://apps.westpointaog.org/memorials/article/12491/.
23. Col. Roffe's biography is taken from the 16th Armored Division Unit Historical Report.
24. *Ibid.*
25. *Ibid.*
26. Col. Greiner biography included in 16th Armored Division Unit Historical Report, 3.
27. Millington, 6-7; The Pilsen Story; See also entries for these dates in Province's *Patton's Third Army*; U.S. Army. 16th Armored Division. Combat Command B. 16th Tank Battalion. After Action Report (280001 Apr 45 to 090001 May 45). Czechoslovakia: 19 May 1945. Hereafter cited as 16th Tank Bn AAR; 64th AIB Unit History; 18th AIB Unit History.
28. Houlihan, VIII-15.
29. Painter, XIII-21; Barrs, XIII-18; 16th Tank Bn AAR, 1-2; Buckheit 16AD, 39; 216AEB History, XII-22; U.S. Army. 16th Armored Division. Combat Command B. After Action Report 28 April 45 to 9 May 45. Czechoslovakia: 22 May 1945. RG407, NARA. [Hereafter cited as 16AD CCB AAR]; 18th AIB Unit History.
30. Houlihan, VIII-17.
31. U.S. Army. 16th Armored Division. Military Police Platoon. After Action Report. Czechoslovakia: 18 May 1945, RG407 NARA. Reprinted in Weaver, VI-3 to VI-4. [Hereafter cited as MP Platoon AAR.]
32. Charles Lemmons letter of 4 May 1945 is quoted in Kathy Hoffman's 2014 biography of her father.
33. U.S. Army. 16th Armored Division, Combat Command B. 64th Armored Infantry Battalion. After Action Report 28 April to 19 May 1945. Czechoslovakia: 19 May 1945. RG407, Archives II, NARA. [Hereafter 64th AIB AAR]; 16AD CCB AAR, 3-4; 64th AIB Unit History.
34. U.S. Army. 16th Armored Division. 216th Armored Medical Battalion. After Action Report. Czechoslovakia: 16 May 1945. RG407, NARA. Reprinted in Weaver, VII-2 to VII-7. [Hereafter cited as 216th Armored Med AAR.]
35. Stanton, 504.
36. Stanton, 334; U.S. Army. 16th Armored Division. 633rd Tank Destroyer Battalion (Self-Propelled). "Original and Final History of the 633d Tank Destroyer Battalion." Fort Bragg, North Carolina: 30 October 1945. [Hereafter cited as "633rd TD BN History."] During World War Two, the U.S. Army organized two types of tank destroyer battalions. Self-propelled battalions mounted anti-tank guns on turreted lightly armored vehicles (M10, M18 and M36). Towed battalions utilized anti-tank guns that had to be towed by a motorized vehicle. The differences were similar to those between self-propelled artillery and towed artillery.
37. *Ibid.*
38. U.S. Army. Third U.S. Army. After Action Report. 3 vols. Germany: 1945, U.S. Army Heritage and Education Center. Carlisle Barracks, Pennsylvania. [Hereafter cited as

USAHEC Archives]; Charles M. Province, *Patton's Third Army: A Chronology of the Third Army Advance August, 1944 to May, 1945* (New York: Hippocrene Books, 1992).

39. For a more detailed discussion of the European Campaign, I recommend the following: Ambrose, Stephen E. *Citizen Soldiers: The U.S. Army from the Normandy Beach to the Bulge to the Surrender of Germany* (New York: Simon & Schuster, 1997); Charles B. MacDonald, *The Mighty Endeavor* (New York: Da Capo P, 1969). MacDonald was a captain in the 2nd Infantry Division during the liberation of western Czechoslovakia and later a U.S. Army historian; Weigley, Russell F. *Eisenhower's Lieutenants: The Campaign of France and Germany 1944–1945* (Bloomington, IN: Indiana U P, 1981); and the U.S. Army's official histories of World War Two, published as the series *The United States Army in World War Two*. I would recommend specifically Gordon A. Harrison's *Cross-Channel Attack*, Martin Blumenson's *Breakout and Pursuit*, Hugh M. Cole's *The Lorraine Campaign*, Charles B. MacDonald's *The Siegfried Line Campaign*, Hugh Cole's *The Ardennes: Battle of the Bulge*, Charles B. MacDonald's *The Last Offensive*, and Jeffrey J. Clarke and Robert Ross Smith's *Riviera to the Rhine*.

Chapter 6

1. *The Army Almanac: A Book of Facts Concerning the Army of the United States*. Washington DC: U.S. Government Printing Office, 1950. Accessed online on 4 February 2014 at http://www.history.army.mil/html/forcestruc/cbtchron/cc/086id.htm; *Order of Battle of the United States Army. World War II. European Theater of Operations. Divisions* Accessed online on 4 February 2014 at http://www.history.army.mil/documents/eto-ob/86id-eto.htm; Maj. Arnold J. Hoebeke, USA, provided an overview of the operations of the 86th Infantry Division and the 343rd Infantry Regiment specifically in his paper *The Operations of the 343d Infantry (86th Division) in the Reduction of the Ruhr Pocket and the Redoubt Area, 28 March, 8 May 1945* (Central Europe Campaign). Advanced Infantry Officers Course 1947–1948. The Infantry School. Fort Benning, Georgia. Posted online by the U.S. Army Maneuver Center for Excellence. Fort Benning Georgia. Accessed online on 5 February 2014 at http://www.benning.army.mil/library/content/virtual/donovanpapers/wwii/stup2/hoebekearnoldj%20maj.pdf. Maj. Hoebeke was Regimental S-4 for the 343rd Infantry at this time; TUSA AAR, 368–384.

2. *Ibid*.

3. TUSA AAR, 370; U.S. Army. 16th Armored Division. 23rd Cavalry Reconnaissance Squadron [Mechanized]. After Action Report 28 April 1945 to 9 May 1945. RG407, NARA. Hereafter cited as 23rd CAV AAR; Schaudt, Howard P. Capt., USA. *The Operations of 23rd Cavalry Reconnaissance Squadron (Mecz) in Pursuit Action with the 86th Infantry Division from Ingolstadt to Wasserburg, Germany*. Advanced Infantry Officers Course 1946–1947. The Infantry School. Fort Benning, Georgia. Posted online by the U.S. Army Maneuver Center for Excellence. Fort Benning Georgia. Accessed online on 5 February 2014 at http://www.benning.army.mil/library/content/virtual/donovanpapers/wwii/stup2/schaudthowardp%20cpt.pdf.

4. TUSA AAR, 370–1.

5. This partial Squadron officer's list was derived from Capt. Schaudt's paper. Despite having reviewed the 23rd Cavalry's records at National Archives II and other sources, I have been unable to identify the Troop Commander for Troop A.

6. Schaudt, 5; Steece interview.

7. Schaudt, 7; Steece interview; 23rd CAV AAR.

8. Hoebeke, 11.

9. TUSA AAR, 371; 23rd CAV AAR; Schaudt, 8–9.

10. 23rd CAV AAR.

11. 23rd CAV AAR; Schaudt, 10–11; 23rd CAV AAR; 23rd CAV Unit History AUG 1945.

12. Schaudt, 10–11; 23rd CAV AAR; U.S. Army. 16th Armored Division. 23rd Cavalry Reconnaissance Squadron [Mechanized]. Unit History. August 1945. RG407, Archives II, NARA. [Hereafter cited as 23rd CAV Unit History AUG 1945.]

13. Schaudt, 11; 23rd CAV AAR.

14. Schaudt, 12–18; 23rd CAV AAR.

15. Schaudt, 12; 23rd CAV AAR; Patterson, My Life, Part 2, 7.

16. Schaudt, 13; 23rd CAV AAR.

17. Schaudt, 13; 23rd CAV AAR.

18. Schaudt, 13–14; 23rd CAV AAR.

19. Schaudt, 13–15; 23rd CAV AAR.

20. Schaudt, 13–14; TUSA AAR, 383; 23rd CAV AAR.

21. *Ibid*.

22. See City of Dorfen website http://www.dorfen.de/stadtgeschichte/blog for more information; 23rd CAV Unit History AUG 1945.
23. Schaudt, 15; 23rd CAV AAR.
24. Schaudt, 15; 23rd CAV AAR.
25. 23rd CAV AAR; Schaudt, 16.
26. *Ibid.*
27. *Ibid.*
28. *Ibid.*
29. *Ibid.*
30. Schaudt, 19; 23rd CAV AAR.
31. 23rd CAV AAR; *My Life*, Part 2, page 7.
32. 23rd CAV AAR; 23rd CAV Unit History AUG 1945.
33. 23rd CAV AAR; 23rd CAV Unit History AUG 1945.
34. Schaudt, 21.
35. 23rd CAV AAR.
36. Schaudt, 21.
37. 23rd CAV AAR.
38. *Ibid.*
39. *Ibid.*
40. *Ibid.*
41. *Ibid.*
42. Yeide, 329.
43. Schaudt, 22; U.S. Army. 16th Armored Division. General Order Number 12. 30 May 1945. RG407, Archives II, NARA. [Hereafter cited as General Order 12.] U.S. Army. 16th Armored Division. Headquarters. Bronze Star Medal Citation, Lt. Col. Raymond G. Adkisson. 30 May 1945. RG407, Archives II, NARA.

Chapter 7

1. TUSA AAR; See also Province's entries for the first days of May 1945.
2. TUSA AAR; Freiherr von Gersdorff, "The Final Phase of the War: From the Rhine to the Czech Border," draft trans. from the German (Oberursel, Germany: U.S. Army, Europe, Historical Division [Foreign Military Studies Branch,] March 1946); Karl Weissenberger, "Battle Sector Xiii (Wehrkreis Xiii) (May 1945)," (Karlsruhe, Germany: U.S. Army, Europe, Historical Division [Foreign Military Studies Branch,] 1946). After the war, U.S. Army historians interviewed hundreds of captured German officers. These historical reports are now kept at the USAHEC Archives.

3. Rudolf Toussaint. "Military Area Prague." Karlsruhe, Germany: U.S. Army, Europe, Historical Division [Foreign Military Studies Branch], written sometime between 1945 & 1954. Copy located at USAHEC Archives.
4. Gerhard Müller, *"The Occupation of Pilsen by the U.S. 16th Armored Division, 16th [Sic] May 1945."* trans. by H. Hintemann. ed. by Col. W. S. Nye (Germany: U.S. Army, Europe, Historical Division [Foreign Military Studies Branch], 1954), USAHEC Archives.
5. *Ibid.*
6. Müller, 4–5.
7. Toussaint, 1–2.
8. Toussaint, 1–2; Czech partisans later reported this to V Corps. See U.S. Army. *V Corps. Operations in the ETO 6 January 42–9 May 45* (Germany: 1945). USAHEC Archives, 450. [Hereafter cited as *V Corps in ETO.*]
9. Toussaint, 1–2.
10. U.S. Army. Seventh U.S. Army. Seventh Army Interrogation Center. Maj. Paul Kubala, Commanding. "Schörner's Evaluation of the Red Army." 3 June 1945. RG 407, NARA.
11. Lt. Col. George Dyer, *XII Corps: Spearhead of Patton's Third Army* (privately published by the XII Corps Historical Association, 1947), 424–6; U.S. Army. Third U.S. Army. XII Corps. 90th Infantry Division. After Action Report, Month of May 1945. RG 407 NARA [Hereafter cited as 90th Infantry Division AAR for May 1945]; John Colby, *War from the Ground Up* (Austin, TX: Nortex P, 1991), 466–9; For 2nd Infantry Division's role, see *Combat History of the Second Infantry Division in World War II* (Nashville, TN: printed for the division by Battery Press, 1946), 150–1; For the 26th Infantry Division's role, see Brig. Gen. William W. Molla's "The Surrender of the 11th Panzer Division." *Yankee Doings* (the newsletter of the 26th Division Association: Dec. 1995), 57–9; Weissenberger, 8; Brig. Gen. Raymond E. Bell, Jr., USA (Ret.) "Giving Up the Ghost." *World War II* magazine. See the September 2005 issue. Brig. Gen. Bell's father, Col. Raymond E. Bell was commander of the 90th Division's 359th Infantry Regiment and was involved with the surrender of the 11th Panzer Division.
12. Edward Taborsky, "Eduard Benes," *Foreign Affairs* (July 1958), 680.

Chapter 8

1. The emergence of the U.S. / Soviet Cold War as demonstrated by the military and diplomatic events in Czechoslovakia in 1945 was the subject of the author's Masters Thesis. Bryan J. Dickerson, "Czechoslovakia 1945: Prelude to the Coming U.S. / Soviet Cold War." (Masters Thesis, Monmouth University, 1999); See also Forrest C. Pogue's "The Decision to Halt at the Elbe." *Command Decisions*. ed. by Kent Roberts Greenfield (New York: Harcourt, Brace & Co., 1959), 374–387.

2. *Ibid.*

3. "SCAF (Supreme Commander Allied Forces) to Bradley [12th Army Group] and 9th Air Force Commanding General 4 May 1945." SCAF Cable No. 335. Found in Nevins, Arthur S. Brig. Gen., USA. Chief of Operations Planning Section. Supreme Headquarters, Allied Expeditionary Force. G-3 (Operations) Division. Personal Papers. USAMHI Archives.

4. TUSA AAR, 392; *V Corps in ETO*; Hobart Gay, Maj. Gen., USA. Chief of Staff. Third U.S. Army. Diary. Personal Papers. USAHEC Archives, 919; U.S. Army. Supreme Headquarters Allied Expeditionary Force (SHAEF). Message from Eisenhower to Bradley, Ref No. FWD-20726 6 May 1945. Outgoing Message File. RG407. NARA; U.S. Army. Twelfth U.S. Army Group. Letter of Instructions No. 22–4 May 1945. RG407. NARA.

5. *Ibid.*

6. *V Corps in ETO*. See Situation Map reprinted on p. 451. A kampfgruppe was an ad hoc combined arms combat formation employed by the German Army in World War Two.

7. *V Corps in ETO*, 450. Col. Mason's Letter of Instruction is reprinted on p. 450.

8. TUSA AAR; *V Corps in ETO*, 450; *Combat History of the Second Infantry Division in World War II*, 150–1; *The First, A Brief History of the 1st Infantry Division, World War II* (Cantigny, IL: privately published the Cantigny First Division Foundation, 1996), 49. This is a reprint of a history printed by the division following WWII; U.S. Army. 97th Infantry Division. 303rd Infantry Regiment. After Battle Report. 12 May 1945. RG407, NARA; U.S. Army. 2nd Infantry Division. 23rd Infantry Regiment. After Action Report for May 1945. Czechoslovakia: 5 June 1945. [Hereafter cited as 23rd Infantry AAR.] Zdenek Roucka, Jaroslav Peklo, and et. als. *Americans in West Bohemia 1945, Exclusive Pictures* (Pilsen, Czech Republic: ZR&T, 2000); U.S. Army. 2nd Cavalry Group. 2nd Cavalry Squadron. After Action Report, May 1945. RG407, NARA; 90th Infantry Division AAR for May 1945; *The Trident Heritage: A Brief History of the 97th Infantry Division and the 97th Army Reserve Command* (Maryland: privately published by the Headquarters of the 97th Army Reserve Command, 1988).

9. *V Corps in ETO*, 450. The V Corps Letter of Instruction is reprinted on page 450.

10. Millington, 7–8; "The Pilsen Story," 33–34; 16th Tank AAR, 2; 64th AIB AAR, 1–2; 16AD CCB AAR, 3.

11. George Thompson. Sgt. Mechanic. Company C / 137th Armored Ordnance Battalion / 16th Armored Division. Phone interview by author 18 January 2000.

12. U.S. Army. 16th Armored Division. After Action Report. 9 June 1945. RG407. NARA. [Hereafter cited as 16AD AAR]; Col. Charles Noble. Commander. Combat Command B / 16th Armored Division. "Noble's Nostalgic Notes: A 16'ner's Experiences in World War II," pp. XXIV-1 through 9 in Dale Weaver's *16th Armored Division History, Patton's Third Army, WWII*; "The Pilsen Story," 34–36.

13. 16th Armored Division AAR; 16AD CCB AAR, 3; 64th AIB AAR, 1–3.

14. *Ibid.*

15. 216AEB History, XII–22.

16. 23rd CAV AAR.

17. 16th Armored Division AAR; Millington, 9; "The Pilsen Story," 34–36; 16AD CCB AAR, 3; 64th AIB Unit History.

18. 16th Armored Division AAR.

19. 16AD CCB AAR, 3.

20. Hamlett oral history, Section 3, 30.

21. 64th AIB AAR, 3–4.

22. 16th Tank AAR, 2.

23. 633rd TD BN History, 4–5

24. 216th Armored Med AAR, VII–6.

Chapter 9

1. Zajicova letter.

2. Vera Fiedlerova, "My Memories on the End of the WW2."

3. Jaroslav Peklo, "The End of War in Pilsen, Bohemia."

4. John Erickson, *The Road to Berlin: Continuing the History of Stalin's War with Germany* (Boulder, CO: Westview P, 1983),

634–5; John MacCormac, "Czech Patriots Take Prague, Then Beg Aid as Foe Attacks," *New York Times*. 6 May 1945: 1+; U.S. Army. SHAEF. Incoming Message File. "Czechoslovak Military Mission (SHAEF) to SHAEF Main, 5 May 1945 (Ref No. Rr-17730)," RG 407, NARA.

5. For more about the Vlasov Army see Catherine Andreyev, *Vlasov and the Russian Liberation Movement: Soviet Reality and Emigre Theories* (Cambridge: U P, 1987). See also Martin Gilbert, *The Day the War Ended: May 8, 1945, Victory in Europe* (New York: Henry Holt, 1995), 78–9; and John Toland, *The Last 100 Days* (New York: Random House, 1966), 576–8; Vlasov and most of his troops were ultimately captured and killed by the Soviets.

6. James Lucas, *Das Reich, The Military Role of 2nd SS Division* (London: Arms and Armour Press, 1991), 192–99. Lucas describes Der Führer Regiment's Prague operation as a rescue mission to save German civilians and wounded from Czech partisans. See also James Lucas, *Last Days of the Reich, The Collapse of Nazi Germany, May 1945* (London: Arms & Armour Press, 1986), 71–94. In both books, Lucas is surprisingly sympathetic to the SS, almost to the point of being an apologist. [Hereafter both works cited by title.]

7. *Americans in West Bohemia 1945.*
8. Zajicova letter.
9. *Americans in West Bohemia 1945.*
10. *Ibid.*; Müller, 8–10.
11. Zajicova letter. Malvina's account is a collaborative effort with her husband Joseph; Joseph Zajic, Citizen of Pilsen, letter to the author, 4 May 1999. Joseph and Malvina were married several years after the war ended.
12. *Ibid.*
13. Quoted in *Americans in West Bohemia 1945.*
14. *Americans in West Bohemia 1945.*
15. Zajicova letter.
16. *Americans in West Bohemia 1945;* Müller, 8–10.
17. Jaroslav Peklo, "The End of War in Pilsen, Bohemia."
18. *Americans in West Bohemia 1945;* Müller, 8–10.

Chapter 10

1. See the Third U.S. Army After Action Report, *V Corps in ETO*, and Lt. Col. Dyer's history of XII Corps for more details.

2. 16th Armored Division AAR; Millington, 12; Noble, XXIV-4; "The Pilsen Story," 35–37; Steece interview; 16AD CCB AAR; 64th AIB AAR, 4; 23rd CAV AAR; 64th AIB Unit History.
3. *Ibid.*
4. Patterson, Part II, 8.
5. 16th Armored Division AAR; Millington, 12; Noble, XXIV-4; "The Pilsen Story," 35–37; Steece interview; 16AD CCB AAR, 3; 64th AIB AAR, 4; 23rd CAV AAR.
6. *Ibid.*
7. *Ibid.*
8. Patterson, Part 2, 8.
9. 16th Armored Division AAR; Millington, 12; Noble, XXIV-4; "The Pilsen Story," 35–37; Steece interview; 16AD CCB AAR, 3; 64th AIB AAR, 4; 23rd CAV AAR.
10. *Ibid.*
11. 216AEB History, XII–22.
12. 16th Armored Division AAR; "The Pilsen Story," 35–37; 16AD CCB AAR, 4; 64th AIB AAR, 4; 64th AIB Unit History, 3–4; General Order 12; U.S. Army. 16th Armored Division. Headquarters. Bronze Star Medal Citation, 1st Lt. Bernard N. Brown. 30 May 1945. RG407, Archives II, NARA.
13. *Ibid.*; Patterson, *My Life*, Part 2, 4.
14. John C. Patterson, Capt., USA. Letter to His Parents, 9 May 1945. Reprinted in Clay Patterson's *Patterson: A Scots-Irish Family*, 222–3.
15. 16th Armored Division AAR; "The Pilsen Story," 35–37; 16th Armored CCB AAR, 4; 64th AIB AAR, 4.
16. *Ibid.*; Mooney interview; "The Pilsen Story," 35–37.
17. Steece interview.
18. *Americans in West Bohemia 1945.*
19. Perkins Account, 3.
20. "Division Hq," II–8.
21. Polish, IX–5.
22. Hamlett oral history, Section 3, 30.
23. U.S. Army. 16th Armored Division. Division Artillery Headquarters. Headquarters Battery. Unit History. 17 March 1944 to 30 May 1945. Czechoslovakia: May 1945. RG 407, Archives II, NARA; 16AD CCB AAR, 3.
24. Zajicova letter; Vera Fiedlerova, Citizen of Pilsen. "My Memories on the End of the WW2," from a letter to the author, 28 June 1998.
25. Peklo, "The End of the War in Pilsen, Bohemia."
26. Malek quoted in Peter S. Green, "American Veterans Return 45 Years After

Liberating Pilsen." United Press International. 5 May 1990. Accessed online at http://www.upi.com/archives/1990/05/05/american-veterans-return-45-years-after-liberating-pilsen/3690641880000/ on 4 December 1990.
27. *V Corps in ETO*, 452.
28. Perkins Account, 3.
29. "The Pilsen Story," 35–37; 64th AIB AAR, 5; 64th AIB Unit History, 4.
30. 16AD CCB AAR, 4; 64th AIB Unit History, 4.
31. Perkins Account, 4.
32. "Division Hq.," p. II-9.
33. 16th Tank AAR, 2; 16AD CCB AAR, 3.
34. 16AD CCB AAR, 3.
35. 16th Tank AAR; 16th Tank History; Noble, XXIV-4; 16AD CCB AAR, 4–5.
36. 16AD CCB AAR, 4.
37. 16th Armored Division AAR; Noble, XXIV-1 through XXIV-15; Mooney interview; 64th AIB AAR, 4; 16AD CCB AAR, 4; 64th AIB Unit History, 4.
38. *Ibid.*; U.S. Army. 16th Armored Division, Headquarters. Citation for Bronze Star Medal. Technical Sgt. John Nicolson. 30 May 1945. RG407, Archives II, NARA; U.S. Army. 16th Armored Division. Headquarters. Citation for Bronze Star Medal, Pfc. Albert Zarback. 30 May 1945. RG407, Archives II, NARA. [Hereafter Zarback BSM Citation.]
39. Malvina letter; "My Memories on the End of the WW2."
40. 16th Armored Division AAR; 16th Tank AAR, 3.
41. *Ibid.*
42. *Ibid.*
43. *Ibid.*
44. The sources for the German surrender of Pilsen are: Generalmajor Müller's "The Occupation of Pilsen By The U.S. 16th Armored Division, 16th [sic] May 1945;" Col. Noble's "Noble's Nostalgic Notes: A 16'ner's Experiences in World War II." Though Noble was not present at the German surrender, he was briefed by his deputy, Lt. Col. Perkins who was there; 16AD CCB AAR, 4; Perkins Account, 4, and *V Corps in ETO*, 452.
45. *Ibid.*; Perkins Account, 4; Perkins wrote of Noble calling on the Germans to surrender. Interestingly enough, Noble did not mention this in his account of Pilsen's liberation; 64th AIB Unit History, 4.
46. *Ibid.*; Lt. Col. Charles Schaeffer, USA (ret.). 2nd Lt. Adjutant. 216th Armored Engineers Battalion / 16th Armored Division. Interview by author, Pilsen, 7 May 2000. [Hereafter cited as Schaeffer interview.]
47. *Ibid.*
48. *Ibid.*
49. Perkins Account, 4.
50. *Ibid.*
51. Schaeffer interview.
52. Perkins Account, 4; A photo-copy of the surrender note was reprinted in *The Sixteener* (Sixteenth Armored Division Newsletter). Summer 2014.
53. Perkins Account, 5.
54. *Ibid.*
55. *Ibid.*
56. Schaeffer interview.
57. Perkins Account, 5.
58. Müller, 10–11.
59. General Order 12; U.S. Army. 16th Armored Division. Headquarters. Citation for Bronze Star Medal. Technical Sgt. Mickey R. Seeley. 30 May 1945. RG407, Archives II, NARA; Zarback BSM Citation.
60. 23rd Cavalry AAR, 10.
61. *Ibid.*
62. 16th Armored Division AAR; 16th Tank AAR, 3–4; 16AD CCB AAR, 4.
63. 16th Armored Division AAR; *Trident Heritage*; "The Pilsen Story," 35–37; 16AD CCB AAR, 4.
64. Lemmons letters of 13 and 16 May 1945 quoted in his daughter's biography of him.
65. *Ibid.*
66. 16th Tank AAR, 4.
67. MP Platoon AAR, VI-4.
68. 396th AFAB AAR; U.S. Army. 16th Armored Division. 396th Armored Field Artillery Battalion. Unit History for 1 May 1945 to 31 May 1945. RG407, NARA. [Hereafter cited as 396th AFAB Unit History May45].
69. 16th Armored Division AAR; "The Pilsen Story," 35–37; 16AD CCB AAR, 4; 64th AIB Unit History, 4–5. The awarding of the Combat Infantry Badge was awarded per 16th Armored Division General Order No. 8. Two officers, three warrant officers and 101 enlisted soldiers of the 64th AIB were not awarded the Combat Infantry Badge as they were not physically present with the Battalion during the battle.

Chapter 11

1. 16th Armored AAR, 12; U.S. Army. 16th Armored Division. Combat Command R. 26th Tank Battalion. After Action Report.

Czechoslovakia: 21 May 1945. RG407, Archives II, NARA.
2. 26th Tank Battalion AAR; 16th Armored AAR, 13.
3. *Ibid.*
4. *Ibid.*
5. *Ibid.*
6. 23rd CAV AAR.
7. 16th Armored Division AAR; 26th Tank Battalion AAR.
8. U.S. Army. 16th Armored Division. Combat Command A. Unit History. Czechoslovakia: 1 June 1945. RG407, Archives II, NARA.
9. *Ibid.*; 23rd CAV AAR.
10. *Ibid.*; 16th Armored AAR, 11; 393rd AFAB AAR; 18th AIB Unit History.
11. *Ibid.*
12. *Ibid.*
13. Eike interview.
14. 16th Armored Division AAR; U.S. Army. 16th Armored Division. Combat Command A. 18th Armored Infantry Battalion. Unit History. 1945? RG407, NARA; Harley Barrs. Armored Infantryman. Anti-tank-Platoon / B Company / 18th Armored Infantry Battalion / Combat Command A / 16th Armored Division. "Recollections." in *16th Armored History*, XIII-18; Lt. Col. Painter "Recollections," p. XIII-21; "The Pilsen Story," 35–37.
15. *Ibid.*
16. 16th Armored AAR, 11.
17. Gene Eike, Staff Sgt. Squad Leader. A Company / 18th Armored Infantry Battalion / Combat Command A / 16th Armored Division. Interview by the author at the 16th Armored Division Association Reunion, Baltimore, Maryland, 16 October 1998. [Hereafter reunion cited as 16th Armored Reunion.]
18. 23rd CAV AAR.
19. 393rd AFAB AAR.
20. 18th AIB Unit History.
21. See *The Trident Heritage* for more about the 97th Infantry Division.
22. For more about the 2nd Infantry Division, see *Second to None*.
23. *Trident Heritage*.
24. George Shultz, Jr., Pfc.. Combat Photographer, Company I / 23rd Infantry Regiment /2nd Infantry Division. author's Questionnaire. February 1998.
25. 16th Armored AAR, 13.
26. 16th Armored AAR, 13; 16th Armored CCB AAR, 4; 216th Armored Med AAR, VII-6.
27. 23rd CAV AAR.
28. 64th AIB AAR, 8.

Chapter 12

1. Prague Radio broadcast quoted in John MacCormac, "Czech Patriots Take Prague, Then Beg Aid as Foe Attacks," *New York Times*. 6 May 1945: 1+.
2. Milka Vildova. Citizen of Stenovice, Czechoslovakia. Interview by the author, Epjovice, Czech Republic, 7 May 2000.
3. Robert I. Gilbert, Lt. Col., USA (Ret.). 1st Lt. Executive Officer. Company F / 2nd Battalion / 38th Infantry Regiment / 2nd Infantry Division. Phone interview by author, 29 March 1998; U.S. Army. SHAEF. Incoming Message File. "Czechoslovak Military Mission (SHAEF) to SHAEF Main, 6 May 1945 (Ref No. Rr-17731)," RG 407, NARA; U.S. Army. 4th Armored Division. Combat Command B. S-2 (Intelligence) Journal. RG407, NARA; See entry for 7 May 1945. This information was sent by CCA to 4th Armored G-2 and the other two division combat commands; 16AD CCB AAR; U.S. Army. SHAEF. Incoming Message File. "Twelfth Army Group to SHAEF Forward, 7 May 1945 (Ref. No. Qx–31923)." RG407, NARA; U.S. Army. SHAEF. Outgoing Message File. Message from Eisenhower to U.S. Military Mission, Moscow, 8 May 1945 (Ref. No. FWD-21001)." RG407, NARA; U.S. Army. SHAEF. Outgoing Message File. Message from Eisenhower to U.S. Military Mission, Moscow, 8 May 1945 (Ref. No. FWD-21006)." RG407, NARA.
4. U.S. Army. 16th Armored Division. Division Headquarters. Assistant Chief of Staff (G-2 Intelligence). G-2 Journal. RG407, Archives II, NARA. See entries for 6 and 7 May 1945; U.S. Army. 16th Armored Division. Division Headquarters. Assistant Chief of Staff (G-2 Intelligence). After Action Report 28 APR to 9 MAY 45. RG407, Archives II, NARA. See entries for 6 and 7 May 1945; CCB AAR; U.S. Army. 16th Armored Division. Division Headquarters. Assistant Chief of Staff (G-2 Intelligence). G-2 Periodic Report #9. 7 May 1945. RG407, Archives II, NARA
5. Ladislas Farago, *Patton: Ordeal and Triumph* (New York: Ivan Obolensky, 1963), 785–6; Ladislas Farago, *The Last Days of Patton* (New York: Berkeley Books, 1981), 49–50; George S. Patton, Jr. *War as I Knew It* (New York: Bantam, 1979), 309; John Toland, *The Last 100 Days* (New York: Random House,

1966)p. 566; After the war, Capt. Fodor would launch a highly popular series of travel guides.
6. "The Pilsen Story," 35–37; 16AD CCB AAR, 4.
7. Jack Gallagher, Sgt. Tank Commander. D Company / 5th Tank Battalion / Combat Command A / 16th Armored Division. Interview by author at 16th Armored Division Association Reunion, Baltimore, Maryland 16 October 1998; "The Pilsen Story," pp. 35–37.
8. Krusheski interviews.
9. Bradley quoted in The *Last Days of Patton*. p. 50, and *Ordeal and Triumph*, 787; *War as I Knew It*, 309; Diary of Hobart Gay, 929; Omar N. Bradley, *A Soldier's Story* (New York: Henry Holt, 1951), 549.
10. *Ibid*.
11. Polish, IX-6. See also Polish, "Worth a Second Thought," Weaver, IX-8; The block quote is taken from Solomon Polish, Warrant Officer. Division Message Center Officer, Division Headquarters (Forward) / 16th Armored Division, letter to the author, 9 June 1998.
12. *Ibid*.
13. *A Soldier's Story*, 549; Diary of Hobart Gay, 929; *Ordeal and Triumph*, 787; Toussaint, "Military Area Prague."
14. "The Pilsen Story," p. 37.
15. Hamlett oral history, Section 3, 31.
16. *Ibid*.
17. *Ibid*.
18. Taborsky, 680. After the war, Taborsky served as Ambassador to Sweden and was serving there when President Benes was ousted by a Communist Coup in 1948. Taborsky subsequently sought asylum in the West.
19. John Deane, *Strange Alliance* (New York: Viking, 1947), 159; The emergence of the U.S / Soviet Cold War as demonstrated by the debate over the liberation of Prague and other military / political events in Czechoslovakia in 1945 was the subject of my Master's Thesis. Bryan J. Dickerson, "Czechoslovakia 1945: Prelude to the Coming U.S. / Soviet Cold War." (Master's Thesis, Monmouth University, West Long Branch, NJ, 1999).
20. *Ibid*.; U.S. Army historian Forrest C. Pogue examined the controversy of Eisenhower's decisions to not capture Berlin and to not liberate Prague in his "The Decision to Halt at the Elbe." *Command Decisions*. In the series *U.S. Army in World War II, The European Theater of Operations*. ed. by Kent Roberts Greenfield (New York: Harcourt, Brace & Co., 1959), 374–387.

Chapter 13

1. *V Corps in ETO*, 454.
2. Huebner's Letter of Instruction 061500B MAY 1945 reprinted in *V Corps in ETO*, 452.
3. Smith interview; Gene Eike, Staff Sgt. Squad Leader. A Company / 18th Armored Infantry Battalion / Combat Command A / 16th Armored Division. Phone interview by author, 29 December 2002.
4. 16th Tank Battalion AAR, 4.
5. 64th AIB AAR, 5.
6. *Ibid*., 6.
7. *Ibid*.
8. *Ibid*.
9. *Ibid*., 6–7.
10. 26th Tank Battalion AAR.
11. 216th Armored Med AAR, VII-7.
12. CCA 16th Armored Unit History, 3; 18th AIB Unit History.
13. 633rd TD BN History, 6–7.
14. 23rd CAV AAR.

Chapter 14

1. For the account of the Pratt Mission, the following sources were utilized: *V Corps in the ETO*, 454–7; the 16th Armored Division AAR, 14–15; U.S. Army. 16th Armored Division. 23rd Cavalry Reconnaissance Squadron. After Action Report. 28 April, 9 May 1945. RG 407, NARA; the Diary of Hobart Gay, 919; and Keith M. Schmedemann. Col., USA (Ret.). Maj. Assistant G-1 (Personnel) Officer. V Corps. Phone interview by author. 6 May 1998. Schmedemann served on the V Corps staff with Lt. Col. Pratt; Bartos, Omar and Ramona Murphy Bartos. "At the Mercy of the Enemy." *World War II* (October 2006): pp. 42–45; U.S. Army. Third U.S. Army. V Corps. Headquarters. Public Affairs Office. Maj. Robert G. Rashid. Press Release. Pratt Mission. May 1945. Reprinted as "Milwaukeean Won Medal for His Role in Surrender." *Milwaukee Journal* (14 September 1945), 1. Hereafter cited as "Rashid, 1."
2. *Ibid*.
3. *Ibid*.; Knoche, Eldon. "Pratt Received Silver Star in WWII." *Milwaukee Journal-Sentinel* (24 October 1995), 4B.
4. *Ibid*.; *V Corps in ETO*, 454.
5. *Ibid*.; Pratt quoted in Rashid, 1. The de-

tails of the Pratt Mission in Prague are primarily from the Rashid press release.
6. Ibid.
7. Ibid.
8. Rashid, 1.
9. Ibid.
10. Ibid.; V Corps in the ETO, 454–7; the 16th Armored Division AAR, 14–15; 23rd Cavalry AAR; Bartos, 42–45.
11. Verber quoted in Rashid, 1.
12. Pratt quoted in Rashid, 1.
13. Rashid, 1; 23rd Cavalry AAR.
14. Pratt quoted in Rashid, 1.
15. Rashid, 1. V Corps in the ETO, 454–7; the 16th Armored Division AAR, 14–15; 23rd Cavalry AAR; Bartos, 42–45.
16. Ibid. The Bartos article incorrectly stated on page 45 that Generalfeldmarschall Schörner had already fled to Bavaria.
17. Verber quoted in Rashid, 1.
18. Ibid.
19. Pratt quoted in Rashid, 1.
20. Ibid.
21. Ibid.
22. Rashid, 1.
23. Ibid.
24. Pratt quoted in Pratt p. 1.
25. Ibid.
26. Ibid.
27. Ibid.; Since the Pratt Mission occurred after the German surrender, the distinction of having advanced the farthest east of any combat operation belongs to another Third Army unit, the 11th Armored Division. On 6 May, patrols of its Troop B, 41st Cavalry Reconnaissance Squadron advanced to the Austrian, Czech border at Horzenschlag, which is about 40 kilometers west of the point reached by the Pratt Mission. See U.S. Army. 11th Armored Division. After Action Report. June 1945? RG 407, Archives II, NARA; U.S. Army. 16th Armored Division. Headquarters. Bronze Star Medal Citation. Maj. Carl J. O'Dowd. 30 May 1945. RG407, Archives II, NARA; U.S. Army. V Corps. Headquarters. Letter of Commendation. 11 May 1945. RG407, Archives II, NARA. Brig. Gen. John L. Pierce added his endorsement to Maj. Gen. Huebner's Letter of Commendation.

Chapter 15

1. Maj. Gen. Huebner's Letter of Instruction for 081700 May 1945 was reprinted in V Corps in ETO, 456.

2. The dropping of the atomic bombs and the subsequent Japanese surrender cancelled the planned invasion of the Japanese Home Islands. The 97th Infantry Division was deployed to the Pacific and did serve for several months on occupation duty in Japan. See Trident Heritage for more about the 97th Infantry Division's unique role in World War Two.
3. Shultz Questionnaire.
4. 16th Tank AAR, 4.
5. Ibid.
6. Steece interview.
7. Smith interview.
8. Noble, XXIV–6; Houlihan, VIII–18.
9. Noble, XXIV–8.
10. 216AEB, XII–23.
11. Painter, XIII–21 to XIII–22; Barrs, "Recollections," XIII–18.
12. Eike interview, 29 December 2002.
13. 633rd TD BN History, 6–7.
14. 23rd Cavalry AAR, 11; Noble, XXIV–8.
15. V Corps in ETO, 464; MP Platoon AAR, VI–4.
16. Mooney interview.
17. Houlihan, VIII–20.
18. 18th AIB Unit History.
19. 18th AIB Unit History.
20. V Corps in ETO, 458; 18th AIB Unit History.
21. 64th AIB Unit History, 4.
22. 18th Armored Infantry Battalion Unit History; 16th Tank Battalion Unit History.
23. Noble, XXIV–9.
24. Noble, XXIV–9.
25. Hamlett oral history, Section 3, 32–4.
26. Steece interview.
27. Lemmons biography.
28. Gen. Robertson's experiences were shared with me by two veterans of his division: retired Lt. Gen. Herron Maples (formerly of the 15th Field Artillery Battalion) and retired Maj. James Smathers (formerly of the 38th Infantry Regiment). See Herron N. Maples, Lt. Gen. USA (Dec.). Maj. S-3 (Operations) Officer. 15th Field Artillery Battalion / 2nd Infantry Division, letter to the author, 16 March 1998; Maples phone interview by author. 31 March 1998; James A. Smathers, Maj., USA (Ret.). Pfc. BAR Rifleman. I Company / 3rd Battalion / 38th Infantry Regiment / 2nd Infantry Division. Phone interview by author, 28 December 2002; Carmine Caiazzo. C Company / 1st Battalion / 9th Infantry Regiment / 2nd Infantry Division, letter to the author. 13 February 1998.

29. U.S. Army. 94th Infantry Division, G-2 (Intelligence) Journal, RG407, NARA. See Entry for 9 September 1945.
30. Hamlett oral history, Section 4, 2.
31. Bryan J. Dickerson, "Ernest N. Harmon and the Challenges of Occupation." *Journal of America's Military Past* (Winter 2000), 53–62; Harmon, Ernest N. with Milton MacKaye and William Rosse MacKaye. *Combat Commander, Autobiography of a Soldier* (Englewood Cliffs, NJ: Prentice Hall, 1970).
32. *Ibid.*
33. Noble, XXIV-11; 16th AD UHR, 2.
34. *V Corps in ETO*, 464.
35. 216AEB History, XII-23.
36. 216AEB History, XII-23.
37. Thompson interview.

Chapter 16

1. Stephen E. Ambrose, *Citizen Soldiers: The U.S. Army from the Normandy Beach to the Bulge to the Surrender of Germany* (New York: Simon & Schuster, 1997), 280–83. Ambrose has taken the U.S. Army figures and put them into tables for each division involved that served with the AEF.
2. Earl F. Ziemke. *The U.S. Army in the Occupation of Germany 1944–1946* (Washington, D.C.: Center of Military History, 1990), 328–330.
3. *Ibid.*
4. *Ibid.*
5. *Ibid.* See also pp. 320–21 for the VE Day troop strengths and occupation force strength.
6. *Ibid.*, 334.
7. Buckheit 16AD, 39.
8. U.S. Army, Third U.S. Army, XXII Corps, 79th Infantry Division, *The Cross of Lorraine: A Combat History of the 79th Infantry Division, June 1942–December 1945* (Nashville, TN: Battery Press, 1986 reprint of 1946 edition) USAHEC Archives. Hereafter cited as *The Cross of Lorraine*, pp. 137–38.
9. *Ibid.* Lt. Col. James W. Dollar, USA (dec.), Letter to the author, 25 April 1998; U.S. Army. 79th Infantry Division. 314th Infantry Regiment. *Through Combat: The 314th Infantry Regiment.* Privately published by the 314th Infantry Regiment in 1945. See pp. 90–91. Accessed online on 6 May 2014 at http://privateletters.net/documents.html. Hereafter cited as *Through Combat.*; 18th AIB Unit History.

10. Dollar, James W. Lt. Col., USA (dec.). 1st Lt. Staff Officer. Headquarters Company / 315th Infantry Regiment / 79th Infantry Division. Letters to the author, 25 April 1998, 20 November 1999 and 2 November 2002.
11. *Ibid.*; 18th AIB Unit History.
12. Eike phone interview, 6 October 2002; Krusheski interviews; Steece interview; Thompson phone interview, 18 January 2000, and email to the author, 23 May 2014.
13. 216AEB History, XII-27 to XII-28.
14. Patterson, My Life, Part 2, 10.
15. Col. Noble biography; Noble, XXIV-11 to XXIV-13; Perkins Account, 7; Perkins obituary; Averitt, 20–21.
16. Hamlett, oral history, Section 4, 2–3.
17. Mooney interview.

Chapter 17

1. 633rd TD BN History, 8–9.
2. *717th Tank Battalion Record.*
3. Buckheit 16AD, 39.
4. 18th AIB Unit History.
5. *Ibid.*
6. Buckheit 16AD, 39.

Chapter 18

1. Greene biography.
2. "My Father, John Leonard Pierce"; Kate Bodine Pierce, "Pierce, John Leonard."
3. See page 86 of the 12th Armored Division History.
4. Col. Noble biography; Noble, XXIV-11 to XXIV-13.
5. Hamlett biography; Hamlett oral history, Section 4, 4–10.
6. Lt. Col. Adkisson's burial information was obtained from http://www.findagrave.com/cgi-bin/fg.cgi?page=gr&grid=8219682.
7. Painter, XIII-22.
8. Barrs, XIII-19.
9. Schaudt's death information was obtained from the Department of Veterans Affairs Grave Locator website.
10. Eike phone interview, 6 October 2002.
11. Krusheski interviews.
12. Lewellen letter, 31 May 2000.
13. Schaeffer interviews.
14. Thompson phone interview, 18 January 2000.
15. Steece interview.
16. Knoche, 4B.
17. Sol Polish, Division Message Center

Officer, Division Headquarters (Forward), 16th Armored Division. "More on the Enigma Secret Cryptographic Device," *Harbor Watch* (July 3, 1998), 8. Sol sent me copies of several of his columns including this one; Polish, IX–6.

18. Lemmons Papers; Randy Allen. "Dean of Policemen to Retire After 35 Years of Gun, Badge." *Kentucky Enquirer* (4 March 1979), 7+. My thanks to Kathy Hoffman for a copy of this article.

19. Patterson, My Life, Part 2, 10–1. Additional details provided by his son's website, www.rose316.com; Patterson, *Patterson: A Scots-Irish Family*, 224–34; U.S. Army. 16th Armored Division. Headquarters. General Orders Number 9. 19 May 1945. RG407, Archives II, NARA; U.S. Army. 16th Armored Division. Headquarters. Bronze Star Medal Citation, 1st Lt. John C. Patterson. 19 May 1945. RG407, Archives II, NARA.

20. "James E. Norvell 1937"; 396th AFAB Unit History May45.

21. Semmelmeyer Tribute.

22. "George B. Pickett, Jr., 1941"; A sampling of his writings include: "What Profiteth a Nation?" *Military Review* (July 1954), 3–6; "Are You Imaginative Military Thinker? *Military Review* (October 1959), 34–7; "Task Force Crombez at Chip'yong-Ni." *Armor* (July–Aug 1952), 34–38; "Tanks in Korea 1950–1951." *Armor* (Nov, Dec 1952), 12–16; For his receiving the Silver Star, see 64th AIB Unit History, 5.

23. Perkins obituary; Averitt, 20–21; Perkins Account, 7.

24. See Footnote 45.

25. Hugh M. Cole. *The Ardennes: Battle of the Bulge.* In the series *The United States Army in World War Two, The European Theater of Operations* (Washington, D.C.: Office of the Chief of Military History, Department of the Army, 1965). See Chapter 12.

26. Symroski biography; Symroski obituary.

27. Smith obituary. *Washington Post* (2 November 2013). Accessed online on 28 October 2015 at http://www.legacy.com/obituaries/washingtonpost/obituary.aspx?pid=167809015; I met Col. Smith and talked with him at length at the Association's 1999 Reunion in Baltimore.

28. Mooney interview; Oscar Jackson Mooney, Jr., obituary. *The Daily Home* (8 December 2015). Accessed online at http://www.legacy.com/obituaries/dailyhome/obituary.aspx?n=oscar-jackson-mooney&pid=176805077& on 9 December 2015.

29. James W. Dollar, Lt. Col., USA (dec.). "Constabulary Constables." *Cold War Times, The Online Newsletter of the Cold War Museum* (November / December 2002), 12–17. [The author of this book served as editor of *CWT* from 2001 to 2003.] Dollar letter, 25 April 1998.

30. Milka Vildova-Yeglin interview.

Chapter 19

1. For an excellent discussion of the Communist Coup and the first twenty years of Soviet Communist domination of Czechoslovakia, see Szulc, Tad. *Czechoslovakia Since World War II*. New York: Viking P, 1971. Szulc was a reporter who covered the Prague Spring.

2. Peter S. Green, "American Veterans Return 45 Years After Liberating Pilsen." United Press International. May 5, 1990. Accessed online at http://www.upi.com/archives/1990/05/05/american-veterans-return-45-years-after-liberating-pilsen/3690641880000/ on 4 December 2015. [Hereafter cited as Green 1]; Peter S. Green, "West Bohemians Celebrate Liberation by American Gis." United Press International. May 7, 1990. Accessed online at http://www.upi.com/archives/1990/05/06/west-bohemians-celebrate-liberation-by-american-gis/9002641966400/ on 4 December 2015. [Hereafter cited as Green 2]; Henry Kamm, "Pilsen Journal: G.I.'S or Russians? Time to Show the Snapshots." *New York Times*, April 11, 1990. Accessed online on 4 December 2015 at http://www.nytimes.com/1990/04/11/world/pilsen-journal-gi-s-or-russians-time-to-show-the-snapshots.html.

3. *Ibid.*

4. *Ibid.*; Peter S. Green's quote is from his 7 May 1990 article.

5. Robert H. Carlson, Maj. (USA) (dec.). 1st Lt. Executive Officer, Cannon Company. 38th Infantry Regiment. 2nd Infantry Division, letter to the author, 24 March 1998; Chylinski quoted in Green 2.

6. Havel quoted in Green 2.

7. Green 1; Green 2.

Works Cited

Official U.S. Army Documents
(Record Group 407, National Archives II, College Park, MD)

U.S. Army. Department of War. Adjutant General's Office. Order AG-320-2 (3-26-1943). 2 April 1943.

U.S. Army. 11th Armored Division. After Action Report. Germany: June 1945?

U.S. Army. V Corps. Headquarters. Letter of Commendation. 11 May 1945.

U.S. Army. 4th Armored Division. Combat Command B. S-2 (Intelligence) Journal.

U.S. Army. Headquarters. Army Ground Forces. Memorandum for the Adjutant General. 322/5 (16th Armd Div) (R) Subject: Reorganization of 16th Armored Division. 1 September 1943.

U.S. Army. 94th Infantry Division. G-2 (Intelligence) Journal.

U.S. Army. 97th Infantry Division. 303rd Infantry Regiment. After Battle Report. Czechoslovakia: 12 May 1945.

U.S. Army. 2nd Cavalry Group. 2nd Cavalry Squadron. After Action Report, May 1945.

U.S. Army. 2nd Infantry Division. 23rd Infantry Regiment. After Action Report for May 1945. Czechoslovakia: 5 June 1945.

U.S. Army. Seventh U.S. Army. Seventh Army Interrogation Center. Maj. Paul Kubala, Commanding. "Schörner's Evaluation of the Red Army." 3 June 1945.

U.S. Army. 16th Armored Division. After Action Report. Czechoslovakia: 9 June 1945.

U.S. Army. 16th Armored Division. Combat Command A. 18th Armored Infantry Battalion. Unit History. Czechoslovakia: October 1945.

U.S. Army. 16th Armored Division. Combat Command A. 5th Tank Battalion. After Action Report. Czechoslovakia: May 1945.

U.S. Army. 16th Armored Division. Combat Command A. Unit History. Czechoslovakia: 1 June 1945.

U.S. Army. 16th Armored Division. Combat Command B. 16th Tank Battalion. After Action Report (280001 Apr 45 to 090001 May 45). Czechoslovakia: 19 May 1945.

U.S. Army. 16th Armored Division. Combat Command B. 16th Tank Battalion. Unit History. 1945.

U.S. Army. 16th Armored Division. Combat Command B. 64th Armored Infantry Battalion. After Action Report 28 April, 19 May 1945. Czechoslovakia: 19 May 1945.

U.S. Army. 16th Armored Division. Combat Command B. 64th Armored Infantry Battalion. Unit History. 1 January 1945 to 31 May 1945.

U.S. Army. 16th Armored Division. Combat Command B. After Action Report for 28 April to 9 May 1945. Czechoslovakia: 22 May 1945.

U.S. Army. 16th Armored Division. Combat Command R. 26th Tank Battalion. After Action Report. Czechoslovakia: 21 May 1945.

U.S. Army. 16th Armored Division. Division Artillery Headquarters. Headquarters Battery. Battery History. Camp Chaffee, Arkansas. 1944.

U.S. Army. 16th Armored Division. Division Artillery Headquarters. Headquarters Battery. Unit History, 17 March 1944 to 30 May 1945. Czechoslovakia: May 1945.

U.S. Army. 16th Armored Division. Division Headquarters. Assistant Chief of Staff (G-2 Intelligence). After Action Report 28 APR to 9 MAY 45.

U.S. Army. 16th Armored Division. Division Headquarters. Assistant Chief of Staff (G-2 Intelligence). G-2 Journal.

U.S. Army. 16th Armored Division. Division Headquarters. Assistant Chief of Staff (G-2 Intelligence). G-2 Periodic Report #9. 7 May 1945.

U.S. Army. 16th Armored Division. Division Headquarters. Bronze Star Medal Citation, Lt. Col. Raymond G. Adkisson. 30 May 1945.

U.S. Army. 16th Armored Division. Division Headquarters. Bronze Star Medal Citation, 1st Lt. Bernard N. Brown. 30 May 1945.

U.S. Army. 16th Armored Division. Division Headquarters. Bronze Star Medal Citation, Technical Sgt. John Nicolson. 30 May 1945.

U.S. Army. 16th Armored Division. Division Headquarters. Bronze Star Medal Citation, Maj. Carl J. O'Dowd. 30 May 1945.

U.S. Army. 16th Armored Division. Division Headquarters. Bronze Star Medal Citation, 1st Lt. John C. Patterson. 19 May 1945.

U.S. Army. 16th Armored Division. Division Headquarters. Bronze Star Medal Citation, Technical Sgt. Mickey R. Seeley. 30 May 1945.

U.S. Army. 16th Armored Division. Division Headquarters. Bronze Star Medal Citation, Pfc. Albert Zarback. 30 May 1945.

U.S. Army. 16th Armored Division. Division Headquarters. General Order Number 12. 30 May 1945.

U.S. Army. 16th Armored Division. Division Headquarters. General Orders Number 9. 19 May 1945.

U.S. Army. 16th Armored Division. Military Police Platoon. After Action Report. Czechoslovakia: 18 May 1945.

U.S. Army. 16th Armored Division. 633rd Tank Destroyer Battalion (Self-Propelled). "Original and Final History of the 633d Tank Destroyer Battalion." Fort Bragg, NC: 30 October 1945.

U.S. Army. 16th Armored Division. 23rd Cavalry Reconnaissance Squadron [Mechanized]. After Action Report (Period 0001, 28 April to 0001, 9 May 1945). Czechoslovakia: May 1945.

U.S. Army. 16th Armored Division. 23rd Cavalry Reconnaissance Squadron [Mechanized]. Unit History. 1 January 1945.

U.S. Army. 16th Armored Division. 23rd Cavalry Reconnaissance Squadron [Mechanized]. Unit History. August 1945.

U.S. Army. 16th Armored Division. 216th Armored Medical Battalion. After Action Report. Czechoslovakia: 16 May 1945.

U.S. Army. 16th Armored Division. 396th Armored Field Artillery Battalion. After Action Report. May 1945.

U.S. Army. 16th Armored Division. 396th Armored Field Artillery Battalion. Unit History. 15 July 1943–31 July 1943.

U.S. Army. 16th Armored Division. 396th Armored Field Artillery Battalion. Unit History. 1 August 1944–31 August 1944.

U.S. Army. 16th Armored Division. 396th Armored Field Artillery Battalion. Unit History. 1 September 1944–30 September 1944.

U.S. Army. 16th Armored Division. 396th Armored Field Artillery Battalion. Unit History for 1 March 1945 to 31 March 1945.

U.S. Army. 16th Armored Division. 396th Armored Field Artillery Battalion. Unit History for 1 May 1945 to 31 May 1945.

U.S. Army. 16th Armored Division. 397th Armored Field Artillery Battalion. Unit History. 1945.

U.S. Army. 16th Armored Division. 393rd Armored Field Artillery Battalion. After Action Report. May 1945.

U.S. Army. 16th Armored Division. 393rd Armored Field Artillery Battalion. Unit History. 1945. "Name Landing Strip Iwan Field." *The Armodier*. 23 September 1944.

U.S. Army. 16th Armored Division. Unit Historical Report. Czechoslovakia: 28 June 1945.

U.S. Army. Supreme Headquarters Allied Expeditionary Force. Incoming Message File. "Czechoslovak Military Mission (SHAEF) to SHAEF Main, 5 May 1945 (Ref No. Rr–17730)."

U.S. Army. Supreme Headquarters Allied Expeditionary Force. Incoming Message File. "Czechoslovak Military Mission (SHAEF) to SHAEF Main, 6 May 1945 (Ref No. Rr–17731)."

U.S. Army. Supreme Headquarters Allied Expeditionary Force. Incoming Message File. "Twelfth Army Group to SHAEF Forward, 7 May 1945 (Ref. No. QX–31923)."

U.S. Army. Supreme Headquarters Allied Expeditionary Force. Outgoing Message File. "Message from Eisenhower to Bradley, Ref No. Fwd-20726, 6 May 1945."

U.S. Army. Supreme Headquarters Allied Expeditionary Force. Outgoing Message File. "Message from Eisenhower to Us Military Mission, Moscow, 8 May 1945 (Ref. No. Fwd–21001)."

U.S. Army. Supreme Headquarters Allied Expeditionary Force. Outgoing Message File. Message from Eisenhower to US Military Mission, Moscow—8 May 1945 (Ref. No. FWD-21006)."

U.S. Army. Third U.S. Army. XII Corps. 90th Infantry Division. After Action Report, Month of May 1945. Germany: June 1945.

U.S. Army. Twelfth U.S. Army Group. Letter of Instructions No. 22–4 May 1945.

Official U.S. Army Documents

(U.S. Army Heritage and Education Center Archives and Library, Carlisle Barracks, Pennsylvania)

Dyer, George. Lt. Col., USA. *XII Corps: Spearhead of Patton's Third Army* (privately published by the XII Corps Historical Association, 1947.

Gay, Hobart Maj. Gen., USA. Chief of Staff. Third U.S. Army. Diary. Personal Papers.

Gersdorff, Freiherr von. Generalmajor, German Army. "The Final Phase of the War: From the Rhine to the Czech Border," draft trans. from the German. (Oberursel, Germany: U.S. Army, Europe, Historical Division [Foreign Military Studies Branch,] March 1946).

Hamlett. Barksdale, Jr., Gen., USA (dec.). Oral History interview. Senior Officers Debriefing Program. Interviewed in 1976 by Col. Jack Ridgway and Lt. Col. Paul Walter. U.S. Army Military History Research Collection. Barksdale Hamlett Personal Papers.

Müller, Gerhard. Generalmajor, German Army. *"The Occupation of Pilsen by the U.S. 16th Armored Division—16th [Sic] May 1945."* trans. by H. Hintemann. ed. by Col. W. S. Nye. (Germany: U.S. Army, Europe, Historical Division [Foreign Military Studies Branch], 1954).

Nevins, Arthur S. Brig. Gen., USA. Chief of Operations Planning Section. Supreme Headquarters, Allied Expeditionary Force. G-3 (Operations) Division. Personal Papers. "SCAF (Supreme Commander Allied Forces) to Bradley [12th Army Group] and 9th Air Force Commanding General 4 May 1945." SCAF Cable No. 335. Found in Nevins Papers.

Toussaint, Rudolf. Gen., German Army. "Military Area Prague." Karlsruhe, Germany: U.S. Army, Europe, Historical Division [Foreign Military Studies Branch], written sometime between 1945 and 1954.

U.S. Army. V Corps. *Operations in the ETO 6 January 42–9 May 45.* (Germany: 1945).

U.S. Army. Third U.S. Army. After Action Report. 3 vols. Germany: 1945.

Weissenberger, Karl. Gen. German Army. "Battle Sector XIII (Wehrkreis XIII) (May 1945)," (Karlsruhe, Germany: U.S. Army, Europe, Historical Division [Foreign Military Studies Branch,] 1946).

Primary Sources and Memoirs

Allen, Randy. "Dean of Policemen to Retire After 35 Years of Gun, Badge." *Kentucky Enquirer.* (4 March 1979), 7+.

Bradley, Omar N. General of the Armies, USA (dec.) *A Soldier's Story.* New York: Henry Holt, 1951.

Deane, John. Gen., USA (dec.) *Strange Alliance.* New York: Viking, 1947.

Denny, Harold. "Road to Prague Lined with Debris." *New York Times.* 11 May 1945: 7.

Dollar, James W. Lt. Col. USA (dec.). "Constabulary Constables." *Cold War Times, the Online Newsletter of the Cold War Museum.* (November / December 2002), 12–17.

Green, Peter S. "American Veterans Return 45 Years After Liberating Pilsen." United Press International. May 5, 1990. Accessed online on 4 December 2015 at http://www.upi.com/Archives/1990/05/05/American-veterans-return-45-years-after-liberating-Pilsen/3690641880000/.

_____. "West Bohemians Celebrate Liberation by American Gis." United Press International. May 7, 1990. Accessed online on 4 December 2015 at http://www.upi.com/Archives/1990/05/06/West-Bohemians-celebrate-liberation-by-American-GIs/9002641966400/.

Harmon, Ernest N. Lt. Gen., USA (dec.) with Milton MacKaye and William Rosse MacKaye. *Combat Commander, Autobiography of a Soldier.* Englewood Cliffs, NJ: Prentice Hall, 1970.

Hoebeke, Arnold J. Maj., USA. *The Operations of the 343d Infantry (86th Division) in the Reduction of the Ruhr Pocket and the Redoubt Area, 28 March, 8 May 1945.* (Central

Europe Campaign). Advanced Infantry Officers Course 1947–1948. The Infantry School. Fort Benning, Georgia. Posted online by the U.S. Army Maneuver Center for Excellence. Fort Benning Georgia. Accessed online on 5 February 2014 at http://www.benning.army.mil/library/content/Virtual/Donovanpapers/WWII/STUP2/HoebekeArnoldJ%20MAJ.pdf.

Hoffman, Kathy Lemmons. "Charles Robert Lemmons." Unpublished Biography. March 2014.

Hubbard, Mont. Col., USA (dec.). Obituary. *Danville Register* (Danville, VA). 17 April 1968.

Kamm, Henry. "Pilsen Journal: G.I.'S or Russians? Time to Show the Snapshots." *New York Times*. April 11, 1990. Accessed online on 4 December 2015 at http://www.nytimes.com/1990/04/11/world/pilsen-journal-gI-s-or-russians-time-to-show-the-snapshots.html.

Kennan, George F. *Memoirs 1925–1950*. Boston: Little, Brown & Co. 1967.

Knoche, Eldon. "Pratt Received Silver Star in WWII." *Milwaukee Journal-Sentinel*. 24 October 1995: 4B.

MacCormac, John. "Czech Patriots Take Prague, Then Beg Aid as Foe Attacks," *New York Times*. 6 May 1945: 1+.

Malone, Mandy, and Norman Tippens. "Obituary, Charles Albert Symroski." *Daily Press*. April 14, 2001. Accessed online on 20 November 2015 at http://articles.dailypress.com/2001-04-15/news/0104150120_1_west-point-fort-riley-headquarters.

Millington, Edgar N. Capt., USA. *The Operations of the 64th Armored Infantry Battalion (16th Armored Division) at Pilsen, Czechoslovakia, 5–7 May 1945 (Central Europe Campaign) (Personal Experience of a Machine-Gun Platoon Leader)*. Advanced Infantry Officers Course 1948–1949. The Infantry School. Fort Benning, Georgia. Posted online by the U.S. Army Command and General Staff College, Fort Leavenworth, KS.

Molla, William W. Brig. Gen. USA (ret). "The Surrender of the 11th Panzer Division." *Yankee Doings* (the newsletter of the 26th Division Association) Dec. 1995: 57–9.

Mooney, Oscar Jackson, Jr., Obituary. *The Daily Home*. (8 December 2015). Accessed online at http://www.legacy.com/obituaries/dailyhome/obituary.aspx?n=oscar-jackson-mooney&pid=176805077& on 9 December 2015.

Patterson, John C. Maj., USA (dec.) Troop Commander. Troop B. 23rd Cavalry Reconnaissance Squadron [Mechanized]. 16th Armored Division. *My Life*. Memoirs dictated to his daughter Faye Ellen Coleman in 2001 and posted online by his son Clay Patterson in 2011 at http://www.rose316.com/images/John_My_Life_-_Part_I.pdf and http://www.rose316.com/images/John_My_Life_-_Part_II.pdf.

Patton, George S., Jr., Gen., USA (dec.) *War as I Knew It*, New York: Bantam, 1979.

Perkins, Percy H., Jr., Col., USA (dec.) Executive Officer. Combat Command B. 16th Armored Division. Personal Account. 1975.

Pickett, George B. Lt. Col., USA, and Edgar N. Millington, Capt., USA. "The Pilsen Story." *Combat Forces Journal*. (April 1951), 33–36.

Polish, Sol. Warrant Officer. Division Message Center Officer, Division Headquarters (Forward), 16th Armored Division. "More on the Enigma Secret Cryptographic Device," *Harbor Watch*. (July 3, 1998), 8.

Schaudt, Howard Capt., USA. *The Operations of 23rd Cavalry Reconnaissance Squadron (Mecz) in Pursuit Action with the 86th Infantry Division from Ingolstadt to Wasserburg, Germany*. Advanced Infantry Officers Course 1946–1947. The Infantry School. Fort Benning, Georgia. Posted online by the U.S. Army Maneuver Center for Excellence. Fort Benning Georgia. Accessed online on 5 February 2014 at http://www.benning.army.mil/library/content/Virtual/Donovanpapers/WWII/STUP2/SchaudtHowardP%20CPT.pdf.

Smith, William W., Jr. Obituary. *Washington Post* (2 November 2013). Accessed online on 28 October 2015 at http://www.legacy.com/obituaries/washingtonpost/obituary.aspx?pid=167809015.

Stakauskas, Betsy. "Charles R. Lemmons, Covington Police Officer." Obituary. *The Cincinnati Enquirer*. 17 September 2001.

Taborsky, Edward. "Eduard Benes." *Foreign Affairs*. July 1958: 669–84.

U.S. Army. 8th Armored Division. 80th Armored Regiment. "Meet the Chief." *Turret Topics* (Newspaper of the 80th Armored Regiment). 21 May 1943. Accessed online on 10 January 2017 at http://www.8th-armored.org/pics/papers/80th-regt-paper.pdf.

U.S. Army. 717th Tank Battalion. History. 1 January 1945 to 31 July 1945. Camp Swift, TX. August 1945. Accessed online at http://cgsc.cdmhost.com/cdm/singleitem/collection/p4013coll8/id/3459/rec/15 on 19 February 2014 from the U.S. Army Combined Arms Research Library.

U.S. Army. Third U.S. Army. V Corps. Headquarters. Public Affairs Office. Maj. Robert G. Rashid. Press Release. Pratt Mission. May 1945. Reprinted as "Milwaukeean Won Medal for His Role in Surrender." *Milwaukee Journal* (14 September 1945), 1.

U.S. Army. U.S. Army European Theater of Operations. History Section. *Order of Battle of the United States Army*. World War II. European Theater of Operations. Divisions. Paris, France: December 1945.

U.S. Department of War. U.S. Army. Field Manual 17–42. *Armored Force Field Manual: Armored Infantry Battalion*. 10 November 1944.

U.S. Department of War. U.S. Army. Field Manual 17–45. *Armored Force Field Manual: Armored Engineer Battalion*. 13 November 1942. Accessed online at U.S. Army Combined Arms Research Library on 21 January 2014 at http://cgsc.contentdm.oclc.org/utils/getfile/collection/p4013coll9/id/792/filename/793.pdf

Ward, Isabell Pierce. "My Father, John Leonard Pierce." Accessed on the D-Day to VE-Day website on 24 January 2014 http://dday.slavnostisvobody.cz/index.php?menu=veterans&submenu=seznam&id=17&lang=en.

Official Histories

The Army Almanac: A Book of Facts Concerning the Army of the United States. Washington, D.C.: U.S. Government Printing Office, 1950. Accessed online on 4 February 2014 at http://www.history.army.mil/html/forcestruc/cbtchron/cc/086id.htm

Cameron, Robert S. *Mobility, Shock, and Firepower: The Emergence of the U.S. Army's Armor Branch, 1917–1945*. Washington, D.C.: Center of Military History, 2008.

The First: A Brief History of the 1st Infantry Division, World War II. Cantigny, IL: privately published the Cantigny First Division Foundation, 1996.

Fowler, Murray H. *Spearhead in the West, 1941–45: The Third Armored Division*. Frankfurt, Germany: Privately published for the 3rd Armored Division by F. J. Heinrich, 1945.

Greenfield, Kent Roberts. Ed. *Command Decisions*. In the series *U.S. Army in World War II, the European Theater of Operations*. New York: Harcourt, Brace & Co. 1959.

Greenfield, Kent Roberts, Robert R. Palmer and Bell I. Wiley. *The Army Ground Forces: The Organization of Ground Combat Troops*. In the series *The United States Army in World War II*. Washington, D.C.: Center of Military History, 1987.

Palmer, Robert R., "Reorganization of Ground Troops for Combat." 261–384.

Palmer, Robert R., Bell I. Wiley, and William R. Keast. *The Procurement and Training of Ground Combat Troops*. In the series *United States Army in World War II: The Army Ground Forces*. Washington, D.C.: Center of Military History, 1991.

Pogue, Forrest C., "The Decision to Halt at the Elbe." 374–387. In the series *U.S. Army in World War II, the European Theater of Operations*. New York: Harcourt, Brace & Co. 1959.

Speed Is the Password: The Story of the 12th Armored Division. Paris, France: Printed by Desfosses-Neogravure in 1945 for *Stars and Stripes* newspaper as part of the *G.I. Stories* series.

Stubbs, Mary Lee, and Stanley Russell Connor. *Army Lineage Series Armor-Cavalry Part 1*. Washington, D.C.: Office of the Chief of Military History, 1969.

U.S. Army. Army Ground Forces. Historical Section. *Reorganization of Ground Troops for Combat*. Army Ground Forces Study No. 8. 1946. Accessed online on 23 January 2014 at http://www.history.army.mil/books/agf/AGF08/index.htm.

U.S. Army. 97th Army Reserve Command. *The Trident Heritage: A Brief History of the 97th Infantry Division and the 97th Army Reserve Command*. Maryland: privately published by the Headquarters of the 97th Army Reserve Command, 1988.

U.S. Army. 2nd Infantry Division. *Combat History of the Second Infantry Division in World War II*. Nashville, TN: printed for the division by Battery Press, 1946.

U.S. Army. 717th Tank Battalion. *717th Tank Battalion Record*. Privately published by the battalion in October 1945. Accessed online at http://digicom.bpl.lib.me.us/ww_reg_his/25/ on 19 February 2014.

U.S. Army. Third U.S. Army. XXII Corps. 79th Infantry Division. *The Cross of Lorraine: A Combat History of the 79th Infantry Division, June 1942–December 1945.* Nashville, TN: Battery Press, 1986 reprint of 1946 edition.

U.S. Army. Third U.S. Army. XXII Corps. 79th Infantry Division. 314th Infantry Regiment. *Through Combat: The 314th Infantry Regiment.* Privately published by the 314th Infantry Regiment in 1945. Accessed online on 6 May 2014 at http://privateletters.net/documents.html

U.S. Army. 12th Armored Division. "A History of the United States Army Twelfth Armored Division, 15 September, 1942–17 December, 1945" (1947). *World War Regimental Histories.* Book 43. Accessed on 2 January 2015 at http://digicom.bpl.lib.me.us/ww_reg_his/43

U.S. Army. U.S. Army European Theater of Operations. History Section. *Order of Battle of the United States Army. World War II. European Theater of Operations. Divisions.* Paris, France: December 1945.

Weaver, Dale, ed. *16th Armored Division History, Patton's Third Army, WWII.* Privately published by the 16th Armored Division Association in 1986.

  Barrs, Harley. Armored Infantryman. Anti-Tank Platoon / B Company / 18th Armored Infantry Battalion / Combat Command A / 16th Armored Division. "Recollections." Weaver, XIII-18. "Division Headquarters & Headquarters Co." Weaver, II-1 to II-9.

  Gontrum, Ralph W. Col., USA. (dec.) "Recollections of a Colonel," Weaver, III-1 to III-2.

  "Headquarters Company, 16th Armored Division Trains," Weaver, IV-1.

  "History of the 16th Tank Battalion." Weaver," History of the 18th AIB." Weaver, XIII-1 to XIII-5.

  Houlihan, Frank J. Lt. Col., USA. 137th Armored Ordnance Maintenance Battalion. 16th Armored Division. "History and Records, 137th Armored Ordnance Maintainance [Sic] Battalion 16th AD 1942–1953," Weaver, VIII-1 to VIII-21.

  "M. Platoon," Weaver, VI-1 to VI-2.

  Noble, Charles, Col., USA. "Noble's Nostalgic Notes: A 16'ner's Experiences in World War II," Weaver, XXIV-1 to XXIV-9.

  Painter, Howard, Lt. Col. USA (Ret.). Company Commander. Company B. 18th Armored Infantry Battalion. Combat Command A. 16th Armored Division. "Recollections." Weaver, XIII-20 to XIII-22.

  Polish, Solomon. "Worth a Second Thought," Weaver, IX-8.

  Smith, William W., Jr., Col. USA (dec.). "A Brief History of the 216th Armored Engineer Battalion, 16th Armored Division 1943–1945." Weaver, XII-1 to XII-28.

Wiley, Bell I., "The Building and Training of Infantry Divisions." 429–498.

Wilson, John B. *Maneuver and Firepower: The Evolution of Divisions and Separate Brigades.* In the Army Lineage Series. Washington, D.C.: Center of Military History, 1998.

Ziemke, Earl F. *The U.S. Army in the Occupation of Germany 1944–1946.* Washington, D.C.: Center of Military History, 1990.

Interviews and Personal Correspondence

Caiazzo, Carmine. C Company / 1st Battalion / 9th Infantry Regiment / 2nd Infantry Division. Letter to the author. 13 February 1998.

Carlson, Robert H. Maj. (USA) (dec.). 1st Lt. Executive Officer, Cannon Company. 38th Infantry Regiment. 2nd Infantry Division. Letter to the author, 24 March 1998.

Dollar, James W. Lt. Col., USA (dec.). 1st Lt. Staff Officer. Headquarters Company / 315th Infantry Regiment / 79th Infantry Division. Letters to the author, 25 April 1998, 20 November 1999 and 2 November 2002.

Eike, Gene. Staff Sgt. Squad Leader. A Company / 18th Armored Infantry Battalion / Combat Command A / 16th Armored Division. Interview by the author at the 16th Armored Division Association Reunion, Baltimore, MD: 16 October 1998.

_____. Phone interviews by author, 6 October and 29 December 2002.

Fiedlerova, Vera. Citizen of Pilsen, Czechoslovakia. Letter to the author, 12 September 1998.

_____. "My Memories on the End of the WW2," from a letter to the author, 28 June 1998.

Gallagher, Jack. Sgt. Tank Commander. D Company / 5th Tank Battalion / Combat Command A / 16th Armored Division. Interview by author at 16th Armored Division Association Reunion, Baltimore, Maryland 16 October 1998.

Gilbert, Robert I. Lt. Col., USA (Ret.). 1st Lt. Executive Officer. Company F / 2nd Battalion / 38th Infantry Regiment / 2nd Infantry Division. Phone interview by author, 29 March 1998.

Krusheski, Edward. Private. Rifleman. A Company / 69th Armored Infantry Battalion / Combat Command R / 16th Armored Division. Phone interviews by the author, 20 June 1998 and 17 January 2000.

Lewellen, Verne. Parts Clerk. 137th Armored Ordnance Battalion / 16th Armored Division. Letter to the author, 31 May 2000.

Maples, Herron N. Lt. Gen. USA (Dec.). Maj. S-3 (Operations) Officer. 15th Field Artillery Battalion / 2nd Infantry Division. Letter to the author, 16 March 1998.

_____. Phone interview by author. 31 March 1998.

Mooney, Oscar Jackson, Jr. (Dec.). Sgt. Battery C / 396th Armored Field Artillery Battalion / Combat Command B / 16th Armored Division. Interview by the author. Pilsen, Czech Republic, 7 May 2000.

Peklo, Jaroslav. Citizen of Pilsen, Czechoslovakia. "The End of the War in Pilsen, Bohemia," from a letter to the author, 10 March 1998.

_____. "The Last Days of War in Pilsen and Prague," from a letter to the author, 8 April 1998.

Polish, Solomon. Warrant Officer. Division Message Center Officer, Division Headquarters (Forward), 16th Armored Division. Letter to the author—9 June 1998.

Schaeffer, Charles T. Lt. Col. USA (Ret.). 2nd Lt. Adjutant. 216th Armored Engineers Battalion / 16th Armored Division. Interview by the author in Pilsen, Czech Republic. 7 May 2000.

_____. Letter to Jaroslav Peklo—20 January 2000.

_____. Phone interview by the author—3 January 2003.

Schmedemann, Keith M. Col., USA (Ret.). Maj. Assistant G-1 (Personnel) Officer. V Corps. Phone interview by author. 6 May 1998.

Shultz, George, Jr. Pfc. Combat Photographer, I Company / 23rd Infantry Regiment / 2nd Infantry Division. author's Questionnaire. February 1998.

Smathers, James A. Maj., USA (Ret.). Pfc. BAR Rifleman. I Company / 3rd Battalion / 38th Infantry Regiment / 2nd Infantry Division. Phone interview by author—28 December 2002.

Smith, William G., Jr., Col., USA (dec.) Battalion Commander. 216th Armored Engineers Battalion / 16th Armored Division. Interview by author at 16th Armored Reunion, 16 October 1998.

Steece, Mark. Armorer. B Troop / 23rd Cavalry Reconnaissance Squadron [Mechanized] / 16th Armored Division. Phone interview by author. 22 February 2014.

Thompson, George. Sgt. 137th Armored Ordnance Maintenance Battalion / 16th Armored Division. Email to the author, 11 February 2013.

_____. Email to the author, 23 May 2014.

_____. Phone interview by author 18 January 2000.

Yeglin, Miloslava "Milka" (maiden name Vildova), Citizen of Stenovice, Czechoslovakia. Phone interview by author, 15 October 1998.

_____. Interview by the author, Epjovice, Czech Republic, 7 May 2000.

Zajic, Joseph. Citizen of Pilsen. Letter to the author, 4 May 1999.

Zajicova, Malvina. Citizen of Pilsen. Letter to the author, 15 April 1998.

Secondary Sources

Adkisson, Raymond C. 1st Lt., USA. *Night Marches: Action of Australian and Indian Units Battle of Sari Bair (Gallipoli) 6–7 August 1915*. Regular Course. The Infantry School. Fort Benning, Georgia. Posted online by the U.S. Army Maneuver Center for Excellence. Fort Benning Georgia. Accessed online on 5 February 2014 at http://www.benning.army.mil/library/content/Virtual/Donovanpapers/wwi/STUP1/AdkissonRaymond%20C.%201LT.pdf.

Ambrose, Stephen E. *Citizen Soldiers: The U.S. Army from the Normandy Beach to the Bulge to the Surrender of Germany*. New York: Simon & Schuster, 1997.

Andreyev, Catherine. *Vlasov and the Russian Liberation Movement: Soviet Reality and Emigre Theories*. Cambridge, England: Cambridge, University Press, 1987.

Averitt, Jack N. *Families of Southern Georgia*. Baltimore, MD: Genealogical Publishing Company, 2007. Reprint of 1964 edition.

Bartos, Omar and Ramona Murphy Bartos. "At the Mercy of the Enemy." *World War II*. October 2006: 42–45.

Bell, Raymond E., Jr., Brig. Gen. USA (Ret.)

Works Cited

"Giving Up the Ghost." *World War II* September 2005.

Buckheit, John, Capt. (USA). "16th AD Was the Last U.S. Armored Division Formed During WWII, and the Last Deployed." *Armor* (July–August 1993), 38–39.

Buecker, Thomas R. *Fort Robinson and the American Century 1900–1948*. Norman: University of Oklahoma Press, 2002.

City of Dorfen, Germany. History. Accessed online http://www.dorfen.de/stadtgeschichte/blog on 4 January 2015.

Colby, John. *War from the Ground Up*. Austin, TX: Nortex P, 1991.

Cole, Hugh M. *The Ardennes: Battle of the Bulge*. In the series *The United States Army in World War Two, the European Theater of Operations*. Washington, D.C.: Office of the Chief of Military History, Department of the Army, 1965.

"Colonel Charles H. Noble." Brians Journey (Brian LaViolette Scholarship Foundation) website http://www.briansjourney.com/soh/pilsen-noble, accessed 14 January 2014.

"Colonel Percy Harold Perkins, Jr., Obituary." *Savannah Morning News* (17 January 1998). Accessed online on 12 February 2015 at http://savannahnow.com/stories/011798/OBITS011798.html.

Dickerson, Bryan J. "Czechoslovakia 1945: Prelude to the Coming U.S. / Soviet Cold War." Master's Thesis, Monmouth University, West Long Branch, NJ, 1999.

_____. "Ernest N. Harmon and the Challenges of Occupation." *Journal of America's Military Past*. (Winter 2000), 53–62.

Erickson, John. *The Road to Berlin: Continuing the History of Stalin's War with Germany*. Boulder, CO: Westview, 1983.

Farago, Ladislas. *Patton: Ordeal and Triumph*. New York: Ivan Obolensky, 1963.

_____. *The Last Days of Patton*. New York: Berkeley Books, 1981.

Faulk, Florine Pierce, and Grace Edman. "Pierce, Frank Cushman," *Handbook of Texas Online* (http://www.tshaonline.org/handbook/online/articles/fpi09), accessed January 24, 2014. Published by the Texas State Historical Association.

Forty, George. *U.S. Army Handbook 1939–1945*. New York: Barnes & Noble Books, 1995.

_____. *United States Tanks of World War II in Action*. New York: Blandford, 1983.

Gilbert, Martin. *The Day the War Ended: May 8, 1945—Victory in Europe*. New York: Henry Holt, 1995.

"Hamlett, Barksdale, Jr." Personal Papers. Manuscripts and Folklife Archives. Department of Library Special Collections. Kentucky Library and Museum. Western Kentucky University. Bowling Green. Accessed online on 27 January 2014 at http://digitalcommons.wku.edu/cgi/viewcontent.cgi?article=2016&context=dlsc_mss_fin_aid.

"Hubbard, Mont." Register of Personal Papers. Virginia Military Institute Archives. Lexington, VA. Accessed online on 12 May 2016 at http://www.vmi.edu/Archives/Manuscripts/Military_History_Manuscripts/.

Knoche, Eldon. "Pratt Received Silver Star in WWII." *Milwaukee Journal-Sentinel*. (24 October 1995), 4B.

Levin, David. "Remembering Camp Shanks." *Hudson Valley Magazine*. (August 16, 2010). Accessed online at http://www.hvmag.com/Hudson-Valley-Magazine/September-2010/Remembering-Camp-Shanks/ on 24 January 2013.

Lucas, James. *Das Reich, the Military Role of 2nd SS Division*. London: Arms and Armour Press, 1991.

_____. *Last Days of the Reich, the Collapse of Nazi Germany, May 1945*. London: Arms & Armour Press, 1986.

MacDonald, Charles B. *The Last Offensive*. In the series *The United States Army in World War II: The European Theater of Operations*. Washington, D.C.: Center of Military History, 1993.

_____. *The Mighty Endeavor*. New York: Da Capo P, 1969.

"Major General Douglass T. Greene." Hall of Fame Listing. Drexel University. Accessed online on 24 January 2014 at http://www.drexeldragons.com/hof.aspx?hof=548&path=&kiosk=.

Patterson, Clay, CPG, FSA Scot. *Patterson: A Scots-Irish Family*. Dandridge, TN: Rose-Crag Publications, 2013.

Patterson, John C. Capt., USA. Letter to his parents, 9 May 1945. Reprinted in Clay Patterson's *Patterson: A Scots-Irish Family*, 222–223.

Pierce, Kate Bodine. "Pierce, John Leonard," *Handbook of Texas Online* (http://www.tshaonline.org/handbook/online/articles/fpi11), accessed January 24, 2014. Published by the Texas State Historical Association.

Province, Charles M. *Patton's Third Army: A*

Chronology of the Third Army Advance August, 1944 to May, 1945. New York: Hippocrene Books, 1992.

Rhode, Gotthold "The Protectorate of Bohemia and Moravia 1939-1945." 305-321. Victor S. Manatey, and Radomir Luza, eds. *A History of the Czechoslovak Republic 1918-1948.* Princeton, NJ: Princeton University Press, 1973.

Roucka, Zdenek, Jaroslav Peklo, et. als. *Americans in West Bohemia 1945—Exclusive Pictures.* Pilsen, Czech Republic: ZR&T, 2000.

Shirer, William L. *The Rise and Fall of the Third Reich: A History of Nazi Germany.* New York: Simon & Schuster, 1959.

The Sixteener. (Sixteenth Armored Division Newsletter). Summer 2014.

Stanton, Shelby L. *Order of Battle, U.S. Army, World War II.* Novato, CA: Presidio, 1984.

Szulc, Tad. *Czechoslovakia Since World War II.* New York: Viking P, 1971.

Toland, John. *The Last 100 Days.* New York: Random House, 1966.

Weigley, Russell F. *Eisenhower's Lieutenants: The Campaign of France and Germany 1944-1945.* Bloomington: Indiana University Press, 1981.

Yeide, Harry. *The Infantry's Armor: The U.S. Army's Separate Tank Battalions in World War II.* Mechanicsburg, PA: Stackpole Books, 2010.

West Point Association of Graduates Online Memorials

"James E. Norvell 1937." Memorial Page. Accessed online on 22 January 2015 at https://apps.westpointaog.org/Memorials/Article/10876/.

"George B. Pickett, Jr., 1941." Memorial Page. Accessed online on 20 January 2016 at http://apps.westpointaog.org/Memorials/Article/12491/.

Semmelmeyer, Herbert W. Tribute written by Donald H. Nelson and accessed online on 30 October 2015 at http://apps.westpointaog.org/Memorials/Article/6306/

Symroski, Charles A. Memorial Page. Written by Ann Symroski and their daughters and Accessed on 19 November 2015 http://apps.westpointaog.org/Memorials/Article/10226/.

U.S. State Department Documents

U.S. State Department. *Foreign Relations of the United States 1939: Volume I General.* Washington, D.C.: GPO, 1956.

"The Acting Secretary of State to the German Charge (Thomsen), March 20, 1939," *FRUS 1939*, 56.

"The Acting Secretary of State to the Minister in Czechoslovakia (Carr), 17 March 1939," *FRUS 1939*, 47.

"The Acting Secretary of State to the Minister in Czechoslovakia (Carr), 20 March 1939," *FRUS 1939*, 55-56.

"The Consul General at Prague (Linnell) to the Secretary of State, 25 March 1939," *FRUS 1939*, 60-61.

"The German Charge (Thomsen) to the Secretary of State, 17 March 1939." *FRUS 1939*, 45-47.

"The German Charge (Thomsen) to the Secretary of State, 18 March 1939." *FRUS 1939*, 51-52.

"The Minister in Czechoslovakia (Carr) to the Secretary of State, 17 March 1939," *FRUS 1939*, 51.

"The Minister in Czechoslovakia (Carr) to the Secretary of State [Extracts], 19 March 1939," *FRUS 1939*, 54.

"Wilbur John Carr." Biography. U.S. Department of State. Office of the Historian. Accessed on 27 June 2014 at http://history.state.gov/departmenthistory/people/carr-wilbur-john.

Index

Numbers in bold italics indicate pages with illustrations

Adams, Maj. Lewis 121
Adjusted Service Rating 162
Adkisson, Lt. Col. Raymond 30, 65–66, 68–73, 76, 126, 171
Alexander, Capt. Russell B. 66, 75–76
Allen, Maj. Gen. Roderick 45
Anderson, Maj. Julian P. 91
Antonov, Gen. Alexei 133
Anzio Invasion 49, 158
Ardennes Counter-Offensive *see* Battle of the Bulge
Armies (U.S.):
  1st 57, 64, 79, 86–87
  2nd 34–35
  3rd 3–4, 60, 62–65, 79–80, 83, 85–88, 94–95, 100, 124, 129–132, 147, 150, 155, 157, 159, 170, 184
  15th 55, 170
Armored Force 12–13, 28, 58, 158
Armstorf (Arestodt) 69
Asch, Czechoslovakia 63
Aschaffenburg, Germany 189
Atlantic Wall 55
Atomic Bombs 163, 167, 170, 174, 177–178
Auburn University 25

Ballman, William R. 35
Baltic Sea 86, 133
Bamberg, Germany 165, 171
Barrett, Capt. "Shorty" 28, 36
Barrs, Harley 6, 23, 34, 55, 123, 152, 171
Bartley, Robert F. 68
Battalions, Armored Engineer (U.S. Army):
  24th 28
  53rd 28
  220th 28
Battalions, Armored Field Artillery (U.S. Army):
  54th 177
  412th 23
  413th 24
  440th 48
Battalions, Engineer Combat (U.S. Army):
  1st 165, 172

20th 165
122nd 62
123rd 62
124th 62
311th 65
327th 173
Battalions, Field Artillery (U.S. Army):
  4th 30
  14th 48
  82nd 48
  186th 165, 174
  254th 65
  281st 65
  331st 65
  332nd 65
  404th 65
  911th 65
  987th 31
Battalions, Other (U.S. Army):
  38th Armored Infantry 49, 178
  83rd Reconnaissance 59
  95th Chemical Mortar 65
  127th Armored Ordnance 165, 172
  311th Medical 65
  839th Anti-Aircraft Artillery (Automatic Weapons) 65
Battalions, Tank (U.S. Army):
  191st 48–49
  717th 17–18, 167
  760th 48
  787th 18, 65, 78
Battalions, Tank Destroyer (U.S. Army):
  807th 65
  820th 110
Battle of Kasserine Pass 46
Battle of the Bulge 44, 54, 59, 64, 80, 87, 125, 127, 149, 158, 178
Beck, Lt. Col. Thoss B. 89–91, 119–120
Bednars, Benjamin *107*
Benes, President Eduard 39–40, 83, 132–133, 158, 180
Bergen-Belsen, Germany 57
Bernstein, Maj. Jack 36
Bissonnette, Roland 122

217

218 Index

Black, Ambassador Shirley Temple 183
Bockhorte, Germany 71
Bohemia, Czechoslovakia 37-43, 79, 89, 95-96, 98, 128, 133, 137, 179, 182-184, 187
Bor, Czechoslovakia 93, *121*, 160
Bradley, Gen. Omar 79, 86, 130-133
Braun, Eva 79
Brisack, Lt. Col. Floyd R. 93, 154
Bromley, Col. Charles V. 16
Brown, 1st Lt. Bernard N. 101, 105
Browne, Lt. Col. Barry D. 26
Buchenwald, Germany 57
Budweis, Czechoslovakia 38, 86, 100, 123, 128, 130, 133
Bunyachenko, Gen. Sergei 96
Burke, Lt. Edward C. 68

Caiazzo, Carmine 157
Calais, Col. C.H. 15
Camp Atterbury, Indiana 174, 194
Camp Barkeley, Texas 45
Camp Bowie, Texas 48
Camp (Fort) Campbell, Kentucky 21, 25, 29
Camp Chaffee, Arkansas 12-14, 22, 24-36, 50-55, 193, 209
Camp Forrest, Tennessee 62
Camp Funston, Kansas 29
Camp Gruber, Oklahoma 177
Camp Kilmer, New Jersey 168, 172-173
Camp Lucky Strike, France 168
Camp (Fort) McCoy, Wisconsin 173, 175
Camp Perry, Ohio 26
Camp (Fort) Polk, Louisiana 48
Camp Roberts, California 50
Camp Shanks, New York 45, 53-54
Camp Wheeler, Georgia 23
Cardwell, Capt. Arjenter B. 58
Carlson, 1st Lt. Robert H. 182
Carr, Ambassador Wilbur J. 41
Casper, 1st Lt. Gilbert 101
Cavalry (U.S.):
1st Cavalry Division 48
2nd Cavalry Group 4, 63, 79, 83, 88
2nd Cavalry Regiment 59
3rd Cavalry Regiement 59
7th Cavalry Regiment 59
14th Cavalry Regiment 58
26th Cavalry Troop 47
86th Cavalry Troop 65
102nd Cavalry Group 149
106th Cavalry Group 68-69, 76
121st Cavalry Squadron 76
Chaffee, Maj. Gen. Adna 13, 32
Chamberlain, Prime Minister Neville 38
Cheb, Czechoslovakia 37, 39, 63, 88, 124, *159*, 194
Chotesov, Czechoslovakia 104-105, *121*
Church of Our Lady of Victory, Prague 37
Churchill, Prime Minister Winston 38, 85
Chylinski, 1st Sgt. Steve 182

Civilian Conservation Corps 48
Clark, Maj. Gen. Mark 46
Colorado State University 172
Companies (U.S. Army):
2nd Signal 29
86th Quartermaster 65
97th Signal 110
583rd Ambulance 94
786th Ordnance Light Maintenance 65
994th Engineer Treadway Bridge 31
998th Engineer Treadway Bridge 18, 91
Corps (U.S. Army):
II 46
II Armored 45
III 64-65, 78
V 79, 85-89, 100, 108, 124, 127-131, 135, 140-141, 146, 148-153, 157, 166, 184
VII 170
XII 63, 79, 86, 88-89, 100, 124, 127, 135, 150, 155
XXII 156-159, 165, 169-170
XXIII 59
XXXVI 51
Covington, Kentucky Police Dept. 31, 174, 194
Cranford, Maj. J.H. 49-50
Cruise, Lt. Col. Edward E. 58
Czechoslovakia 4-5, 36-43, 62, 74, 79, 81-89, 91, 93-96, 100-101, 106, 108, 120, 122, 125, 129-133, 136, 138-139, 144, 149-152, 154-160, 163-165, 167-170, 172, 177, 180-183, 189-190

Dachau, Germany 57
Daladier, Prime Minister Eduoard 38
Dallaire, Staff Sgt. Onits 123
Dalton, Lt. Gerard 139
Danube River 64, 66-67
David, Lt. Richard E. 68
Deane, Gen. John R. 133
Dedmon, Lt. Roy L. 66, 73, 75-77
Denny, Harold 39
Desert Training Center, California 48
Devore, Col. Gerald B. 16
Displaced Persons 61, 136, 147, 150-155, 160, 170
Divisions (Armored) (U.S. Army):
1st 7-9, 13, 158
2nd 3, 7-9, 13, 17, 158
3rd 3, 9, 13, 17, 177
4th 3-4, 9, 13, 16-17, 22, 24, 26, 28, 86, 88, 100, 124, 129, 161-162, 165, 173-174
5th 9, 13
6th 9, 12-13, 32
7th 3, 9, 48-49, 178
8th 9, 13, 20, 24, 28-29
9th 3-4, 9, 24, 57, 87-88, 100, 124, 131, 135, 149, 155, 184
10th 9, 12-13
11th 9, 100, 176

12th 9, 13, 45, 49, 169, 178
13th 9
14th 9, 12, 32, 66-67
20th 9, 13-14, 16-17, 22-24, 26, 28-29
Divisions (Infantry) (U.S. Army):
  1st 4, 46, 79, 87-88, 100, 124, 131, 135, 149, 153, 155, 161-162, 164-165, 171-172
  2nd 4, 6, 46, 83, 87-88, 100, 117, 124-125, 129-130, 135-136, 149, 153, 155, 157, 161, 162, 177, 179, 182-185, 188
  5th 59, 86, 88, 100, 124
  8th 45
  10th (Mountain) 14, 170
  24th 170
  26th 47, 83, 86, 100, 155
  28th 45
  30th 164
  33rd 62
  71st 14, 60
  79th 17, 162-164, 168
  83rd 45
  84th 165
  86th 18, 61-78, 89, 126, 171
  90th 4-5, 62-63, 83, 86, 88, 124
  94th 157
  97th 63, 87-88, 100, 109-110, 117, 124-126, 135, 138, 149, 155, 162-163, 179, 182, 187
  102nd 165
Dobriv, Czechoslovakia 126
Dollar, 1st Lt. James W. 164, 179
Domazlice, Czechoslovakia 96
Dönitz, Grossadmiral Karl 139, 145
Dorfen, Germany 69, 71-73, 77
Drexel University 12, 169
Driscoll, Lt. Victor 75
Drobek, Maj. T.W. 16, 22
Dubcek, Alexander 181
Durham, Capt. Frank 29

Earnest, Brig. Gen. Herbert 83
Eighth U.S. Army Air Force 159
Eike, Staff Sgt. Gene 1, 6, 50, 56, 122, 136, 152, 165, 171, *187*, 188
Eisenhower, Gen. Dwight D. 57, 62-64, 85-86, 100, 127, 130, 132-135, 139
Elbe River 37, 86, 124, 133
Elbeufren-en-Bray, France 57
Elliott, Lt. Col. Philip L. 90
Epjovice, Czechoslovakia *187*, 188
Erskine, Col. David G. 15, 23, 26

Farson, Staff Sgt. John J. 106
Ferguson, 1st Lt. Richard 179
Fiedler, Georg 179
Fiedlerova, Vera 6, 40, 42-43, 95, 107, 112, 179, 184
Fischerhausen, Germany 68
Fitzpatrick, Master Sgt. Joseph 110
Flossenbürg, Germany 63
Fodor, Capt. Eugene 129

Fort Belvoir, Virginia 28, 177
Fort Benning, Georgia 7, 30, 48, 171, 176
Fort Bliss, Texas 48
Fort Bragg, North Carolina 29, 167, 197
Fort Dix, New Jersey 29
Fort Driant, France 59
Fort Knox, Kentucky 7, 13, 17, 21, 25, 27-30, 59, 175
Fort Leavenworth, Kansas 48, 158, 176, 179
Fort Leonard Wood, Missouri 175
Fort Meade, Maryland 29
Fort Riley, Kansas 25, 29, 47, 51, 175
Fort Robinson, Nebraska 39
Fort Sill, Oklahoma 24-25, 46, 48, 170, 176
Fort Smith, Arkansas 12, 32
Fourth Marine Brigade (U.S.) 125
Frank, Reich Minister Karl 80
Freal, Capt. Harris R. 66
Fredendall, Maj. Gen. Lloyd 46
Freising, Germany 68
Fuller, Lt. Col. William H.G. 22, 49-50, 178

Gallagher, Sgt. Jack 130
Gay, Maj. Gen. Hobart 86, 158
Georgia Institute of Technology 48
German Army Units:
  Army Group Center 81-83
  Army Group North 83
  Army Group South 83
  Infantry Leib Regiment 82
  Volkstrum (Home Guard) 87
  Wehrkreis Prague 80, 82, 153
  Wehrkreis XIII 80, 83
  2nd Panzer Division 80, 87, 158
  2nd SS Panzer Division 96
  4th "Der Führer" Panzer Grenadier Regiment 96
  6th Mountain Infantry Division 82
  7th Army 80, 82-83, 87
  11th Panzer Division 80, 83
  13th Engineer Construction Replacement Battalion 87
  19th Infantry Regiment 82
  41st Infantry Regiment 82
  98th Mountain Infantry Regiment 82
  404th Training Division 87
  413th Training Division 87
  665th Engineer Brigade 87
Gestapo 42, 95, 98, 110, 117
Gilbert, 1st Lt. Robert 129
Goering, Feldmarschall Hermann 39, 172
Gontrum, Col. Ralph W. 13-15, 90
Gordon, Col. Richard A. 13, 15, 49, 169
Grafenwöhr, Germany 165
Grafton, Lt. Col. Clealon V. 13, 15
Grand Hotel, Pilsen 118, 126, 132
Gray, Lt. Col. William V. 16
Greene, Brig. Gen. Douglas T. 12, 14-15, 45, 169

Greiner, Col. Edwin C. 59, 90
Groff, Sgt. Herman 29
Group (Field Artillery) (U.S. Army): 190th 166

Haag, Germany 73–75, 77
Hahney, Lt. Col. Everett G. 90
Hamlett, Col. Barksdale, Jr. 45–47, 50–51, 90, 93, 106, 132, 156, 158, 165–166, 170–171
Harmon, Lt. Gen. Ernest N. 156–158, *159*
Havel, President Vaclav 181, 183
Hecken, Germany 71
Hendren, Lt. Col. Irving K. 50, 121
USS *Hermitage* 54–55
Heydrich, Reich Minister Reinhard 42
Hitler, Adolf 5, 38–40, 61, 79, 83, 86, 98, 139, 181
Hitlerjugend 98
Hoebeke, Maj. Arnold J. 66
Hoenfelds, Germany 170
Hoffman, Kathy 6, 31, 183
Holz, Lt. Col. H.P. 13, 15
Houlihan, Lt. Col. Frank 35, 51, 151
Hubbard, Maj. Monte 16, 24, 49, 177
Huebner, Lt. Gen. Clarence 86–88, 128, 135–136, 146, 149, 151
Hull, Secretary of State Cordell 41
Hvezdazy, Czechoslovakia 137

Ifland, Robert 111
Inn River 66, 69, 71
Interrogation of Prisoners of War Team 231, 122
Irwin, Maj. Gen. S. LeRoy 86
Isar Canal 67, 69
Isar River 63–64, 66–68
Iwan, 2nd Lt. Edward S. 35

James I, King 13, 15
Jung, Maj. Walter J. 164

Kaiserlautern, Germany 60
Karlsbad 37, 86–88, 100, 123–124, 128, 131, 133, 135, 150
Kaznejon, Czechoslovakia 156
Kennan, George F. 38, 40–42
Kephart, Capt. Stewart 139
King, Lt. Col. Richard 29
Kinzlbach, Germany 71
Kirchasch, Germany 70
Kitchener, Lt. Ray 112–113
Königgrätz, Czechoslovakia 144
Kolesar, Capt. Joseph 66, 73, 75
Konstantinbad, Czechoslovakia 160
Korean War 169–170, 176, 179
Kozolny, Czechoslovakia 102
Krejcik, Jindra 97
Krelovice, Czechoslovakia 152
Krepinsky, Dr. Kanel 97–98

Krusheski, Edward 6, 23, 119, 130, 165, 172
Kübelwagen 106

La Feuillie, France 55
Lawwill, Maj. Julius K. 68
Le Havre, France 55–56, 167
Lemmons, Charles R. 31, 54, 61, 117–118, 157, 174, 183
Lengdorf, Germany 70, 75
Lewellyn, Vern 1, 6, 27, 189
Lewis, Lt. Col. L.F. 93, 110, 121
Lidice, Czechoslovakia 42
Linnell, Irving N. 41
Lippizzaner Horses 63
Loket, Czechoslovakia 168
Lübeck, Germany 86, 133
Luftwaffe 39, 79–80, 126, 172, 148

M4 Sherman tank *10*, *11*, 21, 55, 101
M5 light tank 10
M7 self-propelled gun 10, 23, *24*, 111, 153
M8 armored car 29–30, 72, 102, 108, 122, 126, 139, *144*
M8 assault gun 30, 68, 71, 76
M10 tank destroyer 10, 62, 72, 198
M18 tank destroyer 10, 62, 94, 198
M24 Chaffee tank 10, 29, 30, 68, 70, 72, 77, 117
M26 Pershing tank 10, 93
M36 tank destroyer 10, 198
MacArthur, Gen. Douglas 170
Maiz, Germany 60–61
Marienbad, Czechoslovakia 152, 155
SS *Marine Eagle* 54
SS *Marine Panther* 54, 56
Marshall, Gen. George C. 85
Masaryk, Foreign Minister Jan 39–41, 170
Mason, Col. S.B. 87–88
Massachusetts National Guard 47
Massie, 1st Lt. Carl B. 110
Mather, Maj. Donald W. 58
McConnell, Maj. Glen 35, 160
McFadden, Lt. Col. Daniel T. 164
McLain, Patrick R. 73
McLaskey, Maj. Gen. Harris M. 65, 76
McNair, Lt. Gen. Lesley J. 46
Merklin, Czechoslovakai 126
Messerschmitt Me-262 104, 126
Metz, France 59
Meyer-Detring, Col. Wilhelm 139–146, *140*, *142*
Military Vehicle Club 185
Millington, Capt. Edgar 132, 177
Minghi, Capt. Lawrence J. 103
Miraculous Infant of Prague 37
Montgomery, Field Marshall Bernard L. 86, 133
Mooney, Sgt. O.J. 1, 6, 25, 105, 111, 153–154, 166, 178–179, 188
Moosinning, Germany 68–69

Index

Morgan, William D. 16, 25
Morrow, Sgt. George 74–75
Müller, Generalmajor Gerhard 80–81, 97, 113, 116
Munich 38–39, 69, 72, 82, 165
Munich Conference 38

National Guard 32, 45, 47, 140, 164, 166, 169, 185
National Redoubt 62, 64, 86
NATO 182, 186
Nicolson, Tech. Sgt. John 111
Nieder-Neuching, Germany 68
Ninth U.S. Army Air Force 122
Noble, Col. Charles H., Jr. 20, 54, 57, 89–91, 102–103, 105–106, 110–111, 113–114, 116, 118–119, 126, 151, 153, 156, 158, 165, 169–170
Normandy, France 3, 36, 44, 49, 55, 59, 80, 125, 140, 161, 166
North Camp Polk, Louisiana 21
Norvell, Lt. Col. James E. 47–49, 57, 92, 118, 175–176
Norwich University 171
Nuremburg, Germany 60–62, 66–67, 85, 89, 94, 165, 172
Nuremburg War Crimes Trials 165, 172
Nyrany, Czechoslovakia 89

Odor, Lt. Col. Raymond W. 17
O'Dowd, Maj. Carl 66, 139, 141, 146
Office of Strategic Services 129
Operation Cobra 46
Operation Olympic 165
Operation Overlord 44
Operation Torch 46
Oregon National Guard 185

Painter, Capt. Howard 22, 33, 55, 60, 123, 171
Panzerkampfwagen III tank 72
Panzerkampfwagen V Panther tank 93
Panzerkampfwagen VI Tiger tank 93
Pasadena Junior College 50
Patterson, Clay 6
Patterson, Maj. John C. 47, 54, 70, 75, 101–102, 165, 174
Patton, Gen. George S., Jr. 3, 13, 46, 62, 80–83, 85–87, 95–96, 100, 127, 129–133, 158, *159*, 164, 170
Pearl Harbor Attack 8, 50
Peklo, Jaroslav 6, 42–43, 95, 99, 107–108, 179, 184
Pennsylvania National Guard 166
Perkins, Lt. Col. Percy H., Jr. 48–49, 57–58, 106, 109–116, 165, 177
Pickett, Lt. Col. George B., Jr. 58, 61, 92–93, 101, 109, 127, 129–130, 132, 137, 176–177
Pierce, Brig. Gen. John L. 44–45, 47, 58, 89, 90, 93, 106–107, 120, 131, 156, 158, *159*, 168–169

Pilsen, Czechoslovakia 1, 3–4, 37, 40–43, 79–89, 93, 95–133, 135–140, 144–150, 153–160, 168, 172–173, 177, 179, 181–189
Pilsen Airport *101–102*, 104, 126, 140
Pilsner Urquell *102*
Pindar, Capt. John A. 66, 68
Plan, Czechoslovakia 122
Polish, Warrant Officer Solomon 6, 29, 54–55, 106, 131, 174
Prague, Czechoslovakia 4, 37–42, 80–88, 95–100, 106, 109, 123–124, 127–145, 151, 153, 156, 179, 181
Pratt, Lt. Col. Robert H. 139–146, *142*, 173–174
Pratt Mission 139–146
Prestice, Czechoslovakia 126
Pretzen, Czechoslovakia 68, 70
Pribram, Czechoslovakia 130, 135, 137
Prisoners of War 31, 61, 63, 116–117, 122, 138, 147, *148*, 152–155, 165, 173
Protectorate of Bohemia and Moravia 40–42, 79–81
Purnell, Lt. Col. Edward K. 16

Ray, Maj. Richard H. 16
Reed, Col. Charles H. 83
Regensburg, Germany 165
Regiments (Armored) (U.S. Army):
20th 16
80th 20
Regiments (Field Artillery) (U.S. Army):
11th 46
12th 46
15th 46
18th 46
84th 25
144th 12
195th 12, 16
Regiments (Infantry) (U.S. Army):
2nd 59
8th 45
9th 157, 188
16th 165
23rd 125, 149, 179
38th 129
301st 157
303rd 125
313th 164
314th 164
315th 164
341st 65, 71
342nd 65–67
343rd 65–67
358th 5, 62
Reims, France 51, 59–60, 135, 139, 150
Remagen, Germany 57, 87
Republic Square, Pilsen 1, 97, 105–107, 109–113, 126, 182–184, 187
Revolutionary National Committee 97–98
Rezmittal, Czechoslovakia 137

Index

Rhine River 3, 57, 60, 158, 184
Robertson, Maj. Gen. Walter 157
Rodelle, Staff Sgt. Meyer **144**
Roffe, Col. A. Worrell 58–59, 90, 158
Rogina, Capt. Matthew H. 121
Rokycany, Czechoslovakia 106, 123, **188**
Ronsberg, Czechoslovakia 126
Rouse, Roby 36
Rufano, Joseph, Jr. 72

St. Bartholomew's Cathedral 111, 187
St. John Neumann 37
St. Lo, France 46
St. Wolfgang, Germany 74, 77
Salerno, Italy 49, 158
USAT *Santa Rosa* 54
Savage, Charlie 1, 189
Schaeffer, Lt. Col. Charles 1, 6, 28, 113–115, 165, 172, **188**
Schaudt, Capt. Howard 30, 66, 78, 171
Schmidt, Capt. Vincent 74
Schofield Barracks, Hawaii 46
Schörner, Feldmarschall Ferdinand 80–83, 96–98, 128, 139, 141–145
Schrafstetten, Germany 70
Schulten, Lt. Col. Leo E. 14, 16, 91
Schulze, Maj. Hermann 164
Schwindau, Germany 75
USS *Sea Pike* 167
Seeley, Technical Sgt. Mickey 116
Semmelmayer, Col. Herbert W. 16, 23–24, 176
Siegfried Line 52
Shultz, George, Jr. 125, 149
16th Armored Division Units:
  Armored Field Artillery Battalions:
    393rd 15–16, 18, 23, 35, 90, 121–123
    396th 15–16, 18, 23–25, 49, 57, 90–93, 101, 105, 110–111, 118, 153, 166
    397th 15–16, 18–19, 23, 25, 49, 51, 54, 56, 90, 92, 120
  Armored Infantry Battalions:
    18th 19, 22–23, 33–34, 49–50, 52, 55, 56, 90, 121–123, 150, 152–156, 164–165, 168, 171, 187
    64th 18–19, 22, 55–56, 58, 60–61, 90–93, 109–112, 116, 118, 127, 130, 132, 136–137, 150, 155
    69th 18–19, 22–23, 25, 35, 58, 90, 92, 119, 130, 155, 165
  Armored Regiments:
    5th 15–18, 167
    16th 15–16, 18
  Division Artillery 15, 19–20, 23, 25–26, 45, 47, 50, 65, 90, 93, 106–107, 166, 170, 175
  Division Band 18
  Division Headquarters 15, 17–19, 58, 60, 89–91, 106, 110, 129
  Division Trains 15, 19, 20, 26, 90, 94, 126
  Military Police Platoon 18–19, 26, 31, 61, 118, 153

Tank Battalions:
  5th 17, 19, 21, 48–49, 55, 90, 121, 130, **148**
  16th 17, 19, 21, 90–93, 101, 103, 109–112, 117, 130, 136, 150, 155–156
  26th 17, 19, 21, 90–92, 119–120, 137, 150
Task Forces:
  A 92, 100, **101**, 102, 105, 110, 112, 129
  B 92, 110–112, 117–118, 136, 150
  Baker 92, 119–120
  Beck 92, 119–120
  Horrocks 92, 119–120
  R 92
Team Casper **101–102**, 104
23rd Cavalry Squadron 17–19, 27, 29–31, 47, 54–56, 61, 63, 64–78, 89–82, 100, 102, 105, 116, 120–126, 138–139, **144**, 146, 150, 156, 165, 171, 173
  Troop A 29, 47, 68–77, 90–91, 121–123, 126, 138
  Troop B 29–31, 47, 66–71, 73, 75, 77, 90–92, 100–105, 126, 138–140, 156, 165, 173–174
  Troop C 29, 66, 68, 71–77, 90–91, 116, 120, 126, 153
  Troop D 17–18, 29, 66, 68–69, 71–73, 76–77, 91, 126, 138
  Troop E 18, 29, 30, 66–68, 70–77
  Company F 30, 66–68, 70–71, 74–77, 91, 138
  Service Troop 29, 66–71, 91
96th Armored Reconnaissance Battalion 15, 18
137th Armored Ordnance Battalion 15–16, 18–19, 26–27, 35, 51, 60, 89–90, 154, 160, 172, **186**
156th Armored Signal Company 6, 19, 27, 29, 55, 106, 131
216th Armored Engineer Battalion 15, 18–19, 27–29, **34**, 35–36, 91–93, 113, 151, 155, 165, 172, **188**
216th Armored Medical Battalion 15–16, 18–19, 26–27, 61, 90, 92, 94, 121, 126, 137, 155
476th Armored Infantry Regiment 15–16, 18, 22
516th Counter-Intelligence Corps Detachment 19
571st Anti-aircraft Artillery Automatic Weapons Battalion 31, 61, 90, 92, 120–121
633rd Tank Destroyer Battalion 31, 61–62, 93, 138, 152, 167
Skoda Works 37, 43, 79–80, **102–103**
Smith, Lt. Col. William, Jr. 6, 13–14, 16, 28, 136, 151, 165, 172, 178
Sosna, Carl 179, 184, 189
Soviet Army Units:
  13th Army 156
  134th Field Artillery Regiment 156
  172nd Infantry Division 156
Soyen, Czechoslovakia 77

Splacene-Porici 116–117
Speakes, Brig. Gen. Stephen 184
Stalin, Josef 85, 180
Staszak, Lt. Stanley M. 70
Steece, Mark 6, 30–31, 55, 66, 101, 105, 150, 156, 165, 173
Stenovice, Czechoslovakia 39, 43, 126
Stod, Czechoslovakia *101*, 104
Stolz, Capt. Morris H. 26
Stribro, Czechoslovakia 100, 153
Struber, Lt. James W. 75
Sturm, Dr. Walter 97
Sturmgeschutz III assault gun 72
Sudetenland 38–39, 99, 106
Sudeten Germans 38–39, 88, 147, 151
Sulislav, Czechoslovakia *101*, 102
Surbey, Maj. Charles R. 35, 52, 56, 160
Symroski, Lt. Col. Charles A. 16, 25, 35, 49, 178

T-34 tank 188
Taborsky, Edward 83–84, 132–133
Tachov, Czechoslovakia *121*, 122–123, 149, 160
Task Force Polk 71, 73, 76
Tennessee National Guard 164
Texas A&M University 45
Texas National Guard 45
Theresienstadt, Czechoslovakia 42
Thompson, Sgt. George 1, 6, 27, 89, 160, 165, 172–173, 183–184, *186*, 188
Thomsen, Hans 42
Toussaint, Gen. Rudolf 80–82, 96, 131, 153
Truman, President Harry S. 85, 180
Twelfth U.S. Army Group 79, 130

Ujejd, Czechoslovakia 136, 150
University of Wisconsin 140
U.S. Army Artillery School 46, 170, 176
U.S. Army Cavalry School 20, 59
U.S. Army Command & General Staff College 20, 35, 48–49, 58, 178
U.S. Army Ground Forces 12–12, 17, 45–47, 50
U.S. Army Infantry School 30, 48, 171
U.S. Army Inspector General 51
U.S. Army Reserve Officer Training Corps (ROTC) 12, 25, 48
U.S. Army Specialized Training Program (ASTP) 25, 30
U.S. Department of State 41–42, 85

U.S. Legation Prague 40–42
U.S. Military Academy 12–13, 20, 23–25, 30, 46, 48, 58–59, 170, 177–178
U.S. Military Mission, Moscow 133
Ustach, Stanley F. 16

V-E Day 147–150
Veltus, Czechoslovakia 137
Velvet Divorce 181
Velvet Revolution 181
Verber, Lt. Otto 139, 141–144
Vildova, Miloslava 6, 39, 42–43, 179, 183, *187*
Virginia Military Institute 24
Vlasov, Gen. Andrei 96, 151
Vltava River 37, 86, 130, 133–134
von Majewski, Generalmajor George 80–81, 97–98, 113–116, 188
von Obstfelder, Gen. Hans 80
von Ribbentrop, Foreign Minister Joachim 40
von Weitersheim, Gen. Wend 83

Waidhaus, Germany 87, 89, 93–94, 106, 120, 122, 184
Walsh, Maj. Eugene P. 14, 16
Walter Reed Army Medical Center 171
Ware, Maj. Philip E. 16
Washington University 171
Wasserburg, Germany 63, 71–77
Weaver, Dale 6
Webb, Col. Thomas V. 59
Weiden, Germany 94
Weiler, Maj. John E. 49, 56–57
Weissenberger, Gen. Karl 83
Weissman, Paul 68
Welchov, Czechoslovakia 141, 144, 146
Welles, Acting Secretary of State Sumner 41–42
Whiting, Lt. Henry H. 72
Williams, Lt. Col. Shelby F. 89–91, 121
Worthington, Lt. Col. James M. 90, 131
Wurzburg, Germany 60

Yeglin, Harold 179, *187*, 188

Zajic, Joseph 98, 112, 179
Zajicova, Malvina 6, 42–43, 95, 97–98, 179
Zarback, Albert 111, 116
Ziervogel, Gen. Max 81

www.ingramcontent.com/pod-product-compliance
Ingram Content Group UK Ltd.
Pitfield, Milton Keynes, MK11 3LW, UK
UKHW030224241224